Praise for *Culture Renovation*

"The best playbooks are a combination of reliable research, relatable examples, and actionable strategies. This is the best playbook I've seen when it comes to creating organizational cultures that create competitive advantage, unlock performance, and rehumanize work."

—BRENÉ BROWN, PHD, AUTHOR OF *NEW YORK TIMES*
#1 BESTSELLER *DARE TO LEAD*

"What's clear is that corporate culture needs an overhaul. What's less clear is how to undertake that massive task. Thank goodness, then, for Kevin Oakes. In *Culture Renovation* he lays out a straightforward framework that any business leader can use to face the future with confidence and to build a great organization from the inside out."

—DANIEL H. PINK, *NEW YORK TIMES* BESTSELLING AUTHOR
OF *WHEN*, *DRIVE*, AND *TO SELL IS HUMAN*

"Your employees are the engine that powers ideas, innovation, and success of your company every day. A strong culture can provide the right fuel to nurture and empower your teams. In *Culture Renovation*, Kevin reinforces how leaders can learn from others and create the environment that enables each employee to make a difference."

—AJAY BANGA, CEO, MASTERCARD

"Today's top talent is seeking employers with a strong purpose aligned with their purpose. They want clear direction for the future and a culture that drives the strongest engagement and best performance and rewards. The company examples and steps that Kevin Oakes provides are the guideposts and evidence for employees to sign on."

—BETH FORD, PRESIDENT AND CEO, LAND O'LAKES

"In today's unpredictable and constantly changing environment, creating an agile and resilient culture is the difference between whether a company thrives or lags the competition. *Culture Renovation* is the blueprint executives need to future-proof the company."

—MARSHALL GOLDSMITH, *NEW YORK TIMES* #1 BESTSELLING
AUTHOR OF *TRIGGERS, MOJO,* AND *WHAT GOT YOU HERE
WON'T GET YOU THERE*

"Culture change is hard but can be such an accelerant to growth, and Kevin Oakes nails it when he says you need a real renovation to unlock your organization's potential. His 18-point guide is a ready road map with key insights on how to create a successful partnership with HR to effect lasting change."

—KATHLEEN HOGAN, CHRO, MICROSOFT

"Happy employees lead to happy customers. When companies put employees first and invest in people and culture, it creates a virtuous cycle that leads to business success. In *Culture Renovation*, Oakes outlines steps that any company can implement to make positive and lasting culture change."

—ASHLEY GOLDSMITH, CHIEF PEOPLE OFFICER, WORKDAY

"Talking about changing a company's culture is common. Doing it—in a sustainable way—is rare. *Culture Renovation* is a must-have primer for making that change happen. Oakes highlights the critical partnership between the CEO and CHRO, and the cooperation between HR and the leaders in an organization. In *Culture Renovation*, Oakes beautifully captures how critical the human resources function has become to create an organizational culture that will thrive over the long term."

—PAT WADORS, CHIEF PEOPLE OFFICER, PROCORE

"People-focused leaders understand an internally healthy culture is the cause of financial success, not the result. In *Culture Renovation*, Oakes outlines 18 proven action steps that any company can implement to make immediate positive culture change and sustain it long term."

"*Culture Renovation* confirms what I've long believed and experienced: It takes an appreciation of the past, and all its lessons, in order to evolve your company's culture for the long term."

"Few things are more important than culture. And no matter how strong and unique your culture, it always can be improved and needs to evolve. With vivid examples, key data, and brisk writing, *Culture Renovation* shows you step-by-step the dos and don'ts of upgrading your culture. I highly recommend it to anyone who cares about culture . . . which should be everyone."

"The importance of corporate culture can simply not be overemphasized. Earlier books made a convincing case that culture drives organization performance and ultimate success. This is the first book to lay out a well-researched, practical road map for how a company refurbishes its culture. Chock-full of down-to-earth, workable solutions, it is destined to be the classic handbook on this extremely vital issue."

"A company's external brand is significantly influenced by its culture; yet few executives pay as much attention to internal sentiment as they do externally. In *Culture Renovation*, Oakes lays out a straightforward, complete framework that all business leaders should internalize if they are interested in building a great organization from the inside out."

"While culture change needs to start at the top, successful leaders understand that to truly renovate culture you need a co-creation mindset throughout the workforce. That means understanding who not only the influencers and energizers are but also the blockers and detractors. In *Culture Renovation*, Kevin details the practices and steps that successful organizations have employed on their journey to create healthy and vibrant cultures. Kevin's magic is that he combines over a decade of quantitative and qualitative research with the world's leading organizations to generate unprecedented insight into successful culture change. His ability to position the ideas in clear compelling steps that make transparent what any leader can—and must—take will make this book an enduring classic."

—ROB CROSS, FOUNDER OF CONNECTED COMMONS AND
EDWARD A MADDEN PROFESSOR OF GLOBAL LEADERSHIP,
BABSON COLLEGE

"That culture matters for company performance is not news. What is new—and important for companies with unhealthy cultures—are the 18 practical steps companies can take to renovate their organizational cultures. Oakes has written a book that is evidence-based and practical on a topic of tremendous importance."

—JEFFREY PFEFFER, PROFESSOR, STANFORD BUSINESS SCHOOL,
AND AUTHOR OF *DYING FOR A PAYCHECK*

"Today's top talent is seeking employers with a strong purpose, innovative vision, and a culture fit. In *Culture Renovation*, Oakes documents 18 proven steps that i4cp's research uncovered as common tactics implemented by high-performance organizations, coupled with case studies that highlight those steps in action. I can't think of a better blueprint for any executive or company to effectively change its corporate culture."

—ELLIOTT MASIE, THE LEARNING CONSORTIUM

"Too many companies post their values on the wall and their websites and expect their employees and customers to magically behave exactly as those words describe. *Culture Renovation* helps clearly define how much more you can achieve when you take the steps to renovate your culture from the inside out, not the outside in."

—ANA WHITE, CHRO, F5

"Culture sets the stage for connecting people to each other and to unleash their own greatest potential. Kevin provides a useful context for thinking about continual growth and evolution whilst navigating ever-changing environments."

—MICHAEL FRACCARO, CHIEF PEOPLE OFFICER, MASTERCARD

"Creating an agile and vibrant culture is key to thriving in today's constantly changing business environment. *Culture Renovation* provides a thoughtful blueprint that any company can follow to evolve culture for high performance—including where to start and how to sustain change over time. It's a practical, insightful guide that should be on any CHRO's go-to list."

—KRISTEN LUDGATE, SENIOR VP, HUMAN RESOURCES, 3M

"The fascinating stories about the intersection between HR and senior leadership—and how important that was in successfully changing a culture—are worth the read alone. But what Oakes lays out in *Culture Renovation* is a go-to manual for any human capital professional interested in improving a company's culture now and maintaining that for years into the future."

—DR. JOHN BOUDREAU, PROFESSOR EMERITUS,
UNIVERSITY OF SOUTHERN CALIFORNIA

"Changing an organization's culture is often attempted, and rarely achieved. In *Culture Renovation*, Oakes leverages research and practical real-life examples to help any organization effectively change culture to compete more successfully in the future."

—CHRISTY PAMBIANCHI, EVP AND CHRO, VERIZON

"The real stories about the intersection between HR and senior leadership—and how important that was in successfully evolving a culture—is worth the read alone. What Oakes lays out in *Culture Renovation* is a must-have manual for making sustainable culture change happen now and in the years to come."

—DEAN CARTER, VP OF HUMAN RESOURCES, PATAGONIA

CULTURE RENOVATION

CULTURE RENOVATION

18 LEADERSHIP ACTIONS
TO BUILD AN
UNSHAKEABLE
COMPANY

KEVIN OAKES

New York Chicago San Francisco Athens London
Madrid Mexico City Milan New Delhi
Singapore Sydney Toronto

3 4 5 6 7 8 9 LCR 25 24 23 22 21

ISBN   978-1-260-46436-8
MHID   1-260-46436-9

e-ISBN   978-1-260-46437-5
e-MHID   1-260-46437-7

Culture Renovation is a trademark of i4cp.

Library of Congress Cataloging-in-Publication Data

Names: Oakes, Kevin, author.
Title: Culture renovation : 18 leadership actions to build an unshakeable
   company / Kevin Oakes.
Description: New York : McGraw-Hill Education, [2020] | Includes
   bibliographical references and index.
Identifiers: LCCN 2020038138 (print) | LCCN 2020038139 (ebook) |
   ISBN 9781260464368 (hardback) | ISBN 9781260464375 (ebook)
Subjects: LCSH: Corporate culture. | Organizational change. | Leadership.
Classification: LCC HD58.7 .O2183 2020 (print) | LCC HD58.7 (ebook)
   | DDC 658.3/14—dc23
LC record available at https://lccn.loc.gov/2020038138
LC ebook record available at https://lccn.loc.gov/2020038139

McGraw Hill books are available at special quantity discounts to use as premiums and sales promotions or for use in corporate training programs. To contact a representative, please visit the Contact Us pages at www.mhprofessional.com.

I finished writing this book the day before Father's Day, so it's only fitting that this book be dedicated to my father, who was my first business partner. Without his guidance and mentorship, I'd probably never have become an entrepreneur, or an author of a business book anyone would have cared about.

CONTENTS

A Blueprint to Renovate Culture

Phase One: Plan

Phase Two: Build

Phase Three: Maintain

FOREWORD

Culture is the underlying fabric that holds an organization together. When the fabric is strong, groups can endure major challenges and thrive during better times. If the fabric is tattered, groups may manage to get by, but employees, projects, and clients fall through the gaps. In cases where the cultural fabric is falling apart, groups and organizations become so dysfunctional that they are a detriment to the health and well-being of their workers, customers, and clients.

As Kevin Oakes describes in the pages that follow, few things are as important to an organization's long-term health as the culture that permeates its daily operations. Yet most companies have not spent enough time building a culture that produces sustainable benefits for the employees, customers, and communities they serve. As a result, employees show up each day and operate at a fraction of their capacity. Often, they go home with less energy than they had when they arrived. When a culture is unhealthy, customers take note. Employees' family members notice and feel the residual ill effects. But it certainly does not need to be this way.

In my estimation, organizations are the single best way for increasing the collective well-being of society. If you think about this for a moment, we spend more waking hours at work than we do engaged in any other activity. Yet for most people, time at work is rated as one of the least enjoyable experiences in a day. This creates an enormous well-being gap—one that leaves limitless social good and potential productivity untapped.

If we close this well-being gap, workers can leave work with more energy than when they arrive. They can be better friends, parents, and spouses when they get home. Employees will get involved in, and contribute more to, their communities. This starts when leaders focus on building a culture that serves a bigger purpose and demonstrably improves employees' holistic well-being.

Leading by Example Is *Not* Optional

After studying and writing books about leadership and well-being for the last 20 years, one central learning emerged: *Creating a healthier culture must start at the top.* If it does not, any initiatives to improve culture and well-being will likely fail. In contrast to programs I have seen on strengths development and employee engagement, which can be very effective in small groups and pockets of organizations, shifting an entire culture for the better is almost impossible if a company's top executives are not involved.

If an organization spends millions on an HR or benefits-driven program intended to build a culture of well-being, but has a CEO who demonstrates he does not value his own well-being, this will quickly undermine almost all these efforts. Especially when it comes to culture, leaders set the tone. If a leader is not demonstrating the values espoused, few will follow, and any downstream efforts will be perceived as an inauthentic waste of time and money. When a leader sees herself as a role model and follows the stated cultural values, employees will believe, follow, and benefit.

This role of the leader is central, and greatly magnified, in the pursuit of true culture renovation. As Kevin describes so eloquently in this book, massive social and culture change *is* possible. Reading the accounts in these chapters actually renewed my faith in an organization's ability to significantly improve. As you will hear, one powerful leadership team can change the trajectory of an important global organization in the span of a few years. Yes, it takes a lot of hard work, heavy lifting, powerful relationships, and a little patience. But if you succeed in the process of culture renovation, it could pay dividends for decades to come.

Simply put, you can build a high-performance culture that demonstrably improves people's lives *in parallel.* As you embark on a path of culture change, I challenge you to measure its effectiveness not only with traditional metrics (e.g., production, quality, retention) but also with outcomes that ultimately matter most to each of us as people.

▶ If employees work for your organization for the next two years, will they be healthier as a result?

▶ Will they be better parents, friends, or spouses because they joined your organization?

▶ Will those employees be more involved in and give more back to the local community?

▶ Can you prove employees have less stress (about work, finances, etc.) because they join your organization?

▶ Do employees feel like they are serving a bigger mission or purpose with your organization?

▶ Can they see if and how they are improving the lives of others every day?

These are rough and informal questions, but I hope they touch on more meaningful elements that can define the future social contract between people and organizations. When you think about renovating a culture, remember that extracting as much as you can out of each employee is no longer the key outcome. Demonstrating how your organization and culture build people up (employees, customers, clients, communities) should be the new gold standard.

Creating organizations and cultures that change the world starts with one leader who takes the initiative, leads by example, and inspires others to follow. As you read the stories and case studies in the chapters that follow, think about how *you* could be that spark that starts a needed fire within your organization. This is change we desperately need.

Institutions should build people up instead of breaking them down. This happens one organization at a time. Inside that organization, it begins with one leader who is determined to start a culture renovation.

Tom Rath
October 7, 2020

ACKNOWLEDGMENTS

There are, of course, many people to thank for the inspiration to write this book and their help throughout the process. I'll start with my co-founder, Jay Jamrog, without whom i4cp would not exist. Jay has been a great business partner, an insightful mentor, and a fearless leader of this organization for decades—long before he ever met me. Over most of that time he's been a culture change critic, but now he has seen the light. I appreciate him challenging my assumptions, and constantly reminding me that he studied everything I think is new decades ago.

I'd like to also thank i4cp's chief research officer, Kevin Martin, for spearheading our research on culture and many of the other research studies that are referenced—either explicitly or implicitly—in these pages. Kevin, with his unbridled enthusiasm, and his team have consistently done great work and are the foundation for what makes i4cp special.

The research team, many of whom contributed to the original culture study and the others cited, continues to produce next practices that high-performance organizations use every day. That team revolves around Lorrie Lykins, our VP of research and managing editor, whose fingerprints are on everything we publish. Other members of that team include Carol Morrison, Joe Jamrog, Kevin Wilde, Tom Stone, and Marianne Menta. Special thanks to Mark McGraw, who tirelessly transcribed many interviews I conducted, and Eric Davis for his superior graphics work in the study and the book, including his influence on the cover.

In addition to Jay and Kevin Martin, I'd like to thank the members of the executive team of i4cp who have been supportive of this effort throughout, a team that includes Jennifer Deutsch, Madeline Borkin, Mark Englizian, Mark Walker, and Norm Thomas. Special thanks to Patrick Murray who has developed numerous tools to support this effort, and Erik Samdahl who has been a primary partner in all aspects of making this book happen, and whose influence on me and i4cp probably doesn't get enough credit (by me or others).

I'd also like to thank so many other members of the team who supported me with ideas, interview subjects, and patience: Adam Mucci, Alex Mattsson, Alyssa McGaha, April Lough, Bryan Baldwin, Carrie Bevis, Chris Holtz, Chris Pascale, David Schmidt, Debra Joseph, Ellie Judd, Hayley Stanton, Jaylen Thompson, Kevin Copestick, Kevin Osborne, Kevin Schulhof, Lindsay Rice, Matthew Boman, Michele DeGabriele, Nina Holtsberry, Patricia Murakami, Pauline Camenos, Ryan Dunn, Stephanie Werner, and Theresa Corrigan.

By the way, if you haven't noticed, we have many Kevins in the company. It's a running joke, and most of us go by nicknames (I'm KO). If your name is Kevin, think twice before applying for a role at i4cp; the joke has gotten old.

As I continue my acknowledgments, I can't forget our board of directors—Andy Dale, Jeff Bussgang, John Boudreau, and Paul Esdale—who have been great partners in helping to build a fantastic organization. As an HR rock star, John has been a great coach for me, and I am forever grateful for his insight and perspective, along with former board member Elliott Masie, who has served as an endless source of innovation and creativity. I also want to recognize our longtime corporate attorney, John Robertson, who has been a constant expert sounding board and guide to me and the company over many years.

And without a doubt, most influential in all of this are our members. We are so fortunate to work with some of the top organizations and most prominent human capital executives in the world . . . many who are featured in this book and in our supporting research studies. The spirit of collaboration and community in the human capital field is unlike that of any other, and their willingness to share their next practices is what made this book possible.

Last, but not least, I'd like to thank my family—Kim, Truman, Ashley, and Audrey—for respecting my writing "process," much of it while sheltered in place, even though I think I can still hear Audrey practicing her ballet on the floor above my home office. My family appreciation extends to my parents—Gordon and Pam—and my two brothers, Brian and Tim. They formed the vocal majority of the all-important book cover artwork team, a process that I never imagined would be as lengthy and garner as many opinions as it did.

One final note: I'd also like to have a shout-out to Amazon for not only (I hope) shipping out many copies of this book, but also for sending me an email recommending it to me as "a book I might like" while I was in the middle of writing it.

That's impressive. And they were right.

RENOVATION VERSUS TRANSFORMATION

Despite the enormous influence of an organization's culture on financial performance, culture is often dismissed as too fluffy, esoteric, or abstract to have much of an impact.

Surprisingly, even the corporate governance process has traditionally overlooked, or at least underestimated, the magnitude of culture's impact on the financial stability of an organization. For years unhealthy cultures have posed tremendous risk to shareholder value, and yet that risk went largely undetected by corporate boards until it was too late. We've seen countless examples of companies that surprised their shareholders with cover-ups, ethical missteps, intentional product manipulation, or safety oversight that decimated market capitalization. "Toxic cultures" are suddenly discovered by the board, the press, and the investors, when of course they've been bubbling under the surface the entire time.

The attitude toward organizational culture has started to evolve. Progressive boards are no longer passive on this issue and are more focused on understanding the culture of the companies they govern. They are now placing more pressure on management for culture insight, metrics, and strategies—and, in many cases, changes. A big part of that is ensuring they receive impartial measures for the cultures they are governing.

"It's the aggregate ecosystem and process around listening—including employee surveys, focus groups, conversations—that's the measure of a good company with a healthy culture," said Irene Chang Britt, who sits on the boards of Dunkin' Brands, Brighthouse Financial, and Tailored Brands, among other organizations. "Leadership can say whatever it wants about the company culture, and the report-out will say what it will. But just having that process in place tells you everything about the culture of the company."

While ethical violations are one of the more pressing reasons organizations have explored changing their culture, it is far from the only reason. The desire to change culture is often triggered by a recent string of poor performances, disgruntled employees, or a new CEO. Acquisitions, and even divestitures, are often catalysts. Culture change is also frequently initiated by disruption to an industry or a desire to focus on digital transformation. It can even be the result of a pandemic or other social or political crisis.

Rarely do companies set out to change their culture when everything is calm and running smoothly, even though that is probably the best time to do it.

Culture transformation is not new. Companies have been attempting this for decades. It's also not unknown—Google the term and you'll get over half a billion hits. While the word "transformation" has long been used to describe culture change, it is not the right description. I've yet to come across a company that has truly "transformed" its culture into something completely different. As I pored over the data and case studies we collected and helped my research team with writing our original report on culture transformation, it suddenly dawned on me: companies that effectively changed their cultures were successful because they were *renovating* what they had, not starting from scratch and completely rebuilding or transforming.

Successful companies recognized that certain elements of their organization, just as in any home renovation, are the core—the foundation of what made them great to begin with. Similar to a house where you want to improve the value, companies recognize that to better compete in the future, to continuously improve shareholder return, and to attract top talent, they need to renovate.

Architectural professionals often advise would-be house renovators that if something is historical, otherwise hard to replace, and in good condition, then keep it. The key is to enhance the house's features and build upon the base. In companies, like in houses, there's often no reason to tear the whole thing down and start over. The unique traits need to be retained, and the history should be honored.

"You really need to figure out what's at the core of your culture—what you want to keep and what you want to evolve and grow," said Pat Wadors, chief people officer of Procore. "Just throwing away your culture is really hard to do, and I wouldn't suggest you do that. In fact, you have to give a nod to your past in order to move forward," advised Wadors.

Microsoft's CEO Satya Nadella agrees with Wadors. Prior to the stunning cultural shift he engineered at the venerable software company, Nadella recognized that—while you can't completely change who you are—to successfully turn around the company's business fortunes he needed to build on the past and renovate the culture.

"If you keep changing who you are, there's no chance," cautioned Nadella. "We learned from our habits in the past, where we feel like, OK, you can't be one company and then suddenly, because you're very successful, do something else. It just doesn't work."[1]

Like Nadella, François Locoh-Donou—who became CEO of F5 Networks a couple of years after Nadella—understood the cultural dilemma many new CEOs often face.

"When I joined F5 as CEO, it was almost 20 years old," said Locoh-Donou. "There was a culture that I inherited, and then there's the culture I envisioned us evolving into."

"The notion of 'culture renovation,' while I wasn't using the term then, is exactly what I was trying to do."

What made you great to begin with wasn't all for naught; in fact, it's probably a story that should be told over and over. Honoring the past is an important step before culture change can be successful, but that's only the beginning.

Why I Wrote This Book

Only 15 percent of companies that embark on culture change are successful. To find out why, my company—the Institute for Corporate Productivity (i4cp)—conducted extensive research and interviewed countless executives. We then distilled our findings into 18 steps—a culture change blueprint—for companies to successfully initiate and maintain a culture renovation.

While the mere thought of changing culture is enough to make many executives groan, the evidence is clear that—done right—it is absolutely worth the energy, time, and resources. In many ways, the stakes have never been higher. Employees want to work for a company that provides a positive holistic experience and serves a greater purpose than simply increasing shareholder value. Boards are demanding greater insight into culture nuances and want to ensure they are governing a productive and ethical culture. Consumers want to support brands that have a culture of giving back to society and a social conscience. The bottom line: organizations with a healthy culture have staying power and an enormous advantage over their competitors.

In Chapter 1, "Does Culture Predict Performance?," I begin with a story about the contrasting paths taken by two well-known Silicon Valley companies. One company had a culture marked by creativity, innovation, and a sense that all things are possible. It had an enormous impact on society and achieved extraordinary financial success. The other company suffered from leadership upheavals, infighting, and changing strategies. The workforce became tired, fearful, and cynical, and the company stumbled for many years as a result.

The different paths of these two companies reflect the bigger picture of how culture impacts performance. As our research shows conclusively, organizations with healthy cultures outperform organizations with lesser cultures in virtually every measure: revenue growth, market share, profitability, and customer satisfaction.

Organizational culture is particularly important today, given the rapid pace of change, globalization, digitization, and other disruptive forces. In Chapter 2, "The Rise of the Unicorns," I describe how technologically innovative companies have created new business models and rapidly taken market share from former market leaders. In response, many longstanding organizations are seeking to become more innovative, agile, or customer-centric. Others are expanding into new markets or countering with strategic acquisitions. For these improvements and strategies to succeed, cultures must change as well.

Even in successful companies, culture is never something to be taken for granted. Markets and society continue to evolve, and companies need to evolve in unison. The goal for leaders should be to future-proof the organization, and corporate culture is the key to making that happen. The reality is that—as the world changes, so must culture. Renovating culture is never quite complete. "You can't freeze culture in a declaration," advises Kathleen Hogan, Microsoft's chief people officer.

The responsibility for changing a culture ultimately rests with an organization's top leaders. As I discuss in Chapter 3, "Culture Renovation Needs to Start at the Top," through their actions, communications, and the values they embody, leaders provide examples for others to follow and set the tone for what is important within the organization. However, the best leaders facilitate a co-creation mindset throughout the organization by enabling and empowering the workforce to renovate successfully. As outlined in this chapter, Microsoft's successful renovation serves as a prime example. Led by Nadella, the company's culture shift has been so effective, I use it as a model for other companies in their attempts to renovate and improve their cultures.

While 18 steps can seem daunting, I divided them equally into three categories: Plan, Build, and Maintain. I'm confident that any organization that studies and implements these steps carefully will reap the benefits of a healthier culture, along with an engaged work-force, better execution, resiliency in the face of challenges, and more loyal customers.

My confidence is not only a function of the data my team and I have analyzed—it reflects extensive examination of many orga-nizations on virtually every aspect of culture and performance. Throughout the book, I document culture insights with original research my company has conducted and stories from familiar orga-nizations. The research and case studies identify not only what works, but just as importantly, what doesn't. Like most of the companies profiled throughout the book, you can be sure that the steps recom-mended will positively impact any organization's culture.

Whether renovating a house or an organization, any successful renovation starts with a detailed blueprint. I hope this book will serve as the blueprint for your next culture renovation.

CULTURE RENOVATION

CHAPTER 1

DOES CULTURE PREDICT PERFORMANCE?

S ilicon Valley has always inspired me. So many innovative companies, interesting people, smart ideas. I get energized every time I'm there.

I shouldn't say every time. On this day in late September 2009, I was not feeling particularly energetic. As I cruised down Highway 101 to Palo Alto, I was actually feeling quite nervous. My company, which I had co-founded just a couple of years earlier and went by the somewhat ominous name of the Institute of Corporate Productivity, was in trouble. Sales had nosedived, and as CEO I had to make the gut-wrenching decision to lay off several employees, including underperforming salespeople. I was in town to try to drum up new enterprise clients because, well, I was now essentially the sales team.

It didn't start like this. My co-founder and I had launched the company in 2007 when the economy was expanding and venture capital was flowing. We nicknamed it i4cp to make it sound more interesting, and we created a logo that was a little edgy for a human resources (HR) research company. I was CEO, and he was our head of research. This wasn't my first CEO gig, but it was a little bit different for me. I was fresh off my first ever series A round of funding, and I was now answering to impatient early-stage-growth investors on my board of directors—a marked change from my previous position as CEO of a public company where I mostly dealt with large institutional investors. With that new venture capital, I had hired a great team and eagerly launched what I thought would be the industry's premier workforce productivity partner to top organizations . . . only to have the economy tank a year later in the 2008 financial crisis. We quickly burned through most of that fresh capital. Now, we were in desperate need of some productivity ourselves.

In addition to being nervous, I also was a little annoyed at myself. I had flown from Seattle to the valley and only had two meetings scheduled, although both were with very large, well-known, iconic technology companies. "Better activity than the previous sales rep," I thought, as I tried to pep-talk myself into optimism.

A few minutes before 10 a.m., I pulled into the parking lot of the headquarters of my first appointment, mentally rehearsing what I wanted to cover in the meeting. As I walked to the main entrance, my private rehearsal was quickly interrupted as I became aware of an unusual ambiance. Everything seemed too quiet. Too serene. As I kept walking, I suddenly had a wave of panic. Is this the right address? I checked my phone and the number on the building, and it seemed to be.

When I opened the door to the lobby, "serene" quickly turned to "cold." A long, dark marble hallway with extremely high ceilings was between me and the receptionist at the far end of the hallway. This wasn't helping to calm the nerves. Were there any windows in this place? It felt like a scene in a low-budget comedy as my footsteps echoed off the marble while I walked toward the desk at the other end of the otherwise empty reception chamber. Despite the racket I was making, the receptionist—a guy in his twenties wearing a tie—never looked up until I reached the desk.

Tie guy acted like I was interrupting his busy morning when I told him whom I was there to meet. He wanted a number to call (don't you have that in your system, I thought?), which I nervously attempted to retrieve. I couldn't find it on my phone, so I pulled out my laptop to locate it. That was a mistake. "Did you really just bring a Dell laptop in here?" he said in a tone like he was seconds away from calling security to ban me from the premises. I sheepishly muttered something, silently cursing myself for my obvious faux pas while also silently cursing pompous tie guy and this ridiculously big marble lobby. After a couple of awkward minutes, I found the number and quickly hid the offending equipment in my backpack, hoping it wouldn't be confiscated by the brand police.

With an obvious look of disdain, tie guy dialed the number and reached the VP that I was there to see. As I waited and took in the coldness of the place, I realized this isn't the Silicon Valley I was used to. I've often experienced a much more friendly, hip, vibrant environment. And nobody wore a damn tie. This place was incredibly uninviting. It reminded me more of an IRS office than a bastion of innovation.

When VP did emerge (wearing a tie as well, leaving me feeling something I'd never before felt in Silicon Valley—underdressed), he opened a door and escorted me out of the lobby into a massive sea of dimly lit cubicles. At least that wasn't unusual. Most tech companies have their own version of "cubeville." What was unusual was that every guy was also a tie guy while most of the women were dressed like they worked on Wall Street. The ambience was a murmur of muffled whispers hovering like a low fog. They all seemed visibly miserable, crouching or sitting low as if they were trying to keep their heads down below the cube-line to avoid detection. The old proverb "The tallest poppies get cut first" suddenly popped into my head.

VP didn't say a word to anyone, and no one said a word to us as we wove our way across this expanse. As we sat in a conference room on the edge of cubeville and I presented what I had rehearsed earlier, I realized I was talking in a tone just above a whisper, and so was VP. It went unsaid, but clearly neither of us wanted to be overheard by the crouching poppies just outside.

The meeting was depressing. VP was half asleep, grim, and lacked any passion. He complained about all the mistakes management had made previously, the myriad of internal issues he was dealing with, and recent poor results. There was no hope for the future. Everything was about the past and clouded in pessimism. "No chance of a sale here at all," I predicted to myself, halfway through the meeting. After a long 45 minutes, I left, eager to get away from this macabre scene. I had plenty of things in life to be pessimistic about; this business needn't be another. I sought out a lunch spot and tried to restore myself with some entrepreneurial enthusiasm.

After lunch I arrived at my second meeting of the day and was immediately struck at the complete dichotomy between what I was seeing now and the morning experience. The parking lot was vibrant, the receptionist cheerful, and I didn't accidentally offend anyone with my brand of laptop. The glass lobby was adorned with a wide variety of trees and plants, and sunlight streamed through. There was nothing serene or cold here. People were flowing in and out of the building through the lobby, most in T-shirts and jeans (finally, standard valley dress attire), and they were smiling, laughing, and boisterous—dare I say joyful. Throughout the area were testaments to the company's growth, products, and purpose. A large screen showed real-time product adoption across the world.

Optimism started to return.

My contact arrived and walked us to our meeting room. The scene "off lobby" was much like the main one. As we wove through the hallways to our meeting room, a half dozen people greeted us along the way. Not a tie in sight. There seemed to be a positive energy at every turn, and people appeared to be happy to be at work—and visible! There was enthusiasm in the air. I had a great conversation with my contact, and he painted a picture of the future that was bright, hopeful, and confident. Not once did he blame someone else for anything. He had big plans and seemed in complete alignment with his boss (the CEO), the strategy, and the long-term vision.

I left the headquarters inspired. I couldn't wait to inject my own company with some of the same energy, joy, alignment, and hope, and to put the past behind us. I could see a future, and I wanted to paint it for my workforce. There would be better days.

A Hypothesis

Fast-forward a couple of years. Our business did turn around. We'd been gaining notoriety, growing our sales, hiring new people. We moved into new, larger offices. We launched an annual conference that eventually became the number one rated conference for HR executives. And we began focusing on next practices in our research, which we defined as people practices that had a strong correlation to market performance but were implemented in only a small percentage of companies. In fact, Next Practices became the name of our conference.

One of our new research projects focused on uncovering next practices in corporate culture. As I worked with my team on the early parts of the study, I immediately thought back to that day a couple of years earlier in Silicon Valley. Those cultures were so different, much like my company is today versus then. As I thought about next practices, I began to think about the impact culture has on market performance, and how the cultural disparity of those two companies was likely an accurate predictor of their financial performance.

I knew the answer, of course, but I quickly put it to a test. What would have happened if I had invested $1,000 into each of those companies the moment I walked out the door? I charted the ticker symbols, and the results were just as I expected. Company #1 would have yielded me nothing, while Company #2 would have more than doubled. Over time, the difference between the two became even more pronounced.

This is a story I've retold many times. I've described that day in Silicon Valley at many conferences and other keynote presentations over the years, and I always ask my audience to guess the companies I'm referring to. Company #2 is one that is often arrived at quickly: that company was Apple. Company #1, however, always proves harder to guess: Hewlett-Packard.

For anyone who knows the tech industry, you know the two companies are quite different. HP was once famous and admired for its culture, which its founders dubbed the "HP Way." The essence of the HP Way could be expressed in a few straightforward objectives: self-financed growth, highly differentiated products, respect for employees, and good corporate citizenship.

But somewhere along its journey, HP lost its way. As the Computer History Museum[1] describes it:

> When Hewlett-Packard split into two companies in late 2015, it was 15 years overdue. Hewlett Packard Enterprise got the computing systems assets and IT services and software businesses, while Hewlett Packard Inc. got the imaging and printing and PC businesses. But which elements of HP's corporate culture would the newly separate companies want to keep? HP's culture, once widely admired, fragmented during the decade and a half of large acquisitions and acrimonious leadership changes prior to the 2015 split.

Acrimonious and frequent CEO swaps certainly played a big part. Once co-founders Bill Hewlett and Dave Packard finally handed over the reins to John Young in 1978, it set off decades of leadership changes and different leadership styles. From Lew Platt's "pragmatic, nothing-fancy" approach[2] in the nineties, to the brash "perfect enough" mantra of Carly Fiorina[3] in the early 2000s, to a style so different under Mark Hurd that it was dubbed "The UnCarly" by Forbes,[4] it was clear that by the time I arrived at headquarters, the workforce had seen it all. The employees were tired, fearful, and cynical. Given all that had gone on, who could blame them for keeping their heads low?

Apple's culture, on the other hand, while often shrouded in mystery, had always possessed a different nuance. The culture reflected the original values created in 1981, and the (mostly) consistent leadership of its founder Steve Jobs until his death in 2011. Terms like "creativity," "innovation," and "excellence" are usually associated with Apple, but so too are sentences from that original value statement such as, "We want everyone to enjoy the adventure we are on together," "We are here to make a positive difference in society, as well as make a profit," and certainly what I felt on that fateful afternoon in 2009, "We are enthusiastic!"

That enthusiasm at Apple—and lack of it at HP—clearly was reflected in shareholder value over the next several years. It has provided me with some great presentation fodder.

In fact, a funny thing happened to me during one presentation that I ironically gave at a conference in Silicon Valley several years later. I told my "tale of two companies" story and did my stock price exercise and gave everyone a lesson in the importance of organizational culture. As I exited the stage, a big burly Australian guy immediately followed me to the podium as the next keynoter.

I was a bit shocked when I heard the emcee's introduction. The burly Australian was from HP. I suddenly had the sinking feeling I'd just made another faux pas in the presence of the iconic company.

My sinking feeling quickly turned to relief the moment he spoke. He loudly and laughingly told the audience, "Well, Kevin told an interesting story at our expense—but I want to tell you all he was absolutely right." Thankfully, he was very good-natured about what I had said. He went on to say HP had many well-documented problems and a huge culture issue in those days. One of his remits was to help change the culture to ensure a better future for the company.

That burly Australian was Adrian Stevens, who ever since that moment has become a friend. Adrian was head of talent management at Hewlett-Packard Enterprise at the time, and he has repeated the same story I told more than once. Culture has been a big focus for HPE since HP split into separate companies, and they've made significant progress since my visit many years ago.

Healthy Culture Traits

I often use specific examples of the impact culture renovation has on performance in presentations and show increases in market cap as the result of culture initiatives. This is when the naysayers typically speak up. Contrarians like to point out the chicken-or-the-egg dilemma by rationalizing, "Hey, if the company is performing well, the stock price continues to go up, options are in the money, and people are getting raises—*of course* the culture is going to be a healthy and happy one." I agree; a well-performing company makes many aspects easier, but it's obvious to me from the data we've collected and the companies I've worked with over several decades that a healthy culture is usually the *cause* of great market performance, not the result.

That doesn't mean there aren't successful companies with poor cultures, or companies that previously had less-than-healthy cultures that improved due to financial success. There are examples of each, but they represent a small minority. When trying to lay the foundation for future financial success, building a healthy culture first is a much easier path.

i4cp's research supports this observation. For years we've conducted research on the people practices of high-performance organizations. Our team of analysts has studied hundreds of different areas of human capital, and we delineate the results based on an organization's market performance versus its competition over the last five years. Our Market Performance Index is made up of four straightforward measures:

1. Revenue growth
2. Market share
3. Profitability
4. Customer satisfaction

We compare the top quartile of high-performance organizations versus the bottom quartile, and report on the differences. We also correlate specific practices to business impact. And when it comes to elements of a "healthy culture," it's crystal clear how they correlate to market performance.

In 2018–2019, we surveyed a total of 7,662 business professionals globally and asked them to rate their own organization's culture. As is obvious by the results displayed in Figure 1.1, market performance correlates with what most people believe are traits of a healthy culture, and the differences with low-performance organizations are pronounced.

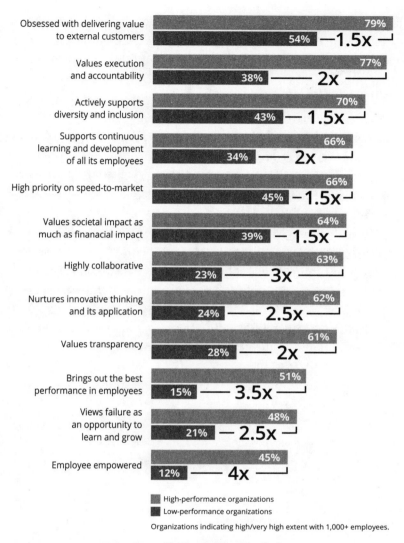

FIGURE 1.1 Traits of a Healthy Culture
Source: i4cp

While most companies would love it if employees described their organization's culture in these terms, the reality is that few companies are excellent at all of them. The vast majority of companies want to improve certain areas of their culture. That's the big reason for this book.

"We want to change our organization's culture" is a statement I've heard many times throughout my career. In a Columbia University study of more than 1,300 executives in major firms, "92 percent said that improving their culture would increase their company's value." Yet "only 16 percent said that their culture was where it should be."[5] Other studies have shown the same phenomenon. In good economies or bad, there is one certainty: changing culture is top of mind for executives at many companies worldwide.

Here's another certainty: culture change is hard. i4cp's research found that a mere 15 percent of companies declare that they have successfully changed their culture.

But of those 15 percent, a clear pattern emerged from our research, which led us to create a blueprint with 18 progressive steps to renovate organizational culture. In the chapters to come, I complement those steps with real-life case studies, data, and stories to bring them to life.

And most importantly, to help organizations raise their performance by improving their culture.

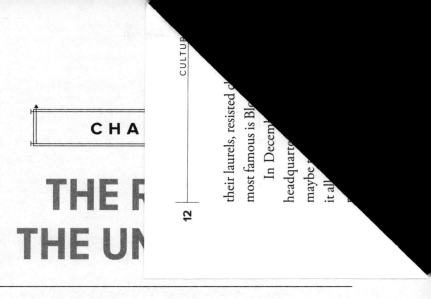

CULTUR

12

their laurels, resisted c
most famous is Bl
In Decem
headquarte
maybe
it all

CHA

THE F
THE UI

In 2013, Aileen Lee invented the term "Unicorn" to refer to start-up organizations with investor valuations of over $1 billion. Lee, a founder and managing partner of Cowboy Ventures, and formerly of famed venture capital firm Kleiner Perkins Caufield & Byers, was preparing an internal report when she came up with the moniker. A summary of the report was published by TechCrunch, and *Unicorn* was borne into everyday business lexicon.

At the time only 39 companies were considered Unicorns.[1] Seven years later the number had ballooned to well over 400. During presentations, I often use a chart showing the proliferation of Unicorns and ask audiences this question:

"What is the one thing that all of these Unicorns have in common besides a value of over $1 billion?"

The answer is they are all disrupting staid businesses and industries. Whether through technology, a new business model, or both, Unicorns are typically focused on disruption, and their valuations reflect the business opportunity that disruption promises. Most companies intellectually understand this, but it's remarkable how slow they are to change. History is littered with companies that rested on

hange, and were too slow to evolve. One of the
ckbuster Video.

ber of 2004, I had the chance to visit Blockbuster's
rs in Dallas. Like Apple, its offices were beautiful, but
too beautiful. There certainly was an air of pretentiousness to
—a visible tribute to Blockbuster's market domination and brand
ecognition.

December of 2004, it turned out, was near a high point for Blockbuster: at that time, it employed over 84,000 people in over 9,000 stores globally[2] and boasted 20 million customers.[3] It had just been spun out from Viacom, and its market cap at the time was near $5 billion.[4] Less than six years later, Blockbuster filed for bankruptcy. As of this writing, there is one Blockbuster store left in the world. Located in Bend, Oregon, it makes money selling apparel emblazoned with the slogan, "The Last Blockbuster on the Planet," and is available to rent for nostalgic slumber parties.

At the time of my Blockbuster visit, I was the president of a publicly traded software company I helped form that year called SumTotal Systems. The company was created by the merger of two previously public companies: Click2learn and Docent. I had been the CEO of Click2learn, the first company Paul Allen founded after Microsoft (the original name was Asymetrix). Paul—may he rest in peace—purchased my company in 1997 with the idea that we would IPO the new, larger entity. We did that a little over a year later, and I quickly became CEO and chairman.

The whole experience for me was trial by fire. I had very rapidly gone from a young entrepreneur who had never raised a round of financing (I bootstrapped my first company with loads of help from my father) to running a public company founded by a software icon. With Paul on our board of directors, meetings were always a tad intimidating, but working with Paul had plenty of perks. Going to lavish parties on his estate with plenty of celebrities in attendance, flying on his custom 757 to sit courtside at Portland Trail Blazers games, and watching the Seattle Seahawks from the owner's suite are indelible memories.

But it wasn't always fun. We garnered more than our fair share of attention for a small company because anything Paul was involved with was covered intensely by institutional analysts and the press. The analysis of our business was extreme—and that only intensified with the sudden dot-com crash of 2000 (and at the time with "dot-com" in our name). Our stock price was often significantly challenged, and we sweated out the threat of being kicked off NASDAQ more than once. We also were one of the first to be affected by the new Sarbanes-Oxley Act and spent a small fortune with consultants who helped us comply with the new reporting requirements. We persevered and pulled through, but the entire experience certainly tested my—and the company's—agility.

Complacency Breeds Failure

Agility is certainly not a word most would associate with Blockbuster.

There's a now infamous story of how Netflix CEO Reed Hastings approached Blockbuster in 2000 to buy his company. This story was told by Netflix co-founder Marc Randolph in his book *That Will Never Work*, which is beautifully summarized by *Inc.* magazine:[5]

> Netflix, which was only a DVD rental-by-mail service in 2000, was struggling. Two years earlier, Netflix executives turned down a buyout offer from Amazon. Although its business model was catching on with consumers, it was far from profitable. An acquisition by Blockbuster would solve its immediate financial problems and would position the company for further growth and eventual profitability.
>
> Netflix executives had been requesting a meeting with Blockbuster's leaders for several months. Suddenly, they received a message that Blockbuster wanted to meet them the following morning, which was less than 12 hours away. With no commercial flights available, Netflix executives

chartered a plane—Vanna White's plane, oddly enough—and arrived in Dallas at the appointed time.

Netflix CEO Reed Hastings was up front about his agenda: "We should join forces," he is quoted as saying in the book. "We will run the online part of the combined business. You will focus on the stores. We will find the synergies that come from the combination, and it will truly be a case of the whole being greater than the sum of its parts."

In response, Blockbuster general counsel Ed Stead asserted that Netflix and many other online businesses would never make a profit. Netflix executives argued the point, until Stead suddenly interjected: "If we were to buy you, what were you thinking? I mean, a number."

"Fifty million," Hastings responded.

At that moment, Randolph wrote that he noticed an odd expression cross Blockbuster CEO's John Antioco's face. "As soon as I saw it, I knew what was happening: John Antioco was struggling not to laugh."

Unsurprisingly, Blockbuster turned down Netflix's offer. It was long ride back to airport for the Netflix team.

Blockbuster's lack of interest turned out to be a blessing. Netflix became a Fortune 500 company, with a market capitalization approaching $200 billion. While it's laughable now to think Blockbuster passed up the opportunity to buy the company for $50 million, a big part of the reason is the arrogance and comfort the entire company possessed—not just Antioco—as it rested on its laurels. I've heard several times that lack of diversity in the senior ranks and board of directors at Blockbuster also played a role. Basically, being so homogenous at the top, the company was unable to see that streaming media would quickly make the DVD rental business obsolete. To Blockbuster's credit it did enter the streaming market; but with an infrastructure and culture that was built around physical stores and physical media, it was clearly too late.

Blockbuster, like many other companies, probably would have benefited by internalizing the observations of the late Andy Grove, president and CEO of Intel: "Success breeds complacency. Complacency breeds failure."

Every successful organization needs to prioritize the ability to spot trends that will change the marketplace and disrupt the way it operates. Truly agile organizations can identify the opportunities that will arise from new technologies, regulatory changes, shifts in customer demographics, and other market developments. And they use those opportunities to innovate in anticipation of future market opportunities.

"The hallmarks of agile organizations are being externally oriented and outcome-driven," says Deb Bubb, an HR executive at IBM. "Agile organizations take insights from their customers and use them to adjust their approach in order to achieve better outcomes."

The 3 A's of Agility

In research we conducted for a study titled *The Three A's of Organizational Agility: Reinvention Through Disruption*, we discovered that high-performance organizations are twice as likely to share and discuss external information about customers, the market, technology, data, and trends with midlevel managers and frontline leaders, as shown in Figure 2.1. And it isn't sporadic with the best companies— they discuss these developments regularly, at least quarterly. I don't know this for certain, but I'd be willing to bet that is not something Blockbuster did on a regular basis.

In fact, I often suggest to companies that they should create a "kill the company" committee internally. By assembling a cross-functional, diverse yet small group whose motive is to brainstorm ways to disrupt the current company, organizations can stay ahead of the Unicorns lying in the weeds and be better prepared for the future. This is one way organizations can create a change-ready culture, and is

This external (outside-in) focus cannot be overestimated in its impact and is reflected in the two variables in i4cp's Agility Effectiveness Index that have the strongest correlations to market performance:

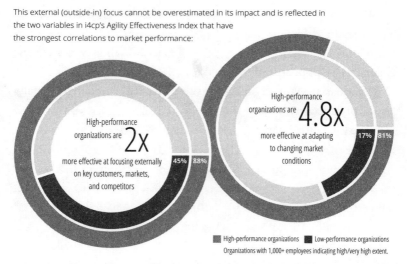

FIGURE 2.1   External Focus of High-Performance Organizations
Source: i4cp

a strategy that can be employed in the first step of our 3 A's of Agility, which are:

1. **Anticipate.** View change not only as expected and manageable, but as a chance to disrupt both within the organization and in the industry.
2. **Adapt.** Break down rigid silos and hierarchies to enable knowledge sharing, continuous learning, and teamwork, and purposefully instill an inclusive, collaborative spirit in the workforce.
3. **Act.** Determine specific areas within the organization that must become more agile. Restructure to minimize hierarchy and bureaucracy as well as empower individuals and diverse, self-directed teams—no matter their proximity—to make decisions and get things done.

How your organization perceives change is a big part of being agile. Would your employees describe change as overwhelming, wearing them down, or destabilizing to what they do normally? If so, you are likely inside a low-performance organization. High-performance organizations are more likely to say change is normal, and in fact part of the business model, as depicted in Figure 2.2. They typically view change as an opportunity to "shake things up" in a positive way on a regular basis. Many organizations feel that regular change actually boosts productivity.

The idea of never letting anything in the organization stay stable for too long to increase productivity was made famous through a research project that dates back almost 100 years. Dubbed the "Hawthorne Effect," it is one of the best-known and most controversial studies ever conducted on workforce productivity. It was named after a series of experiments that took place at the Western Electric factory in Hawthorne, a suburb of Chicago, in the 1920s and '30s. The Hawthorne plant employed about 35,000 people and supplied telephone equipment to AT&T.

While what actually happened remains debated, the lore of the study is interesting. Conducted for the most part under the supervision of Elton Mayo, an Australian-born sociologist who eventually became a professor of industrial research at Harvard, the experiments were intended to study the effects that lighting levels had on employee output. One day, the lighting in the work area for one

How does your organization perceive change?

17% As part of our business model—to be the disruptor
6%
23% As an opportunity—we like things shaken up
9%
44% As normal—expected and manageable
30%
6% As a threat—destabilizes what we do
21%
9% As wearing us down—too much for too long
27%
1% As overwhelming—beyond our ability to manage
7%

+ Positive perception of change

Negative perception of change −

■ High-performance organizations ■ Low-performance organizations
Organizations with 1,000+ employees indicating high/very high extent.

FIGURE 2.2 How Organizations Perceive Change
Source: i4cp

group was turned up and made much brighter, while another group's lighting remained unchanged. The result was that the productivity of the more highly illuminated workers increased much more than that of the control group.

The researchers began to make other changes to select groups (working hours, breaks, etc.), and in most cases productivity improved when a change was made, even when the lights were dimmed. Supposedly, by the time everything had been returned to normal, productivity was at its highest level, and even absenteeism had plummeted.

The studies didn't actually gain notoriety until the 1950s when different researchers concluded that it wasn't the changes in lighting or other physical conditions that affected workforce productivity. Instead, it was because employees felt for the first time that someone was paying attention to the work environment and the workers themselves.

The philosophy that constant change can improve productivity is a fact that is backed up by a great deal of research. Whether workforces like change or not, they need to get used to it. The corporate landscape is under constant change. Almost 90 percent of the companies listed in the 1955 Fortune 500 are nowhere to be found on the same list today.[6] In fact, the life expectancy of a company in the Fortune 500 was originally around 75 years. It has plummeted to less than 15 years.[7]

If you review the market caps of the top five companies over just the first two decades of the twenty-first century, it's fascinating to see the dramatic shift in corporate valuation in a relatively short period of time. At the beginning and through the middle of the 2000s, General Electric had the highest market capitalization of any company. GE's fall since those days has been precipitous. From its peak, the stock price has been cut in half, cut in half again, and then cut in half again. The 80 percent plummet in that time has been historic (Figure 2.3).

The last original member of the Dow Jones Industrial Average, GE, was dropped from the blue-chip index in June of 2018 and replaced by the Walgreens Boots Alliance drugstore chain. Now if I had predicted in 2004 that in less than 15 years GE would be replaced

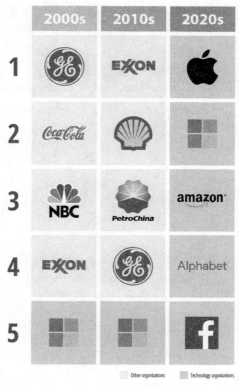

FIGURE 2.3   Top Five Companies by Market Capitalization
Source: Microsoft

on the Dow by Walgreens, I would have been the laughingstock of the business community. But in the two decades since the dot-com crash, there has been tremendous movement in valuations, and the list is now dominated by technology companies. Only one company has managed to keep its hold in this most-valuable pantheon: Microsoft. When it comes to agility, resilience, and ability to change the culture, Microsoft is a remarkable story. But it hasn't been an easy path, even for one of the world's best-known organizations. Of all culture change initiatives in modern history, Microsoft is probably the best example of how to successfully *renovate* your culture. But as outlined in the next chapter, we need to go back several years to truly appreciate the impact of the company's turnaround.

CHAPTER 3

CULTURE RENOVATION NEEDS TO START AT THE TOP

At the turn of the century, Microsoft was on top of the world. Its operating system and applications powered most of the world's computers. Its stock had hit a pre-split all-time high of $119.94 a share at the end of 1999 for a market cap of $583 billion (at the time a record for all companies), and "Microsoft millionaire" was a term commonly used in the industry due to the company's ability to quickly make employees rich through equity grants.

Then, two weeks into the new decade, co-founder Bill Gates announced he was handing over the CEO duties to Steve Ballmer. The news surprised most everyone.

"I was stunned when Bill announced that he was stepping aside to become 'chief software architect' in January 2000, with Steve Ballmer succeeding him as C.E.O.," recalled the other co-founder, Paul Allen. "While Steve had long served as Bill's top lieutenant, you got the sense through the nineties that he wasn't necessarily being groomed for Microsoft's top spot. I'd say that Bill viewed him as a very smart executive with less affinity for technology than for the business side—that Steve just wasn't a 'product guy.'"[1]

Within a year, Microsoft's market cap dropped in half, and employees' stock options—the ticket to becoming a Microsoft millionaire—were now underwater for many and essentially worthless. Microsoft wasn't alone; the dot-com crash affected most companies. But Ballmer was now faced with a reality that Gates never had to endure: a company that was suddenly struggling and needed to reinvent itself.

The story of how Gates and Allen created Microsoft is well-known. But lesser known is how Microsoft's second CEO got involved in the first place.

Ballmer was born in Detroit, and his father was a manager at the Ford Motor Company (Ballmer will only own and drive Ford vehicles out of loyalty). Ballmer graduated valedictorian from Detroit Country Day School and was accepted to Harvard. In 1977, he graduated magna cum laude with a BA in applied mathematics and economics.

While at Harvard, Ballmer was very active. He was a manager of the football team and a member of the Fox Club. He worked on the *Harvard Crimson* newspaper as well as the *Harvard Advocate*. But most fortuitously, he lived down the hall from Bill Gates in their sophomore year. They became good friends and stayed friendly even after Gates dropped out.

After college, Ballmer worked as an assistant product manager at Procter & Gamble for two years, where he somewhat ironically shared an office with Jeffrey R. Immelt, who later became CEO of GE. After briefly trying to write screenplays in Hollywood and then enrolling in Stanford Graduate School of Business, he quit grad school at the behest of Gates to join Microsoft.

Ballmer was employee number 30 when he joined as a top executive in 1980, before Microsoft hit it big with MS-DOS on the first IBM PC. Throughout the next two decades he was in the middle of the company's rise to stardom, but not nearly as well-known as Gates or Allen. While his appointment to the CEO role was a surprise, most insiders could appreciate his devotion. Throughout his career his loyalty to the company was proudly and constantly displayed. Almost everyone would agree that Steve bled and sweat (literally) all things Microsoft.

His style, however, was quite different from Gates's. It certainly was not for the fainthearted and could equally be described as both passionate and violent.

The passion has been forever memorialized in a famous video, usually referred to as the "monkeyboy video," where a sweat-drenched Ballmer runs across stage, arms flailing, screaming: "Whoo! Whoo! Come on, get up, get up, get up! I! Love! This! Company! Yesssss!" According to a review of a biography on Ballmer, one tech columnist likened those gyrations to "a moose being poked with a cattle prod and maybe enjoying it a bit too much." Another suggested Ballmer seemed in need of medical attention.[2] In another famous video, he perspired his way through a chant of "developers, developers, developers." While most outsiders find the videos hilarious, reportedly those who knew him were not surprised. According to the *New York Times*, Ballmer had, after all, once shouted "Windows! Windows!" so furiously at a sales meeting in Japan that he ripped his vocal cords, requiring surgery.[3]

While it was clear Ballmer was Microsoft's top cheerleader, he also was known for a violent streak. In 2004, Ballmer reportedly displayed that violence after hearing news that Mark Lucovsky, an employee, was resigning to join Google.[4]

In legal documents, Lucovsky said: "Prior to joining Google, I set up a meeting on or about November 11, 2004 with Microsoft's CEO Steve Ballmer to discuss my planned departure. . . . At some point in the conversation Mr. Ballmer said: 'Just tell me it's not Google.' I told him it was Google. At that point, Mr. Ballmer picked up a chair and threw it across the room hitting a table in his office." While doing so, he also is reported to have exclaimed of Google's Eric Schmidt, "I'm going to f***ing bury that guy, I have done it before, and I will do it again . . . I'm going to f***ing kill Google."[5] To this day, Ballmer denies ever throwing a chair across a room.

However, I'd be willing to bet anything it's a true story. A former finance executive once described to me a meeting with Ballmer in which she had prepared a large book of research. At the beginning of the meeting he asked, "What's this . . . do we need it for our meeting?" When she said no, it's merely for backup, he picked up the volume of data and threw it across the room. Another employee told me that he and other employees were so amused by a hole Ballmer had punched in the wall after a heated discussion, they put a frame around it.

A Need to Reinvent

While these stories are amusing today, it's important to understand the pressure Ballmer was under when he took the CEO reins. He inherited the most valuable company in the world, but one whose success relied on a near monopoly of desktop computers that ran on Windows, Word, and Excel. That hold on the market was being challenged. Aside from the dot-com crash, the world of technology was rife with disruptions during his tenure: the exploding popularity of the Internet and cloud computing, the complete digitization of media, the introduction of smartphones, and the popularity of tablets to name a few. Microsoft simply couldn't continue to monopolize the end user.

As the years ticked by, it was apparent to almost everyone that Microsoft needed to reinvent itself. It was also apparent that Ballmer was probably not the guy to do it. And after 14 years at the helm, Ballmer admitted that people were probably right, and resigned.

While most would say the Ballmer years were largely wasted, one could argue in hindsight that he was actually quite effective. He tripled annual revenue, from $23 billion to nearly $78 billion, and grew net income to $21.8 billion. He oversaw the launch of the Xbox and Kinect, acquired Skype and Yammer, and introduced new versions of Windows that continue to dominate the PC market, all while maintaining Microsoft's status as one of the world's most valuable companies.

However, the mistakes during the Ballmer regime are impossible to ignore. The company's market share of operating systems fell from 96 percent globally when Balmer took over to 35 percent by the time of his exit. Primary competitors such as Apple and Google carved large markets out of traditional Microsoft strongholds and profited from multiple innovations, many of which Microsoft had already created but failed to execute on. And the stock price during those 14 years was, at best, flat.

"He pretty much oversaw the decline of Microsoft," said Jim McKelvey, co-founder of mobile payments firm Square.[6]

Others were harsher. The *New Yorker*, in a scathing article published immediately after Ballmer's resignation, said, "Ballmer proved to be the anti-Steve Jobs. He missed every major trend in technology."[7] The article went on to say:

> Steve Ballmer, the C.E.O. of Microsoft, finally figured out a way to make some money for himself: he quit. This morning, Ballmer announced that he will retire within the next twelve months. The company's stock surged; Ballmer is now worth about a billion dollars more than he was on Thursday.
>
> Ballmer is roughly the tech industry's equivalent of Mikhail Gorbachev, without the coup and the tanks and Red Square. When he took control, in 2000, Microsoft was one of the most powerful and feared companies in the world. It had a market capitalization of around five hundred billion dollars, the highest of any company on earth. Developers referred to it as an "evil empire." As he leaves, it's a sprawling shadow. It still has cash—but that matters little.

The fall from grace was as precipitous for Microsoft—and almost everyone predicted it would never recover.

"I see Microsoft as technology's answer to Sears," said Kurt Massey, a former senior marketing manager, in 2012. "In the 40s, 50s, and 60s, Sears had it nailed. It was top-notch, but now it's just a barren wasteland. And that's Microsoft. The company just isn't cool anymore."[8]

Externally, the company wasn't cool from a customer perspective, primarily due to a litany of failed products during the Ballmer years. The list is so long and includes such a wide range of both hardware and software products, it's hard to believe so many failures came from one of the most successful companies in history. Not only is the sheer volume of failures impressive, but most were ultimately perfected by Apple, Google, and Amazon.

There's also a long list of failed acquisitions, including aQuantive, Danger, and even Skype, which Microsoft probably paid too much for in hindsight. However, the most famous and worst deal in the Ballmer era was the $7.5 billion acquisition of Nokia in 2014. The deal, the last major act by Ballmer before he departed, was largely done at the insistence of Ballmer. It was squarely focused on his intention of being a dominant player in mobile, but within a year and a half the company ended up writing off around $6.3 billion of the deal and laid off nearly 8,000 employees, costing the company an additional $750 million to $850 million.

Acquisitions, of course, are tricky. And while it's always hard to get unanimous consent from the executive team and the board, there was one notable detractor of the Nokia acquisition among the Microsoft executive team. His name was Satya Nadella.[9]

A Search for a Successor

When Ballmer announced in August 2013 that he would step down within 12 months, the word most commonly used to describe this in news stories was "shocked." There had been almost no speculation of his departure, even though there was a widespread view that Ballmer was not the leader the company needed to navigate the future. The announcement came weeks after the company conducted a major reorganization and delivered an earnings report that showed across-the-board weakness in the business, including dismal sales of the company's new Surface tablet and a lukewarm reaction to the Windows 8 operating system.

In a statement, Microsoft said Ballmer would retire "upon the completion of a process to choose his successor. In the meantime, Ballmer will continue as CEO and will lead Microsoft through the next steps of its transformation to a devices and services company that empowers people for the activities they value most."

Investors applauded the news by sending Microsoft's shares surging more than 7 percent, immediately adding $24 billion to the company's market capitalization. Columnists joked it was the best move Ballmer had made in 14 years. Focus quickly turned to Ballmer's successor.

There were many candidates speculated to be in the running. Prominent external candidates included Alan Mulally (then CEO of Ford and previously Boeing), Stephen Elop (CEO of Nokia and former Microsoft executive), Steve Mollenkopf (COO of Qualcomm), Bill Veghte (COO of HP and former Microsoft executive), Paul Maritz (CEO of VMware and former Microsoft executive), Vic Gundotra (SVP of engineering at Google and former Microsoft executive), and Sheryl Sandberg (COO of Facebook), along with internal candidates including Tony Bates (CEO of Skype), Kevin Turner (COO), Tami Reller (VP of marketing), Julie Larson-Green (EVP of Microsoft's Devices and Studios group), and Satya Nadella (EVP of Microsoft's Cloud and Enterprise Group).

What most news reports missed was that Mollenkopf was the primary target for the role, according to Qualcomm insiders. Microsoft felt it desperately needed traction in the mobile market, and Mollenkopf's expertise and experience as the COO of the world's top mobile chip designer was enticing.

As soon as news of Microsoft's interest became known, Qualcomm acted quickly. It immediately promoted Mollenkopf to CEO to prevent its star executive from leaving.[10] It had been a given that Mollenkopf was in line to eventually succeed CEO Paul Jacobs, the 51-year-old son of former CEO Irwin Jacobs (a Qualcomm cofounder), but that plan was accelerated. As part of the plan, Jacobs moved to the role of executive chairman.

"Our executives are very talented and very sought after," Jacobs said at the time when asked by Reuters whether the promotion was related to an offer from Microsoft. "The timing is a little faster than we originally planned but the key thing is to make sure we kept management continuity."

Less than two months later, on February 4, 2014, Nadella was named CEO. And unbeknown to anyone at the time, one of the most dramatic and successful culture renovations in history began on that day.

The Epitome of Culture Renovation

Nadella was relatively unknown outside of Redmond. Internally, those who did know him felt he had an unusually firm grasp of both the technical and the business side of Microsoft; yet he also had a knack for pushing the tech giant in new directions.[11]

"If you're looking for your most Gates-like president—in terms of really having technology genius plus business genius—Satya seems like the best bet," said Sam Ramji, the former head of open source software at Microsoft.

Nadella, 46 at the time, had been at the company for 22 years, originally joining from Sun Microsystems. He had been leading Microsoft's Cloud and Enterprise group where he was responsible for the firm's ambitious "Cloud OS" effort to move software and storage from on-site computers to the Internet. Previously, Nadella was president of Microsoft's $19 billion Server and Tools Business, where he'd been credited with spearheading the company's push toward cloud computing. Over the years, Nadella had worked closely with both Ballmer and Gates.

Born in Hyderabad, India, Nadella studied electrical engineering at the Mangalore University before moving to the United States to study computer science at the University of Wisconsin–Milwaukee. Nadella's appointment made him the most powerful Indian-born tech executive in the world, according to Reuters. Not lost on the employees, it also made him the first Microsoft CEO to come up through the ranks.

Nadella immediately inspired the organization during his first all-hands meeting and, just as immediately, signaled he would lead the company with a style that was the polar opposite of Ballmer's. Erik Lustig, a former Microsoft director of program management, summed up that first meeting well.

"I was not immediately sure I liked him as the next Microsoft CEO, but I had no specific reason to think he wasn't a solid pick," Lustig recalled in a blog. "I simply thought Microsoft needed to bring in someone from the outside with new ideas about how Microsoft needed to adapt and change. My opinion about whether Satya was the right person for the job changed at his first company all-hands Q&A meeting."

"I may not [be] getting the wording of the exchange exactly right, but you will get the gist," wrote Lustig. "One employee asked the question, 'When will Microsoft gain market share and traction in the mobile space?' Satya's answer in effect was, 'When we build something customers want!' At that moment, I became a believer. His response resonated so strongly with me, and I felt so appreciative that he would have the courage to give that answer to a company where thousands of people had poured blood, sweat and tears into building a product they hoped would in fact not only make Microsoft viable in mobile, but revolutionize mobile experiences. He was genuine in his response, and honest in his feedback. That answer empowered thousands of employees to stop, 'Drinking the Microsoft Kool-Aid,' and be honest about their opinion of the product they were building. It enabled employees to look objectively at the competition, garner a greater respect for the work they are doing, and then bring their best work to the table every day to compete. Satya's approach to candid and honest feedback, from my perspective and point of view, is revolutionizing the Microsoft culture, products, and strategies."

Nadella's style has been described with many different adjectives—calm, introspective, humble, empathetic—all adjectives that no one would ever associate with Ballmer. But Nadella often defines himself differently.

"The one thing that I would say that defines me is I love to learn," Nadella said in his first interview as Microsoft's chief. "I get excited about new things. I buy more books than I read or finish. I sign up for more online courses than I can actually finish. But the thing about being able to watch people do great things, learn new concepts is something that truly excites me."[12]

The importance of learning has been a staple of Nadella's leadership style from the start, and his quotes on the subject are widely cited; in fact, one Microsoft employee told me that virtually every internal PowerPoint presentation begins with a Satya quote. Here are a few examples of his thoughts on learning:

> "Be passionate and bold. Always keep learning. You stop doing useful things if you don't learn."

> "It's not about the failure, it's about learning from the failures. Failure itself cannot be celebrated."

> "The day the learn-it-all says, 'I'm done' is when you become a know-it-all."

> "At Microsoft, we're aspiring to have a living, learning culture with a growth mindset that allows us to learn from ourselves and our customers. These are the key attributes of the new culture at Microsoft, and I feel great about how it seems to be resonating and how it's seen as empowering."

The last quote, recorded in the fall of 2015 prior to a keynote at Salesforce's annual Dreamforce customer event,[13] sums up the core of Nadella's effort to change Microsoft's culture, a goal he seemed to embrace from the very start of his tenure. In fact, just a couple of months later at the December 2015 annual shareholder meeting,

Nadella spoke about the critical importance of culture renovation to the company's future:

"Our ability to change our culture is the leading indicator of our future success."

Growth Mindset

Almost overnight Nadella dramatically changed the culture and, in turn, the business success of the company. He did so by embracing two words that will forever be identified with this turnaround: "growth mindset."

Those two words represent a philosophy that is at the heart of Microsoft's culture renovation. And apart from Nadella, the person most responsible for Microsoft's dramatic cultural shift is probably Carol Dweck, a Stanford psychology professor who popularized growth mindset.

Dweck grew up in Brooklyn, New York, and as a grade-school student, she experienced something that would shape her life. Dweck's sixth-grade teacher seated her students in the room according to their IQ, and according to Dweck, the students who had low IQ scores were not allowed to carry the flag during assembly or perform tasks such as washing the blackboard.

"She let it be known that IQ for her was the ultimate measure of your intelligence and your character," Dweck said. "So, the students who had the best seats were always scared of taking another test and not being at the top anymore."

Dweck was labeled as having the highest IQ. "But it was an uncomfortable thing because you were only as good as your last test score," she reminisced. "I think it had just as negative an effect on the kids at the top [as those at the bottom] who were defining themselves in those terms."[14]

Because of her childhood experience, Dweck was convinced that IQ tests are not the only way to measure intelligence and conducted extensive research on the subject. Dweck discussed that research and her experiences in the classroom while teaching at Columbia, Harvard, and the University of Illinois. After joining Stanford's faculty in 2004, Dweck documented all of this when she published *Mindset: The New Psychology of Success*, in 2007.

Little did she realize how impactful that book would be on one of the world's most powerful companies (and ultimately, many more organizations as a result).

The concept of growth mindset suggests that intelligence and talent are not fixed traits and that the true mark of success is one's ability to learn. People who adopt a growth mindset try hard to understand why they failed, and tend to rebound from setbacks quickly, while those with fixed mindsets believe successes and failures are tied to innate traits and abilities. The key to higher levels of achievement via growth mindset lies in focusing on process more than ability.[15]

The book was initially read by a key initiator of Microsoft's culture renovation: Anupama Nadella, Satya's wife. In 2014, she gave the book to her husband because she thought he might resonate with Dweck's message. That message was rolled out across the company in less than a year. Nadella fully credits Dweck's book with defining his philosophy on company culture.

"I would say that whatever change we've been able to achieve is because the cultural meme we picked was inspired by Carol Dweck and her work around growth mindset," Nadella said. The practice of being "vulnerable enough to say 'I'm not perfect, I'll never be perfect, but I can learn'—that's a good posture to have, to have a living culture that is constantly keeping up with our own aspirations."[16]

Dweck has certainly been impressed with Microsoft's adoption, and has said Microsoft is a "spectacular" example of a large organization with a hunger for new knowledge, and praises Nadella for leading by example. "We've seen a lot of places where leaders preach growth mind-set but don't practice it," she said. "It's not easy to grasp it and implement it, especially in a culture of scientists, who tend to worship natural ability."[17]

Like many great leaders, Nadella tries to simplify the idea. He said, "If you take two kids in school, let's say one of them has a lot of innate capability but is a know-it-all. The other person has less innate capability but is a learn-it-all. You know how that story ends. Ultimately, the learn-it-all will do better than the know-it-all. And that, I think, is true for CEOs. It's true for companies."[18]

At Microsoft, it's a concept that permeates the company. I'm constantly astounded how employees at all levels in the company can eloquently describe the meaning of growth mindset, and—unlike most corporate mantras—without a hint of skepticism or sarcasm. While some may try to poke holes in the science behind growth mindset, Microsoft has done a great job of using it as a rallying theme and reinforcing it throughout the organization. In fact, one of my favorite reinforcements is a small poster that is often located in conference rooms throughout its Redmond campus. The poster poses a simple question:

Is this a fixed mindset meeting or a growth mindset meeting?

Underneath this question are bullet point examples—shown in Table 3.1—of what is meant by both.

TABLE 3.1 Fixed Versus Growth Mindset

FIXED MINDSET	GROWTH MINDSET
Leads to a desire to look smart and therefore a tendency to:	Leads to a desire to learn and therefore a tendency to:
Give up easily	Persist in the face of setbacks
See failure as fruitless or worse	See failures as essential to mastery
Ignore useful negative feedback	Learn from criticism
Feel threatened by the success of others	Find lessons and inspiration in the success of others
Avoid challenges	Embrace challenges with agility

While there is nothing entirely revolutionary about the idea of growth mindset, when it was rolled out within Microsoft it was groundbreaking because of how profoundly different it was from what the company valued in the past. While "knowledge" was often a tool of power, growth mindset shifted that concept to "knowledge sharing is power." This was an acute difference from the Ballmer command-and-control days of leadership and the elitist behavior that most employees viewed as expected and rewarded.

"We went from a culture of know-it-alls to a culture of learn-it-alls," says Chris Capossela, Microsoft's chief marketing officer. "Everything we do now is rooted in a growth mindset."[19]

Nadella said it best in his book *Hit Refresh*:

> Our culture had been rigid. Each employee had to prove to everyone that he or she knew it all and was the smartest person in the room. Accountability—delivering on time and hitting numbers—trumped everything. Meetings were formal. Everything had to be planned in perfect detail before every meeting. And it was hard to do a skip-level meeting. If a senior leader wanted to tap the energy and creativity of someone lower down in the organization, she or he needed to invite that person's boss, and so on. Hierarchy and pecking order had taken control, and spontaneity and creativity suffered as a result. The culture change I wanted was actually rooted in the Microsoft I originally joined. It was centered on exercising a growth mindset every day.

The End of Stack Ranking

While many policy changes have internalized the philosophy of growth mindset, perhaps no change made as much of an impact as when Microsoft decided to scrap the performance review process that had been in place for years.

When making changes to organizational culture, it's important to inspect how the company evaluates performance and what behaviors are being rewarded. Employees are significantly influenced by how their productivity is measured, what criteria will be used to ascertain readiness for future promotions or moves, and of course how they will be compensated. A good performance review process can incent better engagement, improved job satisfaction, more creativity and innovation, and increased discretionary effort among other positive outcomes. A poor performance management process can incent just the opposite, and Microsoft's was legendary for doing just that.

Made popular by Jack Welch in the 1980s when GE was intent on "thinning the herd," Microsoft used a system called "stack ranking." Often referred to as forced distribution or forced ranking, essentially this type of system forces managers to rank the performance of everyone in their group from top to bottom. At GE, Welch would instruct managers to then get rid of the bottom 10 percent, and while this edict wasn't mandated as vocally, within Microsoft that's essentially what happened as well.

Microsoft used a common one-to-five rating, with one being the best and five the worst. Under the system, 20 percent could receive a one, 20 percent a two, 40 percent a three, 13 percent a four, and 7 percent a five. The rankings occurred twice a year, with a midyear ranking used to determine midyear promotions and an end-of-year ranking for compensation and yearly promotion decisions.[20]

"If you were on a team of 10 people, you walked in the first day knowing that, no matter how good everyone was, two people were going to get a great review, seven were going to get mediocre reviews, and one was going to get a terrible review," said a former software developer.[21]

The flaws in this system are obvious. If you applied this concept to the starting five of the 1986 world champion Boston Celtics—widely regarded as having one of the most cohesive starting units ever assembled in the NBA—you would have to jettison a key member of the team, an all-star, just because the system forced you to do so. And teamwork is often what "work" is all about—how well a team cooperates, collaborates, and works together is typically the key to success.

Naturally, there were many tricks managers used to game the system. A popular one was to keep an underperformer around so there was a sacrificial lamb to offer up when review time came. Another was to collude with other managers and swap employees back and forth to time the process. Employees had their own tricks, like avoiding working on teams with the highest performers for fear of falling to the bottom.

But the biggest flaw in the system was that it pitted employees against each other. The primary motivation wasn't to beat Apple or Google; it was to do better than the person in the next office. This created a great deal of political maneuvering, infighting, sucking up to the boss, and just plain old sabotage.

In 2011, Manu Cornet, famous for his satirical cartoons about tech companies, posted a series of humorous organizational charts designed to depict each company's culture. Microsoft's drew the loudest laughs and quickly went viral. The chart consisted of different people on a hierarchy all pointing guns at each other. It was a depiction that resonated with most inside the company.

"The behavior this engenders, people do everything they can to stay out of the bottom bucket," one Microsoft engineer said. "People responsible for features will openly sabotage other people's efforts. One of the most valuable things I learned was to give the appearance of being courteous while withholding just enough information from colleagues to ensure they didn't get ahead of me on the rankings."

While Satya wasn't directly responsible for shifting the performance management philosophy, he certainly was in favor of it. Lisa Brummel, the longtime head of HR under Ballmer, announced that Microsoft was getting rid of stack ranking in November of 2013, just three months prior to Satya's official appointment as CEO. The company replaced it with a no-rating/no-curve system that focused on teamwork, collaboration, growth, and development—all of which fits in better with Nadella's affection for growth mindset.

HR as Partner

While Satya has led the charge on Microsoft's culture renovation, he enlisted the help of a key area of the company from the start: human resources.

In his first year as CEO, Satya successfully convinced Kathleen Hogan, an 11-year veteran of the company, to become Microsoft's new chief people officer, replacing Brummel. At the time, Hogan was a very accomplished business executive running Microsoft Worldwide Services, which included customer service, enterprise support, and consulting with 20,000+ employees. She had no HR experience, but Satya was convinced she could handle the job. He was also convinced that she was the partner he needed to change the culture.

Kathleen told me shortly after she became the head of HR that she was astounded that one of the first words Satya used with her to describe his leadership style was "empathetic." I'm certain she was surprised by this because it was so different than something Ballmer would say. In fact, it's different than what many employees of any company would say. While 92 percent of CEOs report their organization is empathetic, only 50 percent of employees say their CEO is empathetic. This gap in perspective directly affects employee morale—81 percent of employees would be willing to work longer hours if they felt their employer was empathetic.[22]

But as you know already, Nadella is different. Like growth mindset, "empathy" has also been used to define Nadella's CEO tenure, to the point of publications claiming he is obsessed with it.[23]

"The value that I have learned to deeply appreciate and is something I talk a lot about is empathy," said Nadella at an event to promote his book. "I think of empathy as not just as something nice to have but [it] is core to [the] innovation agenda in the company . . . one of the things that I've come to realize is, if I look at what is Microsoft's core business, it is about being able to meet the unmet and unarticulated needs of customers and there is just no way we are going to be able to succeed in doing that if we don't have that deep sense of empathy."[24]

Like Carol Dweck's *Mindset*, another book Nadella subscribes to and had his management team read is *Nonviolent Communication* written in 2003 by psychologist Marshall B. Rosenberg.[25] Nadella handed out copies at his first executive meeting to signal that he intended to turn around a culture most knew as a hostile one, with plenty of infighting and backstabbing. In *Nonviolent Communication*, Rosenberg preaches compassion and empathy as cornerstones of effective communication.

Hogan loved Nadella's style from the start, but if she was going to help Satya effect the kind of culture change he wanted, she knew she had a steep hill to climb. From the beginning, Hogan was very conscious that she did not come from a traditional HR background and the role was critical to the success of the company.

"The steep learning curve kept me humble. I had to surround myself with technical experts in HR who complemented what I didn't bring to the table," she reflected. "I spent time with my industry CHRO peers learning how they onboarded into their roles. I had a lot to learn, and there's lots more to learn."[26]

Kathleen bought into growth mindset from the very beginning.

"Ultimately for us the primary shift includes embracing a growth mindset," she said prior to keynoting my company's annual conference in 2017. "As we've translated that into our company norms, we're moving from a place where employees felt a need to be the single source of knowledge, to a culture of collaboration where employees find more value in working together to best leverage diverse knowledge. This has also included the evolution of our performance system, which today places a premium on collaboration and contributing to the success of others. We're also moving towards a mindset that embraces risk and failure. A shared understanding that risk, failure, and experimentation are the ways to learn and innovate and that not every idea may work every time."

Hogan became such a fan of growth mindset—and Carol Dweck—that she and Dweck penned an article in *Harvard Business Review* together on how leaders are being developed through this philosophy. They wrote that "the CEO is generally the bellwether of a company's culture, and under Satya Nadella's leadership, Microsoft is emphasizing learning and creativity. Nadella believes this is how leaders are made, and that idea is reflected in several programs." Those programs are helping Microsoft with previously unidentified—yet skilled—leaders who are rising to levels they might not have in a traditional development model.[27]

The cultural turnaround at Microsoft under Nadella has been remarkable and swift, as have the business results. In a mere five years since Nadella took over, Microsoft's market capitalization grew from around $300 billion to well over a trillion, and in the process becoming the world's most valuable company. Yet you won't find Nadella talking about it.

"I would be disgusted if somebody ever celebrated our market cap," he told *Bloomberg Businessweek*[28] shortly after the company passed the historic $1 trillion mark on April 25, 2019. Nadella insists it is "not meaningful" and any rejoicing about such an arbitrary milestone would mark "the beginning of the end."

Nadella continues to push the company and consistently cautions employees not to rest on laurels. "At Microsoft we have this very bad habit of not being able to push ourselves because we just feel very self-satisfied with the success we've had. . . . We're learning how not to look at the past."[29]

Hogan completely agrees with this sentiment. "By no means are we declaring victory. We have a ways to go, and we have to earn our aspired culture every day. We have momentum, but we're always trying to close the gap between our aspired culture and the daily experience of our employees. You can't freeze culture in a declaration."[30]

Victory or not, the turnaround has been stunning, and it started at the top.

"There's a long list of other leaders Microsoft could have hired," said Aaron Levie, CEO of Box, which used to go to market by bashing Microsoft but now is a partner. "There aren't a lot of case studies about cultural shifts of the size and scale that Satya is creating."[31]

What Nadella, Hogan, and many others at Microsoft did was remarkable. They followed a blueprint for a culture renovation that should be the model for many other companies worldwide.

A BLUEPRINT TO RENOVATE CULTURE

PHASE ONE

PLAN

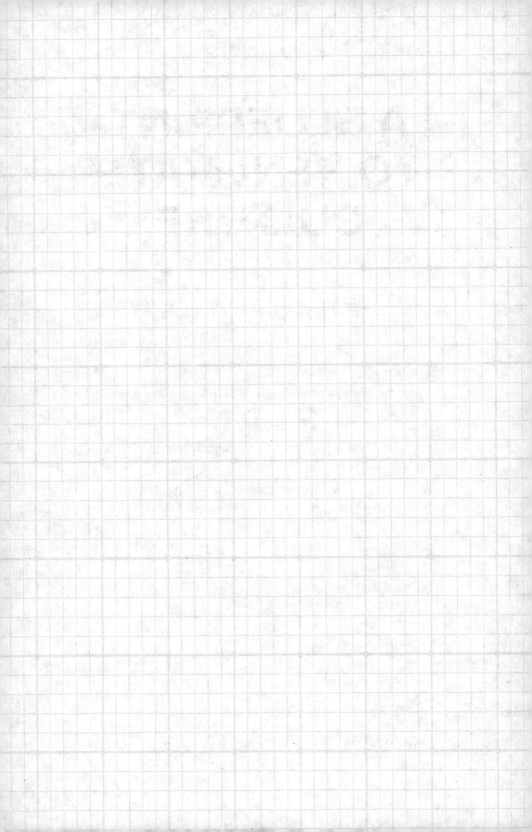

CHAPTER 4

STEP #1:
DEVELOP AND DEPLOY A COMPREHENSIVE LISTENING STRATEGY

Listen to your employees, listen to your customers,
shut the f*** up, and do what they tell you.
JOHN LEGERE, FORMER CEO, T-MOBILE

In 2012, T-Mobile was on the wane. It was losing customers at an alarming rate and had the dubious distinction of being America's fastest-shrinking wireless company.

The company has since undergone an incredible renovation—one that *Fortune* magazine called "a journey that will go down in the annals of corporate history as one of the greatest turnaround stories of all time, rivaling Lou Gerstner at IBM or Steve Jobs at Apple."[1] From 2012 through 2020, T-Mobile led the industry in customer growth almost every year, outgaining Verizon, AT&T, and Sprint combined. As a result, T-Mobile's stock price increased sixfold since the company effectively went public (through a reverse IPO) in 2013. In that same period, Verizon's stock price rose just 9 percent and AT&T's 2 percent.[2]

Credit T-Mobile CEO John Legere for most of this success. His brash attitude embodied the company's *rebel* approach to the industry. While most CEOs tend to skew toward political correctness, Legere's messaging was the exact opposite.

"At most large companies, CEOs are overly diplomatic: They never say anything negative about anyone publicly, and many even avoid speaking a competitor's name," Legere explained. "Public attitudes have shifted about the rhetoric and candor we want and expect from leaders. Look at the 2016 presidential campaign, or at how people like Mark Cuban and Elon Musk communicate. The era when CEOs needed to have every statement cleared by the legal team is over—and good riddance. People want authenticity from leaders, not canned phrases full of legalese."[3]

Legere is a great example of authenticity and the power of transparency. i4cp research has uncovered in several studies that transparency is a top hallmark of high-performance companies, and of effective leaders. The more transparent, generally the better. Yet it's often surprising how many companies systematically and consciously avoid it while at the same time preaching transparency's importance.

"I dress, act, behave, and speak the same as if I'm on CNBC, in the locker room, or out having a drink," Legere adds.[4]

When Legere first joined T-Mobile, he was appalled at the lack of transparency. He talks openly about wanting to have an all-employee meeting on his first day and being told by legal and HR that he should only talk to the senior staff. In his words, the company "was being run like a paramilitary organization." He was shocked to discover that the company had a "no piercings and no tattoos" rule— a rule that was quickly changed when he explained that his older daughter had a pierced tongue and younger daughter had six tattoos, and it was upsetting that they couldn't get a job at the company he was now running.

"When I see something I disagree with, I ask why, and when I hear the answer, I ask why again," says Legere. "It's a leadership technique you can learn from a five-year-old."[5]

Legere's desire to speak his mind needed a broader platform, and social media quickly became a key part of his brash style and leadership strategy. He described how he originally signed up for Twitter, a platform where he eventually developed an audience of well over 6 million followers.

"It happened somewhat accidentally. I was having dinner with my daughter, who thought it would be funny to set up a Twitter account for me. I handed her my smartphone. Minutes after we finished creating the account, T-Mobile's corporate security called to say that someone was impersonating me on Twitter. I assured the caller that it really was me. Our lawyers said it was a terrible idea for me to tweet, but I ignored them."[6]

While there have been plenty of outspoken, charismatic leaders in the past (think Iacocca, Ellison, or Branson), Legere took it to a new level. His tweets about his competition are now legendary. Consistently referring to AT&T and Verizon as "dumb and dumber," Legere never missed a moment to take potshots at his chief rivals. Even the order of which one is dumb, and which one is dumber, is not by accident. In true Legere fashion, the company crowned Verizon the "dumber champion" via a social media event and "research" released on its website after a great deal of promotion.[7]

"When the CEO of Verizon admitted at an investor conference that the company's new video service was 'overhyped,' I posted a link to the story with a tweet saying, 'My God, Verizon, you're making this too easy,'" Legere recalls. He goes on to say, "Then I followed up with 'If @Verizon's "realistic expectations" = spending billions to build a service no one wants/uses, then #NailedIt!'"[8]

He didn't limit himself to Twitter. With over 75,000 followers on Instagram and close to 500,000 followers on Facebook, social media quickly became part of Legere's persona, particularly his quirky yet incredibly effective streaming Facebook show titled "Slow Cooker Sunday." It's hard to imagine almost any other CEO of a Fortune 500 company doing this, but most Sundays throughout his T-Mobile career Legere would live-broadcast a cooking show, starring himself, from his own kitchen or kitchens on the road while he was traveling. With a clever mix of humor, coupled with recipes designed exclusively for a slow cooker (which Legere takes everywhere with him, branded with the T-Mobile logo of course), the show grew so popular it eventually had 5 million viewers and spawned a bestselling cookbook, authored by Legere (with business advice included).[9]

The Value of Being Different

Transparency is clearly a leadership trait that Legere enjoys. But transparency was only part of the equation of T-Mobile's turnaround. The real key was being different.

When Legere joined the struggling wireless carrier, he quickly realized he had to do something radical. The company had just ended a messy attempt to combine with AT&T that fell apart primarily due to opposition from the Justice Department and the Federal Communications Commission. To regain traction in the market, he and his team quickly focused on finding and exploiting weaknesses in Verizon, AT&T, and Sprint to take back market share, and then adopted an in-your-face approach that mirrored Legere's . . . and shook up the industry. The renovation was under way.

"It became clear that the best way to succeed in this industry was to do things as differently as possible from the existing carriers—to do the complete opposite. That was the start of the strategy we named Un-carrier."[10]

Branding themselves the Un-carrier was brilliant. If you are attempting to renovate your company, *naming* your culture renovation has great power. It gives it an identity that everyone—the workforce, the customer base, the press, investors, and even analysts—can rally around and identify. The Un-carrier identity became T-Mobile's mantra to earn a deeper relationship with customers by providing great experiences, which, in turn, reinforced the new identity. T-Mobile even created a manifesto for company operations to drive its focus from a sales-and-promotions emphasis to providing exemplary service and experiences.

T-Mobile's disruption of the industry took the form of several signature moves: getting rid of long-term contracts, enabling Wi-Fi calling, removing global roaming fees, and enabling nonstop music streaming. But long before T-Mobile embarked on this remarkable renovation, it performed Step 1, which is essential to successfully changing a culture: it listened. Top executives didn't assume they knew what employees felt about the culture or what their customers wanted. Instead they listened intently to both.

"It's kind of fun at my age to go back and talk to business-school people," Legere said. "I tell them, 'I can summarize everything you need to know to lead a major corporation. Are you prepared to write this down?' And then they get all ready. I tell them I can summarize how I succeed as a leader: Listen to your employees, listen to your customers, shut the f*** up, and do what they tell you."[11]

Before an organization embarks on a culture renovation, it needs to first understand how the current culture is perceived. In our research, two-thirds of organizations that successfully changed their culture reported that they first gathered sentiment and related data from the workforce to understand how employees viewed the existing culture and ascertain what they'd like the new culture to be.

Too often the senior team assumes it knows what the culture represents. Too often, the team is dead wrong.

Active and current listening today has become mission critical for companies. The rise of the #MeToo movement, blatant and egregious corporate and executive misbehavior, ongoing political rhetoric and divisiveness, continuing concerns about bullying and racial discrimination, and the need for inclusive and psychologically safe workplaces are all contributing to a chaotic work environment. Listening to the workforce can help uncover attitudes and issues bubbling under the surface and provide early warning signals before issues become explosive and drastically affect shareholder value.

Would Boeing have uncovered issues with the 737 earlier had it had a culture of listening? Or Wells Fargo before it was eventually fined billions over setting up fake accounts?

Listening isn't just about preventing scandals, however. It's about developing a true understanding of employee sentiment and the culture in which employees work every day. And it's not that hard. More than ever, employees aren't shy about expressing their opinions. Like it or not, there are tens of millions of comments about employee experiences on Glassdoor, Indeed, Comparably, and other sites or apps, which are the first places most job candidates turn to gain insight on a company's culture. These platforms and tools provide employees a bullhorn to broadcast their opinions in seconds.

The concept of employee listening has been greatly aided recently through technology. Natural language processing (NLP), coupled with machine learning and artificial intelligence, is giving employees a way to share their views in their own voice, rather than through Likert scale questionnaires that simply reflect their level of agreement with statements preordained by someone else. While those types of surveys usually allow employees to offer comments, it's difficult to quickly analyze employee sentiment without having to manually read thousands of survey comments and "bucket" those comments in broad general categories like "communication" or "leadership." Instead, NLP categorizes sentiment in more accurate categories to allow management to see true patterns and identify emerging issues. NLP research enables organizations to gauge employee sentiment in real time to capture how employees feel about current events and activities—a marked contrast to the traditional annual employee engagement survey and a far more accurate method to assess culture.

Think about any opinion or sentiment survey you've ever taken. Did you ever think that your answers were based on your current mood or influenced by a recent event? Most "point in time" surveys suffer from this. Ongoing, frequent surveys weed this out and eliminate "false positives" that can occur in companies around a current hot issue that dissipates a few days later. Effective NLP can provide true ongoing sentiment, not the "issue du jour" that infects the typical annual survey.

Despite the superiority of NLP in identifying employee sentiment, annual employee engagement surveys remain popular. Companies spend hundreds of millions on these surveys annually.[12] Our research shows that 89 percent of organizations reported they used their all-employee engagement survey as a mechanism to measure and/or monitor their organizational culture. But the research also showed no statistical relationship between using the employee engagement survey for this purpose and the firm's ability to achieve a healthy culture.

From the organizations my firm has talked with, it's very clear that over the last few years many companies have abandoned the annual engagement survey for a variety of reasons: it's too slow, cumbersome, expensive, and not actionable enough. When it comes to changing culture, fewer organizations are relying on this traditional tool to accurately gauge employee sentiment because they realize business now moves too fast for it to provide accurate data. Instead, they are moving to more frequent, rapid, and easier methods to gather sentiment and to analyze it more efficiently and effectively in order to act more quickly.

Some companies are even using daily questions to gauge employee sentiment. Amazon, for example, asks its employees one question a day before they log in to the network. The question is often carefully constructed to elicit discussion and healthy debate in the workforce.

One question Amazon has asked in the past, according to an employee: "Is your manager a simplifier, or a complexifier?" This fantastic question immediately makes all managers question their style. It is a good example of how to leverage pulse questions strategically.

In addition to gathering ongoing data, the question-a-day strategy can be used to infuse many different subjects in the workforce around diversity, inclusion, innovation, or other topics management would like the workforce to contemplate. Microsoft employs this method as well, along with frequent pulse surveys. The listening strategy was a key component of its renovation, and early on involved many traditional ways of understanding current culture.

"We spoke with experts, senior leaders and VPs, and numerous focus groups with a wide variety of diverse employee groups to learn about their experience, the culture they desired, what we were passionate about preserving from our history, and what we needed to leave behind," explained Kathleen Hogan.

When they were done, Microsoft had more than 50 different ways to describe its aspirations. Then the leaders did a very innovative thing. They assembled a "culture cabinet" to boil the desired culture down to simple statements and act as evangelists to roll it out. These statements embodied the growth mindset they wanted to embed—being customer obsessed, diverse, and inclusive, and to create "One Microsoft."[13]

"Together, these would allow us to make the difference we wanted to make in the world," said Hogan. Microsoft had a history of taking on bold technological challenges with real impact and giving back to the world, and these were examples of cultural attributes the company desired to retain. But the fear of failure and reluctance to collaborate that characterized a highly individualistic and internally competitive culture—as Nadella called it, "a culture of know it all's"—were attributes Microsoft needed to shed. Says Hogan, "We knew we couldn't just put out dogma or platitudes. It takes time to tap into something people really care about and want to achieve. That power has real teeth. If people recognize your final destination as someplace they want to go, they will help you get there."[14]

A Love Affair

Like Microsoft, T-Mobile also enlisted HR in its culture renovation. While most wouldn't label Legere as an HR cheerleader, HR was instrumental in T-Mobile's turnaround. The HR group picked up the Un-carrier theme and internalized it to reinvent not only the company, but themselves.

Liz McAuliffe, executive vice president of human resources at the time, recounts what it took to inspire and implement renovation in HR.

"To support T-Mobile's disruptive and revolutionary position in the wireless industry, it was obvious what we had to do. We were still an HR function, but we just weren't going to act like it anymore. We became employee obsessed. Just as T-Mobile became obsessed with eliminating customer pain points, we set out to eliminate our employees' pain points."

"We tossed old-school, anachronistic HR practices that fell flat with our workforce and offered little or no value to the business," McAuliffe recalled. "We rebranded HR as #1HR, symbolizing our cohesiveness as a 625-person team and our affinity with T-Mobile's social media presence. We recast our employee-facing teams as HR Crews, with job titles reflecting greater meaning: Employee Success Partner instead of HR Business Partner. We equipped employees with the resources, support, and tools they need for their personal growth and career success, fueling them with more energy and enthusiasm to focus on their customers' needs and operate at the speed necessary to continually innovate. As T-Mobile continues to redefine the wireless industry, we keep innovating for our employees. We won't stop."

To capture the true voice of the employee, T-Mobile's HR team launched an employee-voice program using quick pulse surveys designed to measure engagement in real time. The team also tackled employee feedback by spearheading the elimination of the annual performance reviews in favor of ongoing performance-and-development conversations that are timely and relevant.

While HR's partnership has been critical, T-Mobile's culture renovation would not have happened without Legere's visibility with the workforce.

"I visit T-Mobile call centers," Legere says. "We've got about 18 major call centers in the US, and before I was CEO, I heard that no CEO had gone to physically visit them. I go in, they meet me outside, we take selfies as I stand like a piece of furniture, I tell them about how things are going—but most importantly, I say thank you and help them see that their behavior and their work has driven the culture of the company that's changed the industry and the whole world. It's a bit of a love affair."[15]

That love affair worked. Legere and his team produced one of the most complete renovations of a corporate culture in business history. They succeeded by listening, first and foremost, and then acting on what they heard no matter how much it countered what they had done previously.

"Un-carrier is not just a marketing program," states Legere. "It's a culture. It's the fundamental basis of who we are as a company."[16]

CHAPTER 5

STEP #2:
FIGURE OUT
WHAT TO KEEP

We are not deviating from who we are.
We're building on our values and our foundation.

MIKE ROMAN, CEO, 3M

The biggest part of renovating anything—whether it's a room, a building, or an entire organization—is understanding what stays and what goes. In each, it's important not to let sentiment get in the way of progress—a common misstep. That's a big reason why gathering input from multiple voices is so important; it not only illuminates what the culture is today, but also helps determine the most positive and valued aspects of the company's historical culture to carry forward.

In our research, 57 percent of organizations that were highly successful in renovating their cultures were very intentional in ensuring that the best of the company's existing norms were preserved, and fundamental values and history were woven into the new culture.

This practice is especially important for an organization that has a long and storied history. A good example is 3M, a company that has been in business for over a century and has been in the Fortune 500 most of that time. While most know the name well, few understand the company's roots or even what it really does.

"3M" is based on the company's original name, Minnesota Mining and Manufacturing. The company was launched in 1902 in Two Harbors, Minnesota, and as the name implies, it was originally involved in mining, specifically digging out corundum—a mineral used for grinding wheel abrasives. Shortly thereafter, the company shifted to manufacturing sandpaper products, and that became the company's primary business in the early days. Today, 3M is in the Fortune 100, operates in a variety of industries and consumer markets, and produces over 60,000 products under dozens of different brands. Based just outside of St. Paul, Minnesota, the company generates more than $30 billion in sales and has almost 100,000 employees.

The concept of culture renovation could have been written entirely about 3M. The company's ability to continue to innovate and reinvent itself is legendary, and while much of it is on purpose, some of it has been by chance. As one publication put it, "those three M's might better stand for Mistake = Magic = Money."[1] Few companies have ever created more useful products seemingly by accident than 3M, an amazing historic record that many attribute to the freedom the company gives employees to make mistakes and its appreciation for innovation.

Remarking on 3M's admirable consistency and constant renovation, Bill Hewlett, co-founder of Hewlett-Packard, once said: "You never know what they're going to come up with next. The beauty of it is that they probably don't know what they're going to come up with next either."

15 Percent Time

The five original founders of 3M sound like the start of a bad joke: a lawyer, a doctor, two railroad executives, and a meat market owner. And the irony is, unlike the attitude of 3M today, they had one primary purpose when they established the company: to get rich. But "like so many others who organized mining ventures in the early 1900s," wrote Virginia Huck in *Brand of the Tartan: The 3M Story* (1955), "the founders of 3M apparently incorporated first and investigated later."

As it turns out, the primary product they set out to mine, corundum, was a horrible abrasive. As Huck described in her book, "By the end of 1904, 3M stock had dropped to the all-time low on the barroom exchange—two shares for a shot, and cheap whiskey at that."

Exhibiting the trait that would eventually become its identity, the company admitted defeat and quickly changed course. The company picked up and moved to Duluth to make sandpaper—but the problems continued. The original sandpaper products were poor, and to add insult to injury, the floor of the new office collapsed shortly after 3M moved in from the weight of the company's raw materials. But unbeknown to the owners at the time, the move to Duluth introduced to the company a fortuitous new hire who would eventually establish 3M as the powerhouse it is today.

In 1907, William McKnight, a 20-year-old assistant bookkeeper, joined 3M. Wrote Huck: "His assets were a most brief business school training [five months], inherent determination, and high ambition. No one who saw the quiet, serious boy apply for the job could have possibly predicted that in a very short time he would become the major influence in the success of 3M."

While McKnight reportedly was soft-spoken, he also was direct and efficient. By 1911, he had worked his way up to sales manager. He was known for going into the back room with a client's workmen to personally demonstrate 3M products . . . and at the same time to hear their complaints. As a result, he quickly became aware that 3M's sandpaper was an inferior product. McKnight suggested to management that communication between sales and production needed to improve—and management agreed. They made him general manager in 1914 to fix the problems he was witnessing. Early into his new job, he witnessed another problem: several shipments were ruined by an olive oil leak and went unnoticed by anyone at the company until customers complained. McKnight quickly established a research lab to test materials at every stage of production, creating the company's first quality control mechanism—the first of many creations during McKnight's tenure.

In fact, it was under McKnight that 3M's famous "15 percent time" began. For many decades, 3M has urged its employees to devote 15 percent of their time on the job to doing something beyond their usual responsibilities—such as experimenting with new technology or collaborating with others outside their work areas on new ideas and projects. Some of 3M's most famous products were the direct result of this policy, including Post-it Notes, Scotch Tape, a wireless electronic stethoscope, and many more.

Other companies have popularized this concept, most notably Google's 20 percent time, which is credited with creating Gmail and Google Earth among other products. But it was McKnight's philosophy of "listen to anybody with an idea" that was the original basis for what became 3M's 15 percent rule.[2] It all began in 1920 when McKnight received a letter requesting bulk mineral samples, and McKnight asked the originator of the letter, a Philadelphia inventor named Francis Okie, what he intended to do with the minerals. Okie said he wanted to develop waterproof sandpaper. Realizing that this would be a valuable product, McKnight bought the rights to the idea and hired Okie. By 1921, 3M had released one of its first successful sandpaper products, Wetordry. As Richard Carlton, 3M's director of manufacturing and author of its first testing manual, wrote, "Every idea should have a chance to prove its worth, and this is true for two reasons: (1) If it is good, we want it; (2) If it is not good, we will have purchased peace of mind when we have proved it impractical."[3]

It was Wetordry, and the concept of pursuing ideas, that spawned one of 3M's most successful products.

In 1923, a mechanic at a St. Paul auto body shop was having trouble painting a two-tone car because tapes at the time were poor at masking sections of the car; they left residues and generally didn't work properly. A 3M engineer named Richard Drew, who was testing Wetordry at the shop, stumbled upon the scene and resolved to address the problem. Drew spent the next two years thinking about and experimenting with masking tape before he finally found the right combination of adhesive and backing paper. The tape, which was nicknamed Scotch masking tape, ultimately became one of the most well-known brands ever. It was a hit right off the bat, with first-year sales of $164,279 and rising a decade later to $1.15 million.[4]

Soon after, Drew created an even bigger seller for 3M: cellophane tape. He witnessed a co-worker wrapping his masking tape invention in cellophane and realized if the adhesive were on the cellophane itself it would be moisture-proof. Thus, the Scotch tape we know today was born.

Encouraged by these discoveries, McKnight implored his managers: "Encourage experimental doodling. If you put fences around people, you get sheep. Give people the room they need."

To further ingrain a culture that encourages innovation and experimentation, McKnight developed what became known as the McKnight Principles in 1948—words of wisdom that today are sacred in 3M's corporate culture. The most famous passage celebrates pushing decision making lower in the organization (a key tenet of organizational agility) and celebrates initiative and the importance of making mistakes. He wrote:

> As our business grows, it becomes increasingly necessary to delegate responsibility and to encourage men and women to exercise their initiative. This requires considerable tolerance. Those men and women, to whom we delegate authority and responsibility, if they are good people, are going to want to do their jobs in their own way. Mistakes will be made. But if a person is essentially right, the mistakes he or she makes are not as serious in the long run as the mistakes management will make if it undertakes to tell those in authority exactly how they must do their jobs. Management that is destructively critical when mistakes are made kills initiative. And it's essential that we have many people with initiative if we are to continue to grow.[5]

Even in those early days, culture translated into performance. When McKnight became general manager in 1914, 3M was a $264,000 company; by the time he retired as chairman in 1966, 3M had grown into a $1.15 billion company. More important, management continued to follow McKnight's principles, and 3M kept growing for the next several decades. 3M developed many more famous inventions, expanded globally, broadened its product lines, and was widely admired.

A Commitment to Renovation

Despite its success, in the 1990s, 3M suffered the same ailment many other prosperous companies have run into: it became complacent. The *Los Angeles Times* reported in 1995 that "For decades management books have called 3M a model. Yet the glow of such compliments may have distracted the company, because in this decade 3M allowed old, less profitable products to drag down its earnings growth and stock price."[6] Some called the company "fat and happy."

In true 3M fashion, the company's leaders decided it was time to renovate. In December 2000 they brought on General Electric veteran James McNerney as CEO, the first outsider to run the company in its history. Early in his tenure, McNerney wisely pointed out: "I think we're world-class at the front end of the [innovation] process. If I dampen our enthusiasm for that, I've really screwed it up." McNerney made innovation a core tenent of his leadership, and the market cap improved almost a third during his tenure.

Today, 3M is run by Mike Roman, a veteran of more than 30 years with the company, who was named CEO in 2018. I met with Roman and explored what culture renovation means to him and the company.

"The world's changing around us. If you're not leading change, you're falling behind," Roman told me from his Minnesota home. "That's not something CEOs don't know, but that's a good reminder. That's true for strategy and your competitive value proposition, but it's also true about culture."

Although 3M has an enviable record of long-term success, the mindset of continuous improvement runs deep in the organization. When Roman was named CEO, he wanted to carry on that mantra, and he approached it by renovating what had made 3M great to begin with.

"3M always had this idea of getting better, doing better for our customers, and that brought our culture forward as much as anything the last decade," says Roman. "We've stepped up in a number of strategic areas that are critical to really maintaining the 3M value model, as I call it. It's served us well for 117 years. We built a big business. We've solved problems for customers. We've created a tremendous capability and culture as a result of that.

"We didn't launch a new cultural initiative with consultants or with a small team. We went out and engaged our employees broadly with multiple collaboration tools, listening, post-engagement steps," Roman continued. "We are not deviating from who we are. We're building on our values and our foundation, and we have some fundamental strengths that are really core to who we are. [See Figure 5.1.] Our technology, our manufacturing prowess and capabilities, our global ability to manage multiple business models elsewhere in

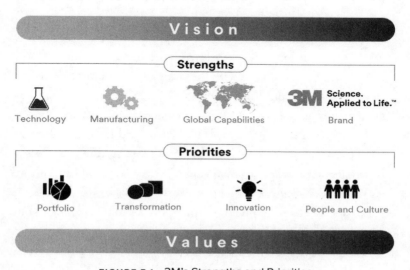

FIGURE 5.1 3M's Strengths and Priorities

many markets, and a brand that means so much to us. But that alone doesn't move it forward.

"We have four priorities. The first priority is managing our portfolio businesses. They are not permanent. We invented masking tape in 1925. We still are a leader in masking tape. Doesn't mean it should be the highest-priority organic investment in our business. We have other areas that are more leading edge. And so we have to think about our portfolio. Sometimes it means making acquisitions, sometimes divestitures.

"The second is we have to transform our company digitally. And this has been a big investment for us. Changing, deploying a new ERP ecosystem, digital tools, automating, bringing in new capabilities. You have to do that to be competitive.

"And then you have to continue to advance innovation. We have to look at how do we stay ahead of competition? How do we solve customers' problems in a fast-changing world of technology? How do we add to our technology capability? So that's kind of the fundamentals of the 3M value model. And as we move further in those leading changes in those areas, it became very clear that people and culture was fundamental to everything we were doing. None of that is successful without putting a foundation of a successful culture underneath everything we do."

Roman was fortunate that he stepped into his role on the same day Kristen Ludgate was named chief human resource officer (CHRO). Ludgate had been with the company for almost a decade in various legal, communications, and HR roles. She became an important partner to Roman as they began to renovate culture.

"Kristen and I decided early on as we stepped into our roles that we had to emphasize this, and we had to think of culture just like any other strategic priority," Roman said. "We don't win if our culture doesn't support all those fundamental strengths and priorities, so it became one of our fundamental four priorities that we think about in strategy."

"For 3M, whenever we needed to recharge the business, we've looked at culture as a tool that goes back decades and decades," said

Ludgate. "So, we're all very excited that other companies now think culture is the *thing to do*. But that's something that we would naturally turn to as an organization. We were in a position of strength, but we also knew we could not sit still. You don't want to wait until you see signs of weakness in your culture to try and change or improve it, especially given the speed of business and how central culture has always been to 3M's success."

"I love your term 'renovation'; I think it's a really nice way to think about it—what renovation is needed. We asked ourselves, how do you intentionally renovate your culture?" said Ludgate. "We knew we had to have a plan to articulate what our aspirational culture is, and then do the hard work of rewiring. But if you want to articulate what it is, you can't have this tiny little group sitting in St. Paul, Minnesota, when two-thirds of your business is outside of the United States. There's a real risk you start on a culture project and you don't actually create anything that's relevant for the majority of your people. I think the only solution to that is the ongoing listening."

Like T-Mobile and others, 3M employed a listening strategy to ensure management didn't assume it knew all aspects of the culture. It sought input from everyone throughout the organization, from the leadership team right on down to production workers.

"We engaged the top leadership team, we engaged our board, we tapped 3Mers from all over the world to sit on focus groups and advisory panels, and we established a cross-functional core team," said Ludgate. "We then took some early thinking out into the organization through crowdsourcing. We've been amazed at the level of response—we received 21,000 ideas from employees in every region about what they loved, what they needed more of, and their ideas for how to advance our culture. That deep listening has been really important. And, of course, deep listening is itself a way to announce a change of culture."

To ensure it didn't do this in an insular way, 3M's leaders looked at other companies for benchmarks. They didn't have to look too far, as it turned out. Amy Hood, chief financial officer of Microsoft, had been on 3M's board since 2017.

"When we activated our culture project, we asked, who do we want to talk to and benchmark with? And there was Amy and Microsoft right there," Roman recalled. "They were at the leading edge, and so we engaged with them. One of the things that we learned early was the importance of activating culture first, not redesigning or innovation, but get a focus on culture. And it served us well. If you look at our cultural elements, they aren't the same as Microsoft, but they resonate similar. I think Microsoft, if anything, got us excited about what we were intuitively thinking we wanted to do."

In addition to benchmarking with others, the principles that William McKnight originally laid out are followed to this day by Ludgate, Roman, and other 3M executives.

"It's the idea that we can try something, and if it's not perfect, we'll make it a little better tomorrow. We need to work on our culture that way," Ludgate says. "We're a science company. The experience of hypothesizing, iterating, learning, and improving—we need to be willing to do that with the processes, policies, and practices that support our culture. We think of this as wiring our culture into our organization, and it's an ongoing evolution."

CHAPTER 6

STEP #3:
SET YOUR CULTURAL PATH

A company can only achieve greatness if its purpose, culture, and brand are in sync.

JOAN AMBLE, BOARD MEMBER AT ZURICH INSURANCE, SIRIUS XM HOLDINGS, AND BOOZ ALLEN HAMILTON

When embarking on a culture renovation, one of the hardest decisions is what path to set for the direction of the company. Ideally, this decision will create something of a North Star that will guide the company's path for decades to come. In the spirit of renovation, the new direction should acknowledge and embrace past successes, but set up the organization to forge new ground into an unknown future.

Typically, the new direction is arrived at through the collective agreement of the senior team and the board. The new direction is usually encapsulated in a few words that are often carefully and painstakingly crafted into a statement—preferably one that is concise, pithy, and easily remembered. If it's done well, it will provide inspiration and direction to employees for generations. Many CEOs and senior teams struggle on this first step. What's the best way to start?

"We created a purpose statement," said Betty Thompson, chief people officer at consultancy Booz Allen Hamilton, in describing how company leaders began their culture renovation. "I know everybody has those, but it was really important for us. We spent a lot of time as a leadership team on it. And ultimately we said our purpose is *to empower people to change the world.*"

The concept of purpose is not new. David Packard of Hewlett-Packard fame shared his thoughts on purpose with a training group in 1960:

> I think many people assume, wrongly, that a company exists simply to make money. While this is an important result of a company's existence, we have to go deeper and find the real reasons for our being. As we investigate this, we inevitably come to the conclusion that a group of people get together and exist as an institution that we call a company so they are able to accomplish something collectively which they could not accomplish separately. They are able to do something worthwhile—they make a contribution to society (a phrase which sounds trite but is fundamental). . . . You can look around and still see people who are interested in money and nothing else, but the underlying drives come largely from a desire to do something else—to make a product—to give a service—generally to do something which is of value.[1]

While today many organizations have vision/mission/values statements, the concept of "purpose" has usurped those traditional statements. When a defined sense of personal and work role purpose is combined with a higher sense of organizational purpose that goes beyond profit, employees become more engaged and performance improves. Engaged companies are proved to be more successful, productive, and sometimes even endearing to society. In fact, a 2010 Burson-Marsteller/IMD Corporate Purpose Impact study found that a strong and well-communicated corporate purpose can contribute up to 17 percent improvement in financial performance.[2]

An Enduring Purpose

Sense of purpose has become an expectation of both current and future employees, and organizations are under pressure to exhibit purpose in their operational practices. Most established companies have a purpose statement, and if it still applies, there is no reason to change it. Some companies, like Johnson & Johnson, have maintained their statements for decades without change, but not all purpose statements are as enduring as J&J's. Some companies outgrow their purpose statements and need to renovate their statements to reflect their new identities.

As an example of this, let's revisit Microsoft. The original "mission" that Bill Gates adopted for the company in 1980 was ambitious, but simple:

A computer on every desk and in every home.

If you are old enough and think back to 1980, you realize that was a lofty goal at the time. It was uncommon for homes to have a computer in the early eighties. Computers were expensive, clunky, and complicated. For Microsoft, it was a decent mission as a young company. But it's also a mission with an end state, something Satya Nadella objected to.

"When I joined the company in 1992, we used to talk about our mission as putting a PC in every home, and by the end of the decade we have done that, at least in the developed world," Nadella told *USA Today*.[3] "It always bothered me that we confused an enduring mission with a temporal goal."

A good purpose does just that; it captures *why* the company does what it does, and it endures through time. Nadella recognized that the company had outgrown its original mission, but he also realized new and existing employees would be attracted to the company if it had a grander purpose. So, one of his first acts in renovating Microsoft's culture was to change the mission to be something bolder and more enduring. He changed it to:

> To empower every person and every organization on the planet to achieve more.

Crafting the right purpose statement is tricky. The trap that many organizations fall into is they feel pressured to create a purpose because that is what is expected. If the purpose is hollow or purely marketing-driven, most will see through it. If the purpose is boring and wordy, it can have the opposite effect; rather than inspiring current and future employees, it can contribute to apathy and sometimes even cynicism. In creating a purpose statement, there are a few guidelines to consider:

- ▶ **It should be relevant.** A purpose statement needs to speak to customers and employees. It should relate to the products and services provided by the company.
- ▶ **It should operate on many levels.** The purpose needs to work on a macro level for large initiatives, as well as a micro level for everyday issues.
- ▶ **It should evoke emotion and differentiation.** A statement should not be so bland that it sounds like it applies to any company. Instead, it should be unique, pithy, and powerful.
- ▶ **It should be enduring.** A good purpose statement should be as relevant in the future as it is today.

Let's look at 10 purpose statements that I think hit the mark:

1. **Merck:** Our purpose is to preserve and improve human life.
2. **Google:** Our purpose is to organize the world's information and make it universally accessible and useful.

3. **Twitter:** To give everyone the power to create and share ideas and information, instantly, without barriers.

4. **Nordstrom:** To give customers the most compelling shopping experience possible.

5. **Tesla:** To accelerate the world's transition to sustainable energy.

6. **Starbucks:** To inspire and nurture the human spirit—one person, one cup and one neighborhood at a time.

7. **TED:** Spread ideas.

8. **Nike:** To bring inspiration and innovation to every athlete in the world. If you have a body, you are an athlete.

9. **Patagonia:** We're in business to save our home planet.

10. **CVS:** Helping people on their path to better health.

Some of these will inevitably resonate more than others. The pithy purpose statements, like TED's "Spread ideas," are easily relatable and help guide employees in making decisions. But let's look at the last one by CVS as an example of decision guiding.

Being True to Purpose

In February of 2014, CVS made a bold and surprising announcement that it would discontinue the sale of tobacco products at its 7,800 US retail locations, a decision that would cost the company about $2 billion annually in lost sales from tobacco shoppers.[4] Larry J. Merlo, president and CEO of CVS, said in a statement at the time the reason was clear-cut: "Put simply, the sale of tobacco products is inconsistent with our purpose."

Others also chimed in.

"As one of the largest retailers and pharmacies in America," said President Barack Obama, "CVS Caremark sets a powerful example, and today's decision will help advance my administration's efforts to reduce tobacco-related deaths, cancer, and heart disease, as well as bring down health care costs—ultimately saving lives and protecting untold numbers of families from pain and heartbreak for years to come."

"This is an important, bold public health decision by a major retail pharmacy to act on the long understood reality that blending providing health care and providing cigarettes just doesn't match," said Dr. Richard Wender, chief cancer control officer at the American Cancer Society.

In a competitive industry, CVS's decision to put purpose ahead of profit could have been very expensive and discouraged investors. But it had the opposite effect. While there was an immediate impact on profit in the quarter that followed the decision,[5] sales rebounded quickly. So did the stock price. One year after the decision, the CVS stock price rose 23 percent versus the previous year, far outpacing Walgreens' stock price, which experienced only a 12 percent increase in the same period.[6]

More important, the decision had a big impact on society. According to CVS, the decision to stop selling tobacco led to a meaningful and measurable decline in cigarette smoking.[7] Within 12 months, in states where CVS Pharmacy had at least 15 percent of the market share, consumers had purchased 100 million fewer packs of cigarettes. Households that purchased cigarettes exclusively at CVS Pharmacy were 38 percent more likely to stop buying cigarettes, and those consumers who bought more than three packs of cigarettes a month were more than twice as likely to stop buying them. The company doubled down on this decision by later announcing a multiyear $50 million initiative to help create the first tobacco-free generation.

To further promote the fact that it is "an innovative health care company driven by a purpose—helping people on their path to better health," CVS announced it would tackle a new challenge on the five-year anniversary of the original decision to stop selling tobacco products: it addressed the growing problem of youth vaping with additional investments and new partners.

All these actions were very strategic. A Gallup Panel study found that while 51 percent of consumers weren't affected by CVS's decision, five times as many consumers said they were more likely to shop the brand (25 percent) because of the company's stance than not (5 percent).[8] CVS cemented the importance of its purpose not only with consumers, but undoubtedly with its own employees as well.

CVS's decision to stop selling tobacco products reflected its internal values. While it came at a short-term cost, the decision differentiated the company from other brands, improved its standing with consumers, and was a big winner with investors. Unfortunately, too many companies, in their attempts to be different, create purpose statements for external consumption that don't truly represent the company internally and are viewed by many stakeholders as disingenuous. Again, a purpose statement can't be a marketing ploy.

Sixty-two percent of consumers want brands to stand for something. And if companies don't live up to their brand promise, the consequences can be swift. Forty-eight percent of US consumers who are disappointed by a brand's words or actions on a social issue complain about it. Forty-two percent of consumers walk away from a brand in frustration if they disagree with the brand on a social issue, and one in five (21 percent) never come back.[9]

The New Corporate Currency

The link between purpose, culture, and brand is unmistakable. We have labeled this "The New Corporate Currency" and created a simple model to highlight this new currency, as shown in Figure 6.1. Twenty-first-century talent, regardless of generational group, wants to associate with organizations that have a strong sense of purpose. Purpose shapes the organization's culture and the employee experience. What employees experience in the workplace will dictate how they feel about the organization and how they share those feelings with colleagues, friends, and acquaintances and in social media. All this shapes the organization's reputation as a place to work—otherwise known as the employer brand. And employer brand has a direct effect on how consumers, investors, and customers—really any external audience—view the company's brand.

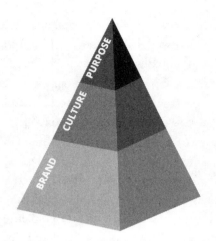

FIGURE 6.1   The New Corporate Currency

"Like the old adage 'the whole is greater than the sum of its parts,' The New Corporate Currency showcases what most savvy senior executives already know: a company can only achieve greatness if its purpose, culture, and brand are in sync," said Joan Amble, board member at Zurich Insurance, Sirius XM Holdings, and Booz Allen Hamilton. "If any one of those elements is not, the corporation's currency can be devalued instantly, and regaining that value can take years . . . and in some instances companies never recover. Getting this right and having the ability to monitor the pulse of the organization on all fronts is an imperative that requires vigilance, constant measurement, and engaged ownership by all."

One company that understands this equation is Mastercard. While most still think of it as a "credit card" company, Mastercard is "a technology company in the global payments industry" with "innovative technology" that sets it apart from competitors.[10] Its stated mission is to connect and power an inclusive, digital economy that benefits everyone, everywhere by making transactions safe, simple, smart, and accessible. With headquarters in Purchase, New York, Mastercard has about 19,000 employees and connections across more than 210 countries and territories.

But what fascinates me about Mastercard is its "decency quotient, or DQ," which the company says drives the culture and everything its people do inside and outside of the company.

The term "decency quotient" is the brainchild of Mastercard's CEO, Ajay Banga, who says the term originated as an off-the-cuff phrase he used one time at a company town hall meeting. Banga was not surprised that the phrase stuck.

"If you put it into language that people can colloquially understand, it becomes much easier for people to embrace," Banga said.[11] They certainly have embraced the concept of decency throughout the organization.

I caught up with Ajay to talk about culture, but also about the remarkable run Mastercard has been on since he arrived at the company. Banga joined Mastercard in 2009 initially as president and COO after he served as CEO of Citigroup Asia Pacific. He was appointed CEO in 2010; and in the decade that followed, the company has seen revenue triple and its market value increase over 14 times. In that time, Banga led a change in the company focus from a payments network to a technology company. Today, Mastercard earns close to half its revenue from emerging payment tech areas, cybersecurity, and data analytics.

But despite Mastercard's technology prowess, it's the human element that has helped propel the company in Banga's estimation.

"The particular attribute of Mastercard's culture that underpins everything is the attribute of being decent," Banga told me. "What we're trying to do is to put decency, and the idea of behaving that way, at the core of everything we do. It's not that we don't want to win. It's not that we don't want to do business, and be competitive, and that we don't watch what our stock price is doing, what our market share is doing, or we don't count the deals we win versus the deals we lose . . . we're commercial people. We care deeply about those topics. But it's the idea of doing the right thing. It's about what you do and *how* you do it. And it's not about who you look like and where you came from. It's about treating everyone with the respect they deserve for the value they bring. It's about having a hand on your back, not in your face. It's the principle of decent behavior at work in the office, with colleagues, with competitors, with clients, with governments, with partners, with whatever you do."

Banga spoke just a week after the death of George Floyd and the race riots that had broken out across the United States.

"Decency plays out in different ways. Right now, it's playing out in the form of how people are responding to how we're behaving to the coronavirus crisis, or how we are behaving more recently to the social change that's spreading across the country. But, unfortunately, those are just today's topics. The fact is decency stands the test of time. However, we also take a lot of pride in doing well. Most employees I speak to, from new employees to people who've been around 5, 10 years or even those who've been here 30 years, they would all use decency quotient to describe the culture, along with the aspect of doing well and having a fighting spirit to win. It's all about doing well and doing good at the same time."

Collective Uniqueness

During the pandemic, several CEOs stated they had become fans of working remotely and pledged to reduce their office footprints to move to a predominantly work-from-home structure. Banga, along with myself, thought some business leaders were rushing ahead too quickly and didn't fully appreciate and acknowledge the diverse home situations that exist in many workforces.

"I hear people say, hey, I can work from home forever. Yeah, if you've got a 5,000-square-foot house, sure you can. But let me introduce you to the majority of our middle-class employees who live in one- and two-bedroom apartments in Singapore and Manhattan and Sydney and Delhi and Mumbai and London. They might live with a mother-in-law and two dogs and two children and a husband. Their life is just bloody *different* than yours. A very important part of being decent is understanding what their lives are. And caring about them and responding to their fears and their concerns as compared to your way of thinking about life."

Mastercard is a very diverse company, which is a reflection on Banga and his deep championing of diversity and inclusion.

"If I had brought into this company my senior management team from Citigroup, who I loved greatly, they're perfect people, and I fired everybody who was here, it wouldn't have worked as well. With that team . . . we have grown up together, worked together, done the same stuff, had the same experiences, and made the same mistakes. We also have the same blind spots. You cannot be innovative when you surround yourself with people who look like you, walk like you, and talk like you. You know that the old saying, 'If it looks like a duck, walks like a duck, and sounds like a duck, it probably is a duck'? The trick is to find not just ducks, but geese and parrots and sparrows and every other kind of gorgeous bird that God created in nature's aviary. And you're not going to get the aviary if you want to be a sparrow surrounded by sparrows.

"Someone asked me, what is it about diversity that you admire the most? And I said, I don't know about admiring it the most, but it's what I call harnessing the collective uniqueness of your people. Together, our collective uniqueness makes us very powerful. That is what I mean, harnessing the collective uniqueness of your people. Your people are your engine, and their diversity, their creativity, their ideas, that's your rocket fuel."

Banga not only understands the power of diversity, but also the interconnectedness of culture and the treatment of employees. This intersection often dictates how the company's brand is ultimately perceived.

"How you treat your employees during this entire period of COVID-19 encompasses everything, ranging from their safety to their well-being. We told our employees very early—literally in the first few days—you're not going to get laid off because of the coronavirus crisis. That's not going to happen. Don't worry about your jobs. You worry about yourself, your family, your colleagues, your clients . . . worry about the stuff that matters. And take this threat off your head so you can actually focus on the rest of it, because so much is going to be challenging about this crisis."

Banga runs his company in the spirit of The New Corporate Currency, and it's no wonder the company has performed so well. Many years of researching high-performance organizations has convinced the i4cp research staff of the significance of culture and employer brand to an organization's market performance.

The importance and impact of these elements, however, is perhaps best summed up by Microsoft's Nadella.

"Being CEO has taught me this—that two things perhaps matter the most: having a very clear sense of purpose or mission that gives the organization real direction; and having a culture that allows you to go after that mission," said Nadella.[12] "One of the key things, I feel, is that just like individuals, companies have an identity. I talk about it even as a soul. It's that collective purpose that a company represents. In Microsoft, we talk about our mission as being empowering every person and every organization on the planet to achieve more. Every one of those words, for me, telegraphs that soul."[13]

CHAPTER 7

STEP #4:
DEFINE THE DESIRED BEHAVIORS

Setting the desired behaviors is critical to renovating your culture, as is walking the walk at the very top. But when the leadership team is obviously truly operating as a team, that's very, very contagious throughout the organization.

—FRANÇOIS LOCOH-DONOU, CEO, F5

Once the path has been established via a strong purpose, a more detailed element of that direction is agreeing on what behavioral aspects of the culture will best support that purpose and require more focus.

Most CEOs I talk with have an idea of what they want more of in their company. "I'd like us to be better at execution . . ." and "I wish we were more innovative . . ." and "We need to be more inclusive . . ." are common refrains. As companies evolve, often the culture drifts away from traits that have been successful in the past, which sometimes causes deficiencies in important core traits.

Understanding your culture type (or more often types) is important. According to a Glassdoor study, 77 percent of adults would evaluate a company's culture before applying for an open position. Fifty-six percent rank an organization's culture as more important than compensation.[1]

Anyone who has worked at different companies knows that cultures can differ dramatically from organization to organization, and often the structure of the organization plays a big part in determining the culture. I've had the privilege of being exposed to many different companies, and the cultural and structural differences are sometimes startling. Organizational structures vary from hierarchical to matrix to flat to (sometimes) holacratic—and everything in between. Other companies have aspects of their culture that define them, from team-based to individualistic; diverse to homogenous; innovative to risk averse; or cutthroat to overly inclusive.

Those cultures manifest themselves in actions throughout the company. Usually, it starts with the leader. For example, Tom Coughlin, former executive vice president of football operations at the Jacksonville Jaguars, was a stickler on time. His philosophy—which dated back to when he was a Super Bowl–winning coach for the New York Giants—was that if you're not five minutes early to a meeting or commitment, you're considered late. To accentuate this, Coughlin had the clocks set five minutes ahead at the Jacksonville Jaguars' facility, which internally became known as "Tom Coughlin Time."[2] He was so serious about punctuality that he often fined players for tardiness. Everyone usually complied, but begrudgingly. Immediately upon his firing in 2019, the clocks were all changed back to normal time.

"That's the first thing I noticed when I got in here," said A. J. Bouye, one of the Jaguar players, the day after Coughlin was let go. "I thought that I was late for meetings. I look up, I had an extra five minutes, so I was good."

Companies often have a rhythm and habits. As opposed to a Coughlin-led organization, you often find cultures where being late to meetings is common, or multitasking during meetings is acceptable. Or you'll see commonality in the way decisions are made. Slow versus fast, consensus versus authoritarian, evidence-based versus instinct. Whatever the cultural norm, it often emanates from the top.

Amazon is a great example of how cultural norms emanate from the top. Famous for its "no PowerPoint" culture, employees who are presenting on a topic instead create several-page narrative memos that are silently read at the beginning of each meeting—kind of like a "study hall" session, according to CEO and founder Jeff Bezos.[3] Bezos created this process early on, and he freely admits that silently reading memos together is the "weirdest meeting culture." Weird or not, it's effective.

"If we don't, the executives—like high school kids—will try to bluff their way through a meeting," Bezos explained. "[The memo is] supposed to create the context for what will then be a good discussion. The reason writing a good four-page memo is harder than writing a 20-page PowerPoint is because the narrative structure of a good memo forces better thought and better understanding of what's more important."

Bezos has additional reasons for this cultural oddity. "Often, when a memo isn't great, it's not the writer's inability to recognize the high standard but instead a wrong expectation on scope," he says. "These employees falsely believe a 'high standard,' six-page memo can be written in just a few days or even hours. In actuality, the process can take weeks. The great memos are written and rewritten, shared with colleagues who are asked to improve the work, set aside for a couple of days, and then edited again with a fresh mind."

While I've not encountered another company with this type of memo culture, there's certainly something refreshing about slowing down to put deep thought into preparing for a meeting—a practice today's hectic environments in many companies often don't allow. Cultural traits are reinforced every day through very overt actions, and every single company has these, whether intentional or not.

Culture Types

In our research on organizational culture, it's clear that you can type-cast cultures. There are many different culture types; our research team settled on 10 as the most common. The percentages in Table 7.1 represent what companies self-labeled as their culture type in a study we conducted. While there certainly are more than 10 culture types, these are a good starting point to identify your organization's current culture and what type of culture you may want in the future. Keep in mind most companies have multiple types (these aren't mutually exclusive), but almost no company exhibits all types.

TABLE 7.1   Culture Types

CULTURE	LEADER TRAITS	EMPLOYEE TRAITS	EXAMPLE
Customer-focused 66.0%	Consultative, trustworthy	Relationship-driven, proactive	T-Mobile
Performance 62.5%	Goal-oriented, relentless	Merit-based, competitive	Netflix
Innovative 52.1%	Entrepreneurial, resourceful	Creative, persistent	3M
Inclusive 47.9%	Sincere, cooperative	Diverse, relationship-focused	Accenture
Collaborative 47.9%	Facilitator, transparent	Open-minded, team-oriented	Twitter
Agile 47.2%	Boundaryless, visionary	Flexible, multitalented	Amazon
Purpose/mission 45.1%	Altruistic, philanthropical	Compassionate, unselfish	Patagonia
Learning 36.1%	Intellectually curious, open-minded	Aspirational, ambitious	Microsoft
Quality 29.2%	Systems-oriented, objective	Accountability, caring	Disney
Safety 26.4%	Procedural, structured	Compliant, risk averse	Shell

Supporting Behaviors

With clarity of what the desired new culture will (and will not) be, the next point of focus is to define the new behaviors that all leaders—from senior executives to middle managers to frontline managers—will need to exhibit (as well as avoid) to support the culture. These behaviors will likely differ depending on the type of culture desired, but it's critical that the behaviors are clearly and constantly communicated, modeled, and embodied by the CEO and senior team. It's also important to measure and reward the desired behaviors among the organization's leaders; at the very least, the behaviors should be components of the company's performance management process.

F5, a global company that specializes in application delivery and security services, is a good example of this. Core to the culture evolution at F5 is something CEO François Locoh-Donou and CHRO Ana White partnered on called BeF5—a set of five behaviors they believe are necessary for the success of the company's long-term strategy, as shown in Figure 7.1.

FIGURE 7.1   Five Behaviors for F5 Success

Settling on those behaviors took time, however. Like many CEOs, Locoh-Donou inherited a strong 20+ year culture that had been in place long before he arrived in 2017.

"My first priority," recalls Locoh-Donou, "was to respect the past. I felt this way because I've seen too many times the movie where the company is very successful, but then plateaus a little bit. A new CEO comes in and immediately starts communicating all the new things the company needs to do to be successful again. That talk track is dismissive of what's been done previously, and it's a very quick way to alienate all the people who have worked hard at the company for many years. The reason the company became prominent is because of them, so it's important to honor that."

Locoh-Donou, who grew up in the West African country of Togo, draws on his heritage when thinking about culture change.

"My philosophy on this is an African one. We very much believe in elders and the wisdom of the people who came before us. So, we are very respectful of the past. And I think if you're renovating or changing your culture, you have to be respectful of the past because otherwise people won't come with you. If you tell them, or even project, that everything they've done previously was wrong, you'll have a hard time bringing them into the future."

If you aren't familiar with F5, it's an interesting story. Founded in 1996 in Seattle, the company originally focused on virtual reality applications, a new and promising niche at the time. But the company ran into a problem that plagued many others: the servers weren't fast enough. To compensate, F5 turned its attention to developing a load-balancing algorithm and brought in investment banker Jeff Hussey to run the company. The original developers left shortly thereafter to pursue their virtual reality dreams, while Hussey remained to build on the algorithm and create what would later become a multi-billion-dollar technology company.

If you're wondering, the company's strange name was inspired by the movie *Twister*.

"A category five was the most stormy of the twisters in the movie and then it gave birth to F5," explained Kara Sprague, executive vice president and general manager of application services.[4] "This was late 90s and the whole idea was about the company coming out of the storm of traffic that was happening in the Internet."

F5 launched its first product in the eye of the storm of the Internet in 1997, a load balancer called BIG-IP that controlled web traffic. When a server went down or became overloaded, BIG-IP directed traffic to other servers. This capability made F5 a hot start-up, which the company leveraged in 1999 by going public on NASDAQ.

After weathering the dot-com bubble burst and shifting focus to the enterprise market, the company found its niche in the security space and eventually as the central control point in the cloud. In 2017, the company hired Locoh-Donou as CEO. Locoh-Donou previously held senior leadership positions at Ciena, a network strategy and technology company, and had a reputation as a very solid technology executive.

Locoh-Donou holds engineering degrees from École Centrale de Marseille and Télécom ParisTech and an MBA from the Stanford Graduate School of Business. He is on the board of Capital One Financial Corporation and is also the co-founder of Cajou Espoir, a cashew-processing facility that employs several hundred people in his native Togo, 80 percent of whom are women. A worldly individual, he was no stranger to the nuances of culture. But from a culture standpoint, Locoh-Donou was surprised at what he found in his first few weeks at F5.

"Generally, what I found is that people were quite loyal to the company, and loyal to one another," he told me in a meeting, which White also attended. "I discovered that people at F5 care about each other—they had a soul, they had authenticity, and they truly wanted to help each other and did so all the time—and they wanted to do the right thing for the company. I found this trait interesting. Companies in the technology industry often have a mercenary culture where people come in for two to three years looking for the big payday and then move on to the next 30 percent salary increase. There often isn't really a strong sense of mission. It was refreshing."

That aspect of the culture was one to be retained, but he discovered there were other aspects that needed change.

"We had come to dominate our market, and I felt that our culture of customer focus, or *customer obsession*, had eroded a little bit . . . that's one of the behaviors we had lost and I wanted to stress it, to bring it back," Locoh-Donou continued. "When Ana joined as our head of HR, we put together the BeF5 behaviors, which were two things: One is codifying the existing culture, but also reemphasizing other aspects of the culture that were very important for the future of the company."

"The help-each-other aspect was always a staple . . . it's really like a family, and one of many reasons I joined F5 from Microsoft," White recalled. "So, one of the first behaviors we codified was *We help each other thrive*. It was a natural behavior we wanted to reinforce, as was, *We obsess over customer needs*."

But Locoh-Donou recognized there was a hurdle to overcome if he were to enact any change in the company. "I don't think we have resistance to change. But we have resistance to the *speed* of change."

"It's important to remember that F5, like a lot of companies, was so successful for so long, they hadn't previously had to endure or drive massive amounts of change," said White. "As François and the team were transforming the company, we were introducing change rapidly in an attempt to be more agile. Speed on decisions was not our strong suit . . . but needed to be. Thus, the behavior of *We choose speed* was born."

"But I would say in all transparency, there was some level of resistance to how much change we were introducing so quickly. And how much speed we were expecting employees to act with. Given that, we realized we needed an overarching guiding principle, and developed *We do the right thing* to sit above the behaviors. We still want to be as agile and nimble as possible, but *We do the right thing* trumps everything else. Employees really appreciated that."

The other behaviors of *We are owners* and *We create a more diverse and inclusive F5* came naturally to Locoh-Donou and White.

"Diversity and inclusion was very important to François, and me. It is key that every employee focused on creating the most diverse and inclusive company possible," White added. "Including it as a core behavior was a unique opportunity to be something really great and differentiate ourselves in the tech industry."

The F5 behaviors are a testament to what culture renovation is all about and are core to what F5 is as a company. Today, those behaviors are the first thing anyone sees entering the gorgeous offices in F5 Tower in the heart of Seattle. More importantly, Locoh-Donou constantly reinforces with leaders what it means to "BeF5" and ensures leaders are doing the same with others. This includes embedding BeF5 into systems and processes, such as performance management reviews, employee recognition programs, and employee learning and development programs.

"What's made our culture renovation successful is leaders leading from the top," observed White. "When we rolled out the new behaviors, we spent a lot of time discussing it as a leadership team. We all agreed that the new behaviors needed to be much more than words on a slide. It's actually the behaviors of the leaders at the top that's really made it work super well."

Locoh-Donou agrees. "The leadership team first and foremost had to model the behaviors . . . and that starts with me. It starts with humility. It starts with being generous . . . it starts by having each other's back. Even though several were previously operating in silos, the team started truly operating as a team and working with each other. Setting the desired behaviors is critical to renovating your culture, as is walking the walk at the very top. But when the leadership team is obviously truly operating as a team, that's very, very contagious throughout the organization."

While it's important to be clear on behaviors, it's also important to constantly reinforce them. "We can all use a nudge occasionally," Locoh-Donou advises, "especially at critical points in day-to-day activities. I tell our leaders to stop and consider the behaviors when making decisions, allocating resources, determining rewards and recognition, making hiring decisions, and communicating. I have learned from Ana and many members of her HR team that it is ideal to pull both small and big levers to reflect the new culture. From training programs, to the way employees are rewarded and recognized, to how new talent is recruited."

Locoh-Donou paused for a second, reflecting on what lies ahead. "There is still a lot to learn."

CHAPTER 8

STEP #5:
IDENTIFY INFLUENCERS, ENERGIZERS, AND BLOCKERS

Organizational network analysis can provide an x-ray into the inner workings of an organization—a powerful means of making invisible patterns of information flow and collaboration in strategically important groups visible.
—ROB CROSS, PROFESSOR OF GLOBAL LEADERSHIP, BABSON COLLEGE

Practically every organization has a well-defined organization chart—a hierarchy the workforce recognizes as the formal chain of command. However, ask almost any employee a simple question: "Is that how work gets done?" and you'll receive a resounding "of course not." When workflow is truly studied, it typically reveals patterns of communication and influence that are very different from the formal hierarchical structures that the company has painstakingly created.

Here's an easy way to think about it. Every organization has "go-to" people whom others in the workforce turn to for answers, comfort, opinions, and guidance. As you are reading this, someone's face probably popped up in your head. Most executives would agree that those people are the lifeblood of the organization. Yet there's a consistent problem in almost every company regarding these critical employees, these invaluable resources, these corporate rock stars.

Most executives don't know who they are.

Don't get me wrong. There are obvious rock stars in every company; they stand out because their influence is so strong and their value is so well-known. But many more are hidden and fly below the radar. They are often buried in the hierarchy, and just as often they are introverts who try hard to stay out of the limelight or are overlooked by most casual observers. But they are there every day, making the company hum and helping the organization thrive.

When renovating culture, it's important to identify these influencers and make sure they are enlisted as proponents of the change because these hidden stars will likely have undue impact on a significant proportion of the workforce. They are the people who provide informal leadership, who span organizational boundaries, and who unleash the latent passion in the workforce.

In fact, it's been estimated that more than 90 percent of change initiatives can be achieved in shorter timescales, and at lower cost, provided that the right influencers are identified and fully involved in all aspects of the change process.[1] Uncovering who those influencers are in the company is not particularly difficult, as long as the right methods are used.

The Power of Organizational Network Analysis

By conducting an organizational network analysis (ONA), those indispensable people are illuminated through a simple survey or through the analysis of interactions on internal communication platforms (like e-mail, Slack, Teams, etc.). The goal is to track and map the company's flow of information, collaboration, and expertise sharing to see who is at the "center of the beehive," and equally to understand who is on the outskirts. More importantly, it's to understand who has influence to promote the culture renovation throughout the company.

The foremost expert today on ONA—most consider him the pioneer of this discipline—is Rob Cross, a professor of global leadership at Babson College. Spanning three decades, Cross's work focuses on applying analysis of social networks to help solve business issues. He has authored three books, the most recent one titled *Driving Results Through Social Networks*. His work has been published in the *Wall Street Journal*, *CIO*, *Inc.*, *Fast Company*, *Harvard Business Review*, *Sloan Management Review*, *Business Week*, *Fortune*, the *Financial Times*, *Time* magazine, and many other publications. Rob is also a good friend and a business partner.

"ONA can provide an x-ray into the inner workings of an organization—a powerful means of making invisible patterns of information flow and collaboration in strategically important groups visible," said Cross. Over two decades of research, Cross and colleagues have found that 3 to 5 percent of people in a typical organization network account for 20 to 35 percent of the value-add collaborations. Typically, half or more are not predicted by leaders ahead of time. Even sophisticated talent management systems overlook most of these central players.

"To be clear, leaders get the top 3 or 4 right," Cross noted. "But then they have surprises come in at 5, 8, 10–12, 17–20, etc. These invisible assets account for huge proportions of how work is getting done and how culture is reinforced or changed."

ONA has traditionally been used to mitigate any issues that could arise with these central figures in the organization. For example, is that person a flight risk? It's certainly possible that someone who is constantly besieged by coworkers may feel overloaded, underappreciated, and maybe underpaid. Often that individual's departure creates internal havoc that was never contemplated.

On the other hand, it's possible that person could be a bottleneck and might be doing work that others should be doing instead. The point is you don't know unless you identify the collaboration points within the organization.

In all companies, strategic success depends on effective collaboration between employees. For example, if client-facing employees and those with roles that are internal and more operational aren't communicating or collaborating frequently, the business suffers. Often entire departments, divisions, business units, and geographies don't collaborate with each other, either on purpose or due to neglect. This is also very common after an acquisition; it can take years for companies joined through acquisition to truly collaborate with each other and to have everyone operating as one organization. This is precisely why many acquisitions fail—because no one thought to analyze whether collaboration was occurring or not.

The goal is not just more collaboration. Rather, it is to align the pattern of collaboration—the lifeline of how the organization is getting work done—with strategic objectives. In some instances, this might mean reducing excessive collaboration. And in others, it could mean connecting silos in the company. To accomplish this, an ONA will reveal:

- ► Where an organization is most siloed
- ► Which units are collaborating well and which ones never communicate with each other
- ► Where the company can optimally invest to immediately impact performance through enhanced collaboration

ONA is often used to identify three types of important network roles:

- ► **Connectors.** The go-to resource for many, connectors support many coworkers in a variety of ways. They often create alignment within a team or department through informal leadership and often are consumed by helping colleagues at any time.

▶ **Boundary spanners.** With ties and relationships that bridge typical organizational boundaries, such as departments, functions, locations, and so on, boundary spanners have a good understanding of the views and concerns of various groups. They often have knowledge of what will work in different parts of the organization and are seen as credible by others.

▶ **Energizers.** By creating enthusiasm and energy around them, energizers instill a sense of possibility in those they interact with. They fuel engagement in conversation and inspire innovation and creativity, as well as unleashing passion deep in the workplace.

These groups are important to uncover in the context of culture renovation. Over half (57 percent) of organizations that successfully renovated their culture conducted an ONA to identify the most influential employees, listen to their perspective, and enlist them as "culture ambassadors" to champion culture change initiatives.

The Role of Culture Ambassador

The concept of culture ambassador is somewhat new, but it is a pivotal role in making change happen.

"I'm a believer now in the concept of culture ambassadors, but I certainly wasn't when we first set out to change our culture," Tim Richmond confessed to me one morning. Tim is chief human resource officer of AbbVie, a Chicago-based biopharmaceutical company that employs 30,000 people in 75 countries. AbbVie was spun out of Abbott Labs in 2013 and is a public company trading on the NYSE. At its inception, AbbVie had a very rare opportunity: act as a large start-up company and create a culture from scratch.

The CEO asked Richmond to oversee this effort.

"We often talk about the value of top-down leadership and messaging when embarking on a culture renovation, but there's a lot of influence from the bottom up that I probably underappreciated," Richmond said. "As we were establishing our culture, I had some people in the company approach me to say we should create these culture ambassadors around the world. Every country should have at least one, every site, every laboratory, and even every work group.

"I remember asking, do we really need to have this right now? But I've learned over time that you listen to good people who have good ideas and ask, well, what would that mean? How would it work? It turns out it was a huge catalyst for change. Because you think you have great ideas from headquarters . . . and sometimes we do . . . but if you are in another country it often doesn't apply. In my career I've been on an international assignment, and you get something from headquarters, and you think, I have no idea what this is. We have no idea how to use it. But the concept of a local ambassador is someone who works at the local level to take the broad enterprise ideas and create from it whatever is important to them."

As a spin-off company, AbbVie had a blank canvas on which to paint new cultural norms.

"We had the opportunity to chart our own course when we became a stand-alone company at the beginning of 2013," said Richmond. "It was up to us to establish our independence and build our future, and it was essential that we succeed—for our employees, our shareholders, and, most importantly, our patients."

Richmond continued: "Creating our culture was so essential to our business success that it was established as one of our top four business priorities. We knew that a positive culture—one with highly engaged employees—impacts business performance for the better and would enable us to deliver on our business objectives. We took advantage of the unique opportunity to intentionally design, and systematically work to bring about, a culture that would enable us to achieve industry-leading performance."

From day one, AbbVie culture has been instilled in the day-to-day working lives of all employees. Like F5, AbbVie emphasizes the importance of behaviors, believing that how employees work with each other to achieve results matters just as much as achieving the company's goals. In the spirit of renovation, AbbVie established a culture that balanced "the best of the old with an eye to new philosophies," according to Richmond. This included aligning new business strategies and culture drivers that would feel uniquely *AbbVie*.

A core part of this process, according Richmond, was when AbbVie gathered top leaders in the organization to prioritize focus areas and to obtain early buy-in and commitment. Armed with research and insights, the company zeroed in on (1) raising awareness about the culture it intended to build and (2) equipping employees with the skills needed to behave in ways that would be fully consistent with that culture. Overall, the purposeful establishment of culture has been a huge success at AbbVie. The company successfully executed on its strategy, and the shareholder return has been significant since the company debuted on the NYSE on January 2, 2013, outperforming most indexes and competitors.

"This high-performing culture enables us to deliver on our business objectives," said Richmond. "To sustain our business performance in the long term, a strong culture with engaged employees is critical. Engaged employees perform better and lead to greater business results; they are intricately linked."

Passive ONA Versus Active

To understand who is best suited to be a culture ambassador, or a member of a culture cabinet, companies can conduct an ONA in stealth mode by analyzing communication patterns of popular technology platforms like e-mail, calendar data, Teams, Slack, or other tools. Often referred to as "passive" ONA, this technique has a couple of issues. One is that it can easily pick up false signals since it tends to focus on the volume of communication or interaction between parties versus the quality or context. For instance, it's hard to ascertain the strategic importance based on e-mail volume when there is a flurry of messages about this weekend's social plans or when the latest funny meme goes viral internally or an inbox gets buried in bureaucratic travel expense approvals.

The bigger issue is that passive analysis won't illuminate the key ingredient of *influence*. To understand that better, most organizations turn to "active" ONA that is done through surveys. In those surveys, typical questions are:

▶ Please identify colleagues in your group who are important to your ability to achieve your work goals.

▶ Please indicate whether greater access to (i.e., more time and attention from) each person below would help you be more effective at work.

▶ Please place a check next to the names of people below whom you consider to be important sources of open, energizing interactions for you at work.

This, according to Cross, is how you uncover the real influencers and energizers that will initiate change and make it last. It also allows you to identify a mechanism to make desired communication flow more efficiently throughout the company.

"A traditional approach to cultural change that cascades messaging from the top down often misses the hidden cultural influencers that really matter, the ones that are deeper down in the organization," said Cross. "In one study we conducted which utilized ONA to map this, we found that the top 50 leaders could directly influence 31 percent of the population just by looking at their network connections. But by shifting our focus to the people who were truly connected internally, the top 50 influencers could reach almost twice as many people. The disproportionate impact of these top influencers might easily have been lost without conducting an ONA."

In any culture change initiative, uncovering the true influencers and energizers could be the difference between success and failure.

"Leaders have always known that they should involve others in cultural change, but without an analytic view it becomes difficult to see whose opinion yields the greatest insight and results," Cross adds. "This is one reason why the large-scale participatory processes that were popular in the nineties died off, due to the work and time involved to get consensus."

As important as influencers and energizers are to culture renovation, it's equally important to understand where blockers exist. Cross has often used ONA to help organizations illuminate those likely to derail the effort.

"Everyone has been a part of change efforts that falter because of resistance," Cross noted. "Often the resistance stems from a small set of opinion leaders with strongly held positions on either side of a practice, norm, or belief. People might mumble that this department or team is holding us up. But the reality is often driven by a small set of key influencers in networks.

"Why would any leader let these disagreements passively slow or derail change efforts or bring them into full group forums where emotions and positions solidify? We would never handle conflict on our teams this way—but our lack of granularity in understanding cultural rifts and the best and most efficient way to heal them leads us to actions that exacerbate the problem."

Sometimes it takes extraordinary events, a crisis even, to unveil the influencers, energizers, and blockers in the organization. How individuals respond to unexpected change is often not known until everyone is in the heat of the moment. Few companies I know of experienced this quite as suddenly or jarringly as Sony Pictures.

Country Versus Company

Monday morning, November 24, 2014, should have been like any other day at Sony Pictures in Culver City, just a few miles west of downtown Los Angeles. But instead it was historic—and horrific.

As employees logged on to their computers, they were immediately assaulted by gunfire—luckily just the recorded sound of it, not the real thing—and the image of an ominous red skeleton on the screen with "Hacked By #GOP" written across its forehead. Underneath the skeleton was a very poorly written message:

> **Warning:**
>
> We've already warned you, and this is just a beginning.
>
> We continue till our request be met.
>
> We've obtained all your Internal data Including your secrets and top secrets.
>
> If you don't obey us, we'll release data show below to the world.
>
> Determine what will you do till November the 24th, 11:00 PM(GMT).

Underneath were website addresses outside of the company that contained many internal sensitive documents, with messages threatening to release them if Sony Pictures did not comply with the group's demands. Computer after computer was systematically infected throughout Sony's headquarters, all carrying the same message. The IT department at Sony moved quickly and made the drastic decision to shut down the entire network, including overseas. Before it did, the malware wiped out 3,262 of Sony's 6,797 personal computers and 837 of its 1,555 servers.[2]

"Our head of IT was a smart, sharp, and strong people-oriented leader, but he also had the technical skills to really know what to do in this kind of situation," George Rose, the head of HR at the time, told me years later. "As soon as he heard about the breach, the first thing he did was—thankfully—shut everything down. It would have been far more damaging had he not done that."

As it turns out, this was not a one-day event. The GOP, which stands for Guardians of Peace, had been accessing Sony's network for several weeks and had already stolen most of Sony's data and deleted the original copies from Sony computers.

Sony's network was down for days as IT tried to repair the damage. The company had no voice mail, no e-mail, no Internet access, and no production systems. Employees were relying on fax machines and whiteboards to do their jobs. Someone found a few old BlackBerrys in a storage room and gave them to executives so they could at least exchange text messages. They even resurrected some old machines to cut physical payroll checks in lieu of electronic direct deposit.

Initially, Sony didn't understand the extent of the breach. In fact, the company's first statement on November 24 could have gone unnoticed by many: "We are investigating an I.T. matter."[3] A more accurate statement would have been: *We've just suffered one of the worst cyberattacks in history, and it was executed by a hostile foreign government with the primary purpose of destroying our company.*

Within a week, the extent of the breach became clear, and more than a dozen FBI investigators were on the scene. The hackers had taken everything. Contracts with actors. Film budgets. Sales reports. Salary data. Retirement and termination plans. Medical records. Social Security numbers. Passport data. Personal e-mails. Passwords. Home addresses. Five entire movies, four of which had yet to be released. Over 170,000 messages between top executives including then CEO Michael Lynton and Motion Picture Group chairman Amy Pascal.

Many of the e-mails were downright embarrassing and were quickly reported by the press. One was from producer Scott Rudin to Pascal about Angelina Jolie regarding the actress's desire to direct. "Kill me please. Immediately," he said when he learned she was studying films of potential directors for a "Cleopatra" film in development. "I'm not destroying my career over a minimally talented spoiled brat," he said in another e-mail. Another revealed that Mark Cuban was not happy with the $30,000 he was getting per episode for *Shark Tank*, a show distributed by Sony Pictures Television. Another revealed Pascal spent $66,350 on a two-day trip for car services, air travel, and a suite at the St. Regis hotel to attend the premiere of *Fury*, starring Brad Pitt and Shia LaBeouf, in Washington, DC.[4]

It wasn't long before the primary suspect in the hack was uncovered: North Korea. The reason? A movie Sony was set to release on Christmas that year—a dark comedy called *The Interview*.

The movie starred Seth Rogen (who also coproduced it) and James Franco as a pair of bumbling journalists. The duo scores the interview of a lifetime when they are invited to North Korea to meet with Supreme Leader Kim Jong-un. After arriving, they are soon contacted by the CIA and tasked with assassinating him instead. Like many of Rogen's movies, it's frat boy humor, but it had a twist rarely seen in cinema: the very visible death of a living political leader.

The depiction of Jong-un's death was hotly debated internally. Studio executives pressured Rogen to tone it down, which he did. A little. The movie ultimately ends with a graphic, slow-motion sequence where Kim is killed when his helicopter explodes, engulfing his body in a fireball. An earlier cut of the scene had shown his head exploding.

North Korea had complained about the film for months, with the threats getting more dire each time. In June, the North Korean government called the film an "act of war" and had promised a "merciless" retaliation against the United States if the film was released. Rogen didn't take the threats very seriously at first, tweeting, "People don't usually wanna kill me for one of my movies until after they've paid 12 bucks for it."

Rogen's tone changed markedly as time went on. After the hack on headquarters, there were additional terrorist threats as the movie's Christmas premiere loomed closer. They warned Sony it should not show the movie in theaters, or there would be consequences. Spooked by this, most major theater chains canceled the movie, but a few independent theaters around the country showed it anyway. The movie ended up being released early to digital soon after. Sony made only $12.3 million worldwide in box office ticket sales, but it made another $40 million in digital rentals (Sony's most successful digital release) for a modest profit on the movie's $44 million budget.

But the damage had been done. Actors were upset, and lawsuits were filed. Pascal was out just a few weeks after the attack. Rogen called the entire episode "a horrible experience."[5] Sony's employees undoubtedly would agree.

According to the *Los Angeles Times,* the ordeal was seen as a wake-up call to boardrooms and corner offices around the country and "did more to raise national security cyber-awareness than any other single event," said John Carlin, assistant attorney general at the Justice Department for national security.[6] "It was a real game-changer," said cybersecurity expert Peter Toren, who used to work in the Justice Department's computer crime and intellectual property section. "It wasn't the typical cybercrime by thieves in search of credit card information to sell—it was an enemy nation causing as much damage, chaos and humiliation as possible."

Culture at Sony Pictures certainly was significantly altered as a result. Employees were disturbed about the amount of personal information that was stolen. Most had to go through the tedious process of changing account numbers, passwords, and even passports. Many lived in fear for several months, wondering when the next hack would take place. Ultimately a class-action lawsuit was filed, and Sony agreed to pay up to $8 million to employees who claimed their personal data was stolen.[7]

Rebuilding Culture

As head of HR, George Rose was in the middle during the entire time. Now retired, he and I reminisced about what it was like to rebuild the culture in the aftermath.

"Initially, everyone was afraid. Literally. They were walking around uncertain about what was going to happen to them," remembers Rose. "And I think the universal feeling was the common bond. Everyone faced similar sets of challenges. For management, since we couldn't control the press and we couldn't control what was being disseminated about us, written about us, thought about us, was to overcommunicate. And we told employees, this is what we need to do to get back. This is what we need to do to get it right. This is what you should focus on and pay attention to."

Rose points to some key leadership actions that started the company on a path to recovery.

"There are a couple of things that happened that really helped," he said. "First, Michael Lynton went on CNN to do an interview, which I thanked him for doing afterward, and told him it was very courageous. On CNN, he expressed—in a very explicit way—that the criticisms we were receiving were unfair. He did this in the midst of everybody, including the president, saying that we had done bad things (by canceling the movie release) and that we weren't upholding the First Amendment, among other things. People internally were so down after the news conference with Obama saying that we had made a mistake that having Michael so strongly refute this on CNN was motivating to them. It was really helpful and constructive.

"The second thing was David Boies wrote a letter to the media (cautioning them against using information that hackers have leaked). He basically said you've played perfectly into the hands of the attackers. You've really created a circumstance where you've made it much more difficult than it otherwise might be by not respecting these things as being private property, but seeing them as public domain that could be shared, should be shared everywhere.

"That was motivating for our people. And as a senior team, we reminded people of that . . . that this was an effort to destroy the company and that you should, as best you can, ignore what's being written. Focus on the tasks at hand and have everyone across the organization similarly directed. I think it gathered people in a way that we otherwise hadn't experienced before. Sony culturally was not necessarily a highly integrated company. We really pushed the highly personal communication effort that needed to take place to sustain the effort of keeping people's focus and discipline toward the task of getting back together and into improving the cultural environment."

Rose said the crisis brought out the best in some people.

"We had to stand up and tell people I know this is difficult, but let's find a way together to see if we can solve for this. I think the majority of people elevated. And it was really encouraging and positive to see so many people contribute ideas, have the energy and the stamina and the will to overcome the personal challenges that they faced. The culture change that took place after that was the result of their efforts."

"I think the culture that we created from this is much stronger," observed Rose. "Better teamwork, communication across the organization, sharing of people and skills and capabilities, knowledge and insight . . . the culture was certainly better and stronger in the aftermath than it was previously. It was there, but it was kind of a skill that hadn't been exercised. And once we started practicing it, the more we continued to hone that, the better it got. It changed the culture. It really helped us become a more integrated organization than we had been previously. Overall, I think it was better because we had all gone through something that no one could fully appreciate, but that really gave us a chance to improve organizationally."

A crisis illuminates leadership, and Sony certainly experienced that.

"Amy Pascal, kiddingly but seriously, said at a holiday party afterward as she was thanking everyone, 'Who would have ever thought that our IT function and our HR function were the two organizations that would have led us through this challenging period?' I really appreciated her saying that," reflected Rose.

"There were some people that really elevated and delivered extremely well . . . and others that did not. Like the COVID-19 crisis, you see the quality of leadership when you're in the midst of it. Our attitude was we were either going to figure out a way to get through this or who knows what was going to happen to the company.

"When you're faced with that, you really see what people are made of. The character of people stands out."

CHAPTER 9

STEP #6: DETERMINE HOW PROGRESS WILL BE MEASURED, MONITORED, AND REPORTED

> The way I think about it—is our culture providing
> a competitive advantage? Is it enabling execution
> of our strategy? The flip side is risk, particularly
> risk related to conduct.
> —BOB HERZ, FORMER CHAIRMAN OF FASB
> AND BOARD MEMBER AT FANNIE MAE AND MORGAN STANLEY

The National Association of Corporate Directors (NACD), which has been setting the standard for responsible board leadership for 40 years, published a remarkable report in 2017 titled "Culture as a Corporate Asset." In it, the association laid the groundwork for improvements to corporate oversight for years to come.

"Boards should set the expectation with management that regular assessments of culture will include qualitative and quantitative information and incorporate data from sources outside the organization." The report also stated that "in many organizations, culture does not get the level of boardroom attention it deserves until a problem arises. We believe this has to change. Oversight of corporate culture should be among the top governance imperatives for every board, regardless of its size or sector."[1]

Certainly, the impetus for the NACD's report was the increasing frequency with which corporate scandals drastically cut the share price of public companies, many times overnight. Too often, organizational culture was to blame. The authors had to look no further than the Wells Fargo account fraud, the Volkswagen emissions scandal, sexual harassment at Uber, and the revelations of sexual misconduct that plagued many companies in the wake of the #MeToo movement. After the report was published, the scandals continued, highlighted by Boeing's "culture of concealment"—which the US House of Representatives cited as a contributor in the 737 Max crashes—and WeWork's spectacular downfall enabled by its "toxic culture." according to multiple publications.

Undoubtedly, and sadly, we will see more.

Too often the boards were surprised by these scandals because there were no warnings. I've often felt that a corporate board's impression of the company culture is 90 percent filtered through the eyes of the CEO, with the remaining 10 percent derived from interaction with the CFO and a few other key executives. It's rare that a board member spends significant time with anyone below the executive level or participates in any internal meetings outside of an occasional all-company meeting (and even that is rare).

It's hard to blame corporate directors for this. They are typically very busy people, many with full-time executive roles in prominent organizations and other commitments. They parachute into and out of board meetings and barely have time to digest the board materials ahead of time.

Directors intellectually know that they should govern the organization's culture more closely, and they will sometimes discuss it in board meetings. But much of that discussion hinges on anecdotal information. They also intellectually know that the CEO's impression of culture might not be accurate or may be too rosy, but they don't have any mechanism to check this. Today, there is very little impartial evidence used by boards to measure and monitor organizational culture—the most that boards can usually point to is whether the annual employee engagement survey scores are increasing or decreasing or if attrition is too high.

Bob Herz was one of the members of the NACD's Blue Ribbon Commission that wrote the "Culture as a Corporate Asset" report. As the former chairman of the Financial Accounting Standards Board and board member at Fannie Mae and Morgan Stanley, Herz understands the link between culture and performance.

"The way I think about it—is our culture providing a competitive advantage? Is it enabling execution of our strategy?" Herz relayed to my chief research officer one day. "The flip side is risk, particularly risk related to conduct and risk in executing the business strategy. I think risk and strategy are the two sides of the coin—you have to make sure the culture is both driving a can-do attitude of innovation and speed to market, while also providing guardrails to protect against potential downsides."

Ultimately, the reason for a culture renovation is to enable the organization to execute on its go-forward strategy. Because this change can sometimes take years, it's important to define up front what the indicators of a successful renovation should be and to put in place mechanisms to monitor progress. Two-thirds (66 percent) of organizations that have undergone a highly successful culture renovation reported that clear measures and indicators were defined and agreed to up front at the executive level. This is an impressive statistic, particularly when buttressed against a more sobering number: 90 percent of organizations that indicated that their culture change initiative was unsuccessful did not set up measures at the beginning to monitor the change.

Most companies struggle with *what* to analyze (the measurement) as well as how to gather the data (the method). Successful organizations typically settle on a core set of measurements they want to review on a regular basis but use multiple methods to gather that data and continuously monitor the state of the organization's culture.

Common Measures

There are many measurements companies can use to check "Is it working?" Core business metrics are always a good measure, as are items such as customer feedback, policy violations (increasing or decreasing), lawsuits, and so on. I won't cover every metric an organization can use—some of them are very industry dependent—but I do want to outline some common and important human capital measurements.

Attrition

One of the most common culture measurements in use today, concern about attrition is ubiquitous in every organization, and most are trying to measure if employees are leaving for better opportunities and/or dissatisfaction with their current job. While we often use "attrition" loosely, the more precise term to use is "unwanted attrition." Exploring attrition can quickly get complex, but most senior teams want to know what level of unwanted or voluntary attrition they have, particularly of critical talent or people in pivotal roles.

While many companies want to benchmark their unwanted attrition with other like organizations, that usually provides incomplete information. The causes of turnover, even within the same industry, are often unique to the DNA of a single organization. No two company cultures are identical, nor are the reasons for turnover. And getting at the elusive unwanted turnover statistics of voluntary attrition versus retirements, relocations, health issues, family considerations, or a variety of other reasons an employee leaves voluntarily can be tricky.

The best benchmark to use is historical attrition *within* the organization, and the only metrics that matter are when the organization dives deep into the demographics. Are we losing more people today than before from one division, department, or geography? Is our new hire turnover rate too high? What is our high-potential attrition rate (probably the most expensive type of attrition)? Are we losing people at a certain time in their tenure, or perhaps they are plateauing at a certain level? What is our attrition trend with women in leadership positions, underrepresented populations, by age category, level, location, and so on? Is turnover happening among people in pivotal roles that require hard-to-replace skills, or is it concentrated in areas where the skills are easily duplicated and in roles that are not critical to business success?

The list goes on. Understanding these metrics deeply is often referred to as "quality of attrition." Analyzing quality of attrition starts to build a clearer picture of whether the turnover levels and trends in your company are cause for concern.

Inclusion

While most understand diversity, the concept of inclusion can be more elusive, and measuring it can feel impossible. While it's often said that if diversity is being invited to the party, then inclusion is being asked to dance. In reality, the concept of inclusion (and belonging, which is often referred to as a deeper level) is a complex but extremely important trait for top companies. More inclusive cultures generally perform better.

Inclusion is usually measured through surveys to gather sentiment analysis. Since inclusion is often inconsistent across demographics, more sophisticated organizations measure and analyze how inclusive each segment of the workforce feels. This can also be done with social sentiment analysis on external sites. Often an "inclusion lens" is used when reviewing free-form comments from current and ex-employees on Glassdoor or similar venues. Other forms of inclusion measurement include focus groups and exit surveys. Unconscious bias training is typically a staple of creating a more inclusive culture, and measuring the availability, frequency, and completion rates of training can also provide more insight into the inclusiveness of the culture.

Employee Referrals

Talent acquisition professionals agree that employee referrals are one of the best sources for top candidates. They are also a sign of a healthy culture; high-performing organizations are three and a half times more likely to have employees refer candidates than low-performing organizations. Additionally, those same high performers are also twice as likely to have employee referral programs that are consistently measured for effectiveness.

A concern that is sometimes voiced by diversity professionals is that relying too heavily on employee referrals promotes homogeneity, and diversity suffers. Although I've heard that concern more than a few times, it's probably overblown. It's a pretty simple satisfaction equation: if employees like the organization, they are more likely to recommend it to a friend, especially if there is no monetary reward for doing so, which can sometimes skew intent.

Talent Mobility

Research shows that organizations with strong talent mobility perform better than their competitors. This is primarily because they don't allow managers to hoard talent, and they more quickly develop their high-potential talent, and overall talent, while improving collaboration across the company. In fact, top organizations say retention of high-potential employees is the leading catalyst for focusing on talent mobility.

Top companies generally are more deliberate with mobility. They are more likely to reward managers for developing and rotating their direct reports and are more likely (four and a half times more than low performers) to report that the criterion for talent mobility is transparent to their entire organizations.

Rehires

If the belief is that anyone who leaves the company for a different organization is a traitor, it will send a strong signal to the rest of the organization that the company cares more for itself than the individual. When employees successfully "boomerang" back to the company, the signal is far different: the grass may not be greener out there, but it's nice to know the company isn't interested in burning bridges.

Rehires aren't just a positive signal; they also are a cost-effective recruiting tool. The cost of hire is measurably lower, as are other elements such as time to onboard and time to full productivity. Too few companies, however, actively reach out to departed employees after a few months. They should—many times, the grass was not greener.

Hotline Activity

Most organizations have mechanisms to report unethical or inappropriate behavior confidentially and/or anonymously. Monitoring this activity helps the organization understand if employees feel comfortable reporting this behavior and what types of behavior are commonplace.

Intel takes this a step further with a "warm line," a confidential web contact form that allows employees to express concerns with their current job that they aren't comfortable talking about with their manager. "The warm line was built on the premise that we're trying to shift the burden of discovery upstream," said Ed Zabasajja, director of HR and one of the data scientists responsible for developing it, "and really be proactive about understanding what factors or reasons are driving an employee to even consider leaving. And then we can perhaps have the opportunity to intervene and design a solution that helps them to stay."

In analyzing warm line cases across the organization, Intel discovered that retaining employees is often about issues other than money. "Lack of career progression" and "issues with a manager" are the two most cited retention issues among the thousands of Intel employees that have used the warm line, with compensation ranking fifth.

EAP Usage

Employee assistance programs help employees navigate legal, financial, and mental health issues, as well as substance abuse and family issues. While usage is often low, these programs have been estimated to deliver a $6.47 return on investment for every $1 spent.[2] During the coronavirus pandemic, more than half (57 percent) of the diversity and inclusion leaders we surveyed said they were ramping up communications to heighten awareness of EAP offerings. This was used as a strategy to prepare for returning to the workplace and to cope with coworker deaths due to COVID-19.

Monitoring the usage of an EAP can provide cultural clues into the overall well-being of the workforce. Holistic well-being—which encompasses physical, emotional/mental, financial, community, career, and social/relational health—is more popular today in top companies. In fact, high-performance organizations embrace holistic well-being at a rate four times greater than low-performing organizations. The attention to emotional and mental health is expected to continue to rise in organizations long term, although most organizations aren't addressing this very well. In fact, only 15 percent of all organizations feel they are highly effective in addressing employees' mental health needs, though the percentage more than doubles in high-performance firms.[3]

Employee Net Promoter Score

Most organizations utilize Net Promoter Score (NPS) to gauge customer satisfaction, but few have transferred that concept to their own employee base. Employee Net Promoter Score (ENPS) seeks the same thing as NPS: would your current or past employees recommend your organization as a place to work? Some even extend this measurement to employment candidates.

The main question is simple: "On a scale of 0 to 10, how likely is it that you would recommend this company as a place to work?" From this, companies can segment respondents into promoters (9–10), passives (6–8), and detractors (0–5). This metric is best done anonymously, and best used when tracked over time to better understand trend data.

Common Methods

Like measures, there are a variety of methods to use to uncover culture change metrics. Some of the more popular ones include focus groups, engagement surveys, pulse surveys, and sentiment analysis.

Focus Groups

Employee focus groups are commonly used when discussing organizational culture, and for good reason: it's been shown that 52 percent of people believe what employees say about their company versus what the company's official communications say.[4] Focus groups are a nice complement to surveys, providing qualitative context to the quantitative data gathered from a survey.

The focus group concept has been morphed by some companies from an information-gathering concept into an "action learning" or proactive exercise called a "hackathon." If you aren't familiar with hackathons, they typically involve employees working long hours, often through the night, to redesign products or processes. The idea is a collective design thinking endeavor that produces innovative solutions. Some companies have used this concept to hack their culture. For example, Ford used a culture hackathon to discover:

- ▶ What do employees love about the current culture and want to see fortified?
- ▶ What about the culture needs to be fixed?
- ▶ What is not present in the current culture that employees want to see in the future?

Dialogue based on the answers set the tone for a two-day event, where employees worked in randomly selected teams to

#hackFORDculture and generate ideas to fortify elements of the culture they loved and fix elements that weren't serving the company well.[5]

Engagement Surveys

The oldest form of culture measurement, these surveys are designed to measure the discretionary effort—usually referred to as the engagement—of the workforce, along with overall job satisfaction. While there are distinctions between an engagement survey and a climate or culture survey, most organizations combine elements of all under the umbrella of an engagement survey. Traditionally done once a year or every other year, as mentioned earlier, engagement surveys are falling out of favor as a measure of culture in organizations for a few core reasons. For one, they have become quite expensive. The engagement survey market is big business, and companies are paying far too much to administer an annual or biannual survey to the workforce. Second, they have become quite bureaucratic, and results and remedies are slow to emerge—and sometimes they never emerge at all. And lastly\\, they are typically one snapshot in time versus a regular pulse to see patterns emerge over shorter increments.

While the year-over-year benchmarking data can provide longitudinal clues to the health of the culture, if the organization is relying solely on the engagement survey—which many are today—as a measure of culture health, it's likely a false proxy. Organizations need to use this as just one data source and combine it with the other sources of sentiment.

Pulse Surveys

These have become increasingly popular versus engagement surveys due to their frequency. Pulse surveys provide a more realistic view of the organization and are shorter, which employees appreciate. The pace of these ranges from as infrequently as quarterly to weekly, and even daily for some organizations. Some organizations are more interested in consistent questions and longitudinal data, while others prefer to cover different topics over time.

Publishing one question a day is an interesting way to subtly reinforce messages to the workforce and ironically avoid "survey fatigue," which longer surveys introduce. As referenced earlier, at certain companies workers receive a daily survey with questions like whether they have had too many meetings lately or if their manager has thanked them in the past week. Weekly is more common. Workday, the human resources and finance software maker, sends out employee surveys at the end of every week on what the company calls "Feedback Fridays." At PepsiCo, the beverage giant invites employees to identify systems that prevent them from getting work done quickly via a tool known as the "process shredder."[6] Pulse surveys are quickly supplanting the longer annual survey in many organizations.

Sentiment Analysis

As discussed earlier, the use of natural language processing tools, powered by AI and machine learning for ongoing monitoring and analysis of internal and external sentiment, is one of the more effective methods to monitor culture. I believe NLP is likely to become a preferred practice in monitoring culture. NLP allows employees to share their observations using their own words, not answers listed for them in a Likert scale. Moreover, employees often have issues that prewritten questions or answers don't cover, which can be better identified with NLP. Most companies don't have time to read thousands of open-ended comments and try to categorize those comments by type manually. For all these reasons, Likert surveys will undoubtedly diminish over time as NLP technology becomes more mainstream.

Effective NLP looks for patterns of sentiment, and it typically bifurcates "good" from "bad" sentiment before parsing by sentiment subject. This can happen in real time so that employee sentiment can be captured frequently and more accurately represent the employees' true voice. This allows cultural patterns to be uncovered over time and prevents false positives that can often plague the traditional annual employee engagement survey. It's not uncommon for an annual survey to pick up the "crisis of the moment" only to have that dissipate in a few days. Ongoing surveys mitigate that, and sentiment analysis, because it doesn't need to be time-bound, can be an "always-on" method of gathering feedback.

Culture Measurement at Ford

Ford Motor Company is one company that has embraced sentiment analysis as a core component of a cultural measuring system.

When Jim Hackett was named CEO of Ford in mid-2017, at his introductory news conference executive chairman Bill Ford promised that Hackett would be a "cultural change agent" and that "he will continue to transform the culture of Ford." Together, Ford said he and Hackett aspired to make the company embody a "culture of caring about each other, about ideas flowing freely."[7]

Those ideas were certainly needed. Few industries are under as much pressure as the traditional auto manufacturers, and there are few US companies as long on tradition as Ford. With well over a century of rich history, and an auto market undergoing transformation like never before, Hackett knew the company needed a culture renovation, and he outlined that need in the Foreword for our culture renovation study:

> With a 115-year history of automotive manufacturing excellence, we are transforming Ford into the most trusted company for smart vehicles in the smart world. As part of this transformation, I want to be careful not to lose some of the innovations that our founder, Henry Ford, originally put in place that today we may take for granted.
>
> In 1918, for example, Henry Ford opened a production plant in Dearborn, MI that—at its peak—had over 100,000 people working in it. Due to the enormity of that bet that he placed, I presume he woke up every day thinking "I have to make this project work" vs. thinking about how to define

the culture of the workplace, but he certainly understood the link between culture and productivity.

Industrial companies, more than tech companies, must have productivity to pay for a space like Henry created. The pay-it-back speed is what productivity is; that's the effectiveness of your workers and your supply chain. He bet everything on that plant, and productivity was like gold to him. Because of that, he had to build an industrial culture that maximized the work output.

Today, like many successful companies, we are pursuing two states in parallel. The first is the traditional business where we've consistently achieved industrial precision and productivity excellence. The question now is how do we achieve even greater success through cultural excellence?

The second is a business where we are building innovative, but imprecise, products that are difficult to predict. The question for this business is a bit different: how do we iterate fast and learn, and how can we work collaboratively and more effectively?

The two states Hackett describes echo the same situation many CEOs of larger companies face when their company and market are disrupted. How can we innovate for the future while preserving the current revenue streams that are rooted in the past? Former CEO Hackett knew that answer lay in successful renovation, and the company has done a lot of renovation work on its culture over the past few years. That work included building a culture strategy room at its headquarters, hosting culture hackathons all around the world, creating a culture cabinet with employee volunteers, defining new company values, and redesigning all people processes to ensure culture is central to how Ford hires, trains, and evaluates employees.

With their focus on culture change, Ford expected to see differences in key areas—such as breaking bureaucracy, testing new ideas to overcome complex problems, and prioritizing customer experience. But it was hard to ascertain if the efforts were having any impact.

Traditionally, Ford would rely on surveys to measure its efforts, with a lot of weight on an every-other-year engagement survey. Concerned about its effectiveness, the HR team interviewed employees to see if they shared that concern. The team heard repeatedly that the workforce didn't mind being surveyed but wanted quicker, more actionable surveys, and managers wanted more automated help to know what to do with the results. As a result, the company shifted to smaller pulse surveys.

But after extensive external and internal research, the company felt that surveys would paint only part of the culture picture. Instead, leaders started looking for data from places where employees were already naturally discussing culture and began collecting and analyzing passive data sources to create a more holistic story. Those data sources included written messages on community whiteboards, anonymous reviews left on Glassdoor, enterprise meeting chat logs, and comment streams on internal news articles.

Utilizing an AI-based platform to analyze text, Ford experts trained the machine learning engine to automate this analysis across languages and specific terms used within the company. The company parses this data by region or demographics (like age) to determine whether sentiment of early-career professionals is different from that of people who have been with Ford for years. It isn't interested in identifying specific people, but rather, knowing what high-level culture topics are trending at any given time. The HR team often takes the trends it spots and uses dashboards to report on results to leadership. While this work is often complex, it helps leaders understand what employees really need and want.

While Ford has begun the habit of publicly releasing some of the data gathered in pulse surveys, that is a practice not employed by most organizations—although that will probably change. In addition to the pressure described earlier from the NACD, corporations are increasingly sensing pressure from investors and regulatory bodies to publicly disclose information and metrics on the health of a company's culture.

Human Capital Reporting Requirements

On August 26, 2020, the US Securities and Exchange Commission (SEC) voted three to two to adopt new data reporting requirements that affect all US-based public companies. These disclosure requirements had not undergone significant revisions in over 30 years, and for the first time included a mandate on publicly reporting human capital metrics. These metrics involved any human capital measures or objectives that the company focuses on in managing the business, to the extent they are material to an understanding of the registrant's business.

Prior to this change, the only human capital metric public companies were required to disclose was the number of employees. Going forward, public companies will be disclosing a mixture of human capital metrics if they are deemed material (a simple way to think of materiality is if a reasonable person would find the information important in making a decision to buy or sell a particular company's stock). This is purposefully vague, and the SEC acknowledged that the exact measures or objectives will depend on the nature of the company's business and workforce. The SEC identified some non-exclusive examples, which included very broad measures that address the development, attraction, and retention of personnel.

Earlier, in January 2019, the International Organization for Standardization (ISO) issued ISO 30414, which provided more specific guidelines for internal and external human capital reporting. ISO 30414 provides guidelines on core HR areas such as organizational culture, recruitment and turnover, productivity, health and safety, and leadership.

"Workforce reporting is about rethinking how organizational value should be understood and evaluated and allowing for more data-driven decision making across workforce management," said Dr. Ron McKinley, chair of the ISO technical committee that developed the standard.[8] "What's more, by providing a number of relevant key metrics that are recognizable on an international scale, multinational companies can more easily transfer human capital information, better control their international HR activities and provide greater transparency for all their stakeholders," he said.

The ISO standards for HR cover the following areas:

Compliance

- Number and type of grievances filed
- Training hours on compliance and ethics
- External dispute resolutions
- Number, type, and source of external audit
- Findings and actions arising from these

Costs

- Total workforce costs
- External workforce costs
- Ratio of the basic salary and remuneration for each workforce category
- Total costs of employment
- Cost per hire
- Recruitment costs
- Turnover costs

Diversity

- Workforce diversity with respect to age, gender, nationality, disability, job family, job level/hierarchy, qualification, diversity of leadership team

Leadership

- Leadership trust
- Span of control
- Leadership development
- Percentage of leaders/talents who have formal mentors or coaches

- Percentage of leaders who have the formal function of mentors or coaches

Occupational Health and Safety

- Lost time for injury
- Number of occupational accidents
- Number of people killed during work (fatality, death, or mortality rate)
- Training hours on health and safety at work versus total amount of training hours
- Number of employees who participated in the training/total numbers of employees

Organizational Culture

- Engagement, satisfaction, commitment
- Retention rate
- Productivity, including revenue, turnover, profit per employee
- Human capital return on investment

Recruitment, Mobility, and Turnover

- Number of qualified candidates per position
- Quality per hire
- Average time to fill vacant positions; time to fill vacant critical business positions, internal/external recruitment
- Transition and future workforce capabilities assessment
- Percentage of positions filled internally
- Percentage of critical business positions filled internally
- Percentage of vacant critical business positions in relation to all vacant positions

Employee Bench Strength

- Turnover rate

- Involuntary turnover rate
- Involuntary critical turnover rate
- Voluntary turnover rate (without retirement)
- Exit/turnover reasons/leaving employment by reason

Skills and Capabilities

- Total developing and training costs
- Learning and development: percentage of employees who participate in training compared with total number of employees per year; average training hours per employee; number of training participants differentiated in training categories
- Internal mobility rate
- Workforce competency rate
- Succession planning

Workforce Availability

- Absenteeism rate
- Full-time equivalents
- Number of employees
- Contingent workforce; independent contractors; temporary workforce
- Number of full-time and part-time employees

HR Experience Wanted

With these new requirements, and the increased attention on culture, boards are recognizing a glaring lack of HR skills at the director level. Several are beginning to change that. Current or former CHROs, particularly female, are one of the most sought-after profiles when board seats open up, for both public and private companies. ABM Industries, ADP, AlaskaAir, BrightView Holdings,

Facebook, Manpower, Red Robin, Shutterfly, Spartan Motors, Tesla, Vail Resorts, and Zumiez are just a few examples of companies that have a former or current CHRO on the board.

"For decades, boards most frequently recruited CEOs and chief financial officers for director roles," wrote Rochelle Campbell, who leads NACD's Board Recruitment Services.[9] "In more recent years, however, board recruiters have seen a shift toward skills being sought in director candidates who have served as a CHRO." From 2005 to 2017, the number of HR executives on US public company boards almost tripled, from 84 to a record 243, according to Equilar, the executive compensation and corporate governance data analysis firm.[10]

"The board searches I've been part of the last two or three years, in just about every case, among the qualities we've listed as a preferred skill or a particularly strong 'what counts factor' is HR experience," said Dave Brandon, chairman of Domino's and board member of Herman Miller, DTE Energy, and PetSmart. "I believe it's much more on the radar because that voice around the table and their perspective is going to make your board perform better."

Brandon also says that some boards are becoming both more agile and hands-on in how they are collaborating with HR and other talent leaders.

"The other thing I've observed is boards are creating—if not permanent committees—ad hoc committees in which they're assigning two to three board members to work with the HR lead and/or the CEO on particular HR related initiatives," Brandon observed. "The point being it's not just about recruiting HR folks to join boards, it's also directing attention from existing board members to important topics such as social responsibility, inclusion and diversity, employee engagement, and culture management. I see far more focus and engagement as it relates to deploying this expertise around the director's table, which 5 or 10 years ago you wouldn't have seen."

Increasingly, corporate boards are waking up to the importance of governing culture as rigorously as they govern other elements of the organization. The concept of a formal culture subcommittee is one that some publicly traded companies, such as Citi, have already put in place.

The charter for Citi's Ethics, Conduct and Culture Committee states that the purpose of the committee is to oversee management's efforts to foster a culture of ethics and appropriate conduct within the organization. The committee's role is one of oversight, recognizing that management is responsible for continuously reinforcing and championing Citi's sound ethics, responsible conduct, and principled culture throughout Citi's employee population. The committee is composed of at least three nonmanagement members of the board. The charter goes on to say that the committee shall have direct access to, and receive regular reports from, management and has the power to conduct or authorize investigations into any matter within its scope of responsibilities.[11]

Most board members I've talked with expect to see more of these specific culture subcommittees in the future and more HR talent recruited for open board positions. They mainly just want to ensure they have better cultural insight.

"Corporate boards want to know if they're sitting on quicksand," said Jamie Gorlick, a partner at WilmerHale and board member of Amazon and Verisign. "They want to know how well their companies are run, and what the spirit of the people in the company is. This came up during the MeToo complaints, when many board members said to themselves, *I had no idea that this was the kind of community that we were supposedly overseeing.*"

A BLUEPRINT TO RENOVATE CULTURE

PHASE TWO

BUILD

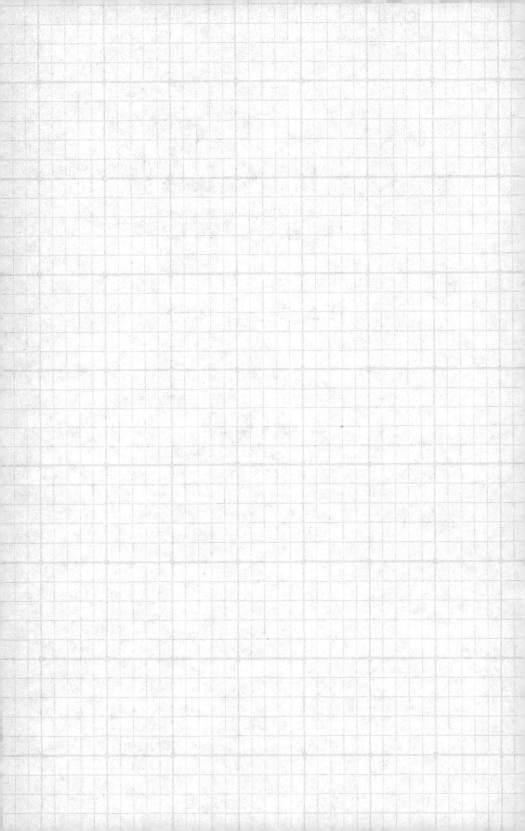

CHAPTER 10

STEP #7:
CLEARLY COMMUNICATE THAT CHANGE IS COMING

For the last 20 years, and all around the world, we CEOs have invested untold millions into the question: "What does it take to have an engaged workplace culture?" We've bought books, retained consultants, rolled out surveys, looked deep into the hearts and minds of the people who work for us. We know how crucial it is to having talent who love working for us and who will offer discretionary effort and innovation. And introductions to their friends. And yet we're still screwing it up."

—GARRY RIDGE, CEO, WD-40

Almost 80 percent of organizations that successfully renovated their culture had a lead architect who made that change happen. In each of those organizations, that lead architect had the same position—CEO. While more than three-quarters (78 percent) of organizations that had a successful culture change started top-down, it's important to establish a co-creation mindset within the organization, something I'll address more specifically later. But it's clear that when it comes to communication about the culture change, the message needs to come consistently and frequently from the top.

I think most CEOs would admit that launching a culture renovation can be a bit unnerving. As outlined in Steps 1–6, it's important to establish the foundation and have the various elements of the planning phase complete and secure. But once it's time to begin building the new culture, it's equally important to be clear on the messaging. We found that 26 percent of respondents cited "there was lack of clarity about the type of culture we desired" as an inhibitor to success in changing the culture.

Despite all the thoughtful research and careful planning, there's no getting around the fact that the initial communication to the workforce is critical—and it needs to be a clear message.

To kick off a culture renovation, the CEO must articulate the purpose of the organization (whether new, old, or renovated), and that purpose must resonate with employees. It needs to make sense to the workforce and be pithy so that it can be remembered and recited without hesitation. The purpose needs to be instilled with the renovation spirit: expressing a genuine respect for the past while building for the future. The initial communication also should be clear on what the new culture initiative seeks to change, what the future looks like, why the culture change is so vital to the success of the business now and looking ahead, and why all stakeholders should care.

You can't ignore past mistakes. But to be effective, the message delivered by the CEO must recognize what made the company great to begin with, honor past innovations, and focus on the future. Leaders of successful culture change initiatives primarily communicated a customer-oriented focus and the importance of shifting or disrupting their markets to better serve their customers as the primary driver for change. They didn't harp on past mistakes as the reason for culture change (such as poor past financial performance, low employee engagement, public relations issues, scandals, competitive threats, etc.). Many times, that's impossible to ignore, but it doesn't need to be dwelled upon. The tone needs to be "Here's where I envision us in the future" versus "We've had a lot of problems, so something needs to change." Essentially, it's a proactive strategy versus a reactive strategy—an important nuance not to be overlooked.

This is sometimes hard to do for new CEOs. Very often they were brought in, or promoted to the CEO role, because there were previous problems. While it's constructive to deal directly with individuals or groups that were at the root of problems, admonishing the entire company for those issues is sure to get any culture renovation off on the wrong foot. Similarly, attempting to change the organization without clear messages and reasoning behind it is likely to result in confusion and chaos.

There's a famous business parable on dysfunctional organizations that touches on this and is always instructive to revisit:

> After firing the longtime CEO, the board brings in a new CEO to turn around a failing organization. The very first day after sitting down at his new desk, the new CEO finds a sealed manila envelope in the top drawer from the previous CEO. Written on it are simple instructions:
>
> When things get tough, open this.
>
> Well, after just a couple of months into the job, it's clear that things are pretty tough—this turnaround is not going to be easy. The stock price has declined, sales are down, key people are quitting, and employee engagement is at rock bottom. So, the new CEO takes a deep breath, opens his drawer, and eagerly rips open the manila envelope. Inside are three smaller envelopes, labeled 1 (open me first), 2 (open

me later), and 3 (open me last). He opens #1 and it reads: "Blame your predecessor."

The new CEO promptly calls a press conference and explains that the previous CEO had left him with a real mess, and it was going to take a bit longer to clean up than expected. Industry analysts, reporters, and shareholders all seem to agree. The stock price goes up a little, and the company seems headed toward the road to recovery.

However, the good feelings are short-lived. After just another few months, sales continue to decline, the stock price slumps even further, and employees keep leaving. Faced with a tough earnings call coming up, the CEO reaches inside and finds the second envelope, and rips it open. It reads: "Reorganize."

The CEO quickly takes out the org chart and rearranges several boxes. The next week is filled with firing some long-tenured managers, consolidating a few divisions, and cutting expenses anywhere possible. He announces all of this on the next earnings call. Wall Street applauds, saying "it needed to be done," and the stock starts recovering.

But it doesn't last. Now about a year into the new job, things are as bad as they've ever been. The reorg seems to have made things worse, the remaining good people are leaving, and the stock price hits a new low. Staring at another tough earnings call on the calendar, the CEO remembers he still has an envelope left. He anxiously opens it. It reads: "Prepare three envelopes."

That story always brings a smile, but it's far more truth than fiction.

A Maniac Pledge

Optimistic, clear, future-forward communication has been the ticket for successful culture change, but not every CEO does this well.

A great example of one who does is Garry Ridge, an energetic and charismatic Australian who has been living in the United States for decades and overseeing one of its best-known brands.

Ridge is president and CEO of the WD-40 Company headquartered in San Diego, California. It makes the ever-popular WD-40 lubricant (found in 8 out of 10 US households), as well as several other lesser-known products: 3-IN-ONE oil, Solvol, Lava heavy-duty hand cleaner, X-14, Carpet Fresh, Spot Shot, and 1001 and 2000 Flushes household cleaning products. Ridge, who took over as CEO in 1997 after serving in several other roles the previous 10 years, has seen the stock price increase sevenfold during his tenure, with the company's market cap growing well north of $2 billion. And he's done it by building an amazing culture based on very simple concepts to energize and inspire his workforce. With just under 500 employees, the company boasts a 93 percent employee engagement rate and an average tenure of 10 years.

The company was founded in 1953 as the Rocket Chemical Company and has a long and storied history. Its staff of three initially set out to create a line of rust-prevention solvents and degreasers for use in the aerospace industry. Working in a small lab in San Diego, they created the original secret formula—so secret it is still locked in a bank vault—and it remains the same formula in use today. In 1969, the company was renamed after its only product, WD-40, and it went public in 1973. The stock price increased 61 percent on the first day of listing. Since that time, WD-40 has grown by leaps and bounds, and it is now virtually a household name, used in numerous consumer and industrial markets such as automotive, manufacturing, sporting goods, aviation, hardware and home improvement, construction, and farming.

Dozens of times, I've shown a can of WD-40 to audiences over the years and asked, "How many of you have this in your household?" Almost every hand inevitably shoots up. I also ask, "And how many of you have lost the little red straw that went with it?" As you would guess, most admit they have (the company says it's by far the biggest complaint about the product, and a flaw it has since corrected). Then

I ask, "Who knows where the name WD-40 comes from?" Despite its immense popularity, very few can answer this question.

"WD" stands for "water displacement," which is the basis for the secret formula. "40" is more interesting—it was the original inventors' fortieth attempt to get that formula right. That "40" represents an important trait of WD-40's culture—that mistakes are not only tolerated, but celebrated, and failure is merely part of the learning process. This is a very big tenet of Ridge's leadership style and very familiar to all his employees.

In fact, Ridge is so serious about the commitment to learning, that he insists everyone at the company take the "WD-40 Maniac Pledge," a solemn vow to become, in his words, a "learning maniac." The pledge reads:

> I am responsible for taking action, asking questions, getting answers, and making decisions. I won't wait for someone to tell me. If I need to know, I'm responsible for asking. I have no right to be offended that I didn't "get this sooner." If I'm doing something others should know about, I'm responsible for telling them.[1]

While WD-40 might seem an atypical setting for such a pledge, it's clear that Ridge is not your typical leader. He has proved that exemplary leadership can take any business, no matter how mundane, and make it flourish. It centers on something every CEO inherently knows, but most fail to execute on: engaging the workforce.

When asked about other leaders, Ridge admits he's baffled. In a provocative blog post directed at CEOs (Ridge is often provocative) and cleverly titled "Are You an Accidental Soul-Sucking CEO,"[2] he questions why we have so much trouble engaging the workforce:

> For the last 20 years, and all around the world, we CEOs have invested untold millions into the question: "What does it take to have an engaged workplace culture?" We've bought books, retained consultants, rolled out surveys, looked deep

into the hearts and minds of the people who work for us. We know how crucial it is to having talent who love working for us and who will offer discretionary effort and innovation. And introductions to their friends. We even know how to quantify all this stuff.

We are at the leading edge of a historic conversation. Our predecessors—the generations who ran the factories and cracked the whips—would look at us and our workplaces in awe. We know better than anyone at any time in the history of humans what it takes to create a workplace where people want to come to work, joyfully invest their efforts and talents into a cause greater than themselves, and go home happy to children who are learning from their examples.

And yet we're still screwing it up.

Ridge provides often-cited engagement numbers as proof—such as more than 50 percent of employees are actively looking for other jobs—and offers that "Amazon Prime and Costco have a better customer retention rate with their discretionary paid memberships than employers throughout the world have with their employees." He goes on to cite that employees who are either nonengaged or actively disengaged cost their organizations between $960 billion and $1.2 trillion globally.

The problem, according to Ridge, is that the responsibility for engagement is conventionally assigned to the direct supervisors of employees and the organizational development team. He argues that this responsibility should reside at the CEO level and it might be the CEO who is unwittingly causing disengagement.

"While your OD department might be working so diligently to refine the behaviors of your managers to staunch the flow of your expensively acquired talent, it might be your office that is sucking the joy, vision, and dedication from your tribe."

At WD-40, Ridge calls his employees a "tribe," one example of many unique words Ridge uses internally to get the attention of his workforce. Ridge has even harsher words to get the attention of other CEOs.

"Why do I use the expression 'soul-sucking'? That's how it feels, especially when an organization that promotes itself as being committed to an engaged culture is led by a CEO who is unfocused, unserious, unkind, or simply doesn't get it. It's more than simply clumsy leadership. It's a breach of promise. And it makes your entire tribe feel depleted and dispirited."

Ridge often talks about how critical it is to have a clearly defined purpose that speaks to the hearts and minds of employees to create an engaged culture. As an example, he cites Larry Fink, chairman and CEO of BlackRock. In his 2018 annual letter to CEOs Fink wrote: "To prosper over time, every company must not only deliver financial performance but also show how it makes a positive contribution to society. Without a sense of purpose, no company, either public or private, can achieve its full potential. It will lose the license to operate from key stakeholders. Demonstrate the leadership and clarity that will drive not only [your] own investment returns but also the prosperity and security of [your] fellow citizens."

At WD-40, purpose is critically important to what, on the surface, could seem like a bland group of products.

"Purpose motivates people to feel part of something where they believe that they are making a difference," Ridge said. "When our tribe members at WD-40 come to work, they ask themselves, 'What am I going to do today?' Their answer: 'I'm going to create something positive for someone. I'm going to solve a problem. I'm going to make something work better. I'm going to create an opportunity. I'm going to cause a positive lasting memory for someone.'

"That's much more motivating than saying, 'I'm going to go to work today and I'm going to sell a can of chemicals.' Don't you think?"

WD-40 actively celebrates many things, including the clever ways the product is utilized and the problems it solves. Over the years, WD-40 users have written thousands of testimonial letters to the company sharing their often unique, if sometimes just plain weird, uses for that yellow and blue can. Some of the more interesting stories include the bus driver in Asia who used WD-40 to remove a python snake that had coiled itself around the undercarriage of his bus. Or when police officers used WD-40 to remove a naked burglar trapped in an air conditioning vent.

A greater purpose helps drive WD-40, as do the company's values. Positive values are important inside the company; without them, Ridge says, employees will require micromanagement and consistent course correction and ultimately can't be trusted to make decisions on their own. A strong culture based on values allows employees the freedom to innovate and create market-differentiating, competitive ideas. WD-40's company values are:

- ▶ We value doing the right thing.
- ▶ We value creating positive, lasting memories in all our relationships.
- ▶ We value making it better than it is today.
- ▶ We value succeeding as a tribe while excelling as individuals.
- ▶ We value owning it and passionately acting on it.
- ▶ We value sustaining the WD-40 Company economy.

"The worst thing that can happen in an organization is someone getting really good results and violating values," writes Ridge. "Inevitably, people conclude that 'it's results at all costs and values don't matter.' That will kill your company over the long term. It demoralizes your people, depletes energy, squanders confidence, burns up the sense of belonging inside your culture. It creates friction among tribe members. People start doing really bad things; they hurt each other and your customers, just to get results."

Because of Ridge, WD-40's culture is the exact opposite. For example, employee engagement scores consistently are above 90 percent, and almost all (98 percent) say they "love to tell people they work at WD-40." Nearly all the employees (99 percent) believe their "opinions and values are a good fit" for the organization, and 93 percent report that the organization "encourages employees to continually improve in their jobs." Another 97 percent indicate they're "clear on the company's goals," with 93 percent saying they're "excited about" the direction that WD-40 is headed in.

Ridge attributes these consistently high engagement levels—and the organization's stellar business results—to a culture that fosters fearless employees.

"Fear is the most disabling emotion we have," observes Ridge. "Yet bad things happen in companies. It's just a fact of life. When your people are afraid to try new things, make a mistake now and then, despite the best of intentions, fear precludes creativity and freedom. At WD-40 Company, we have a tradition called 'The Learning Moment.' It's the positive or negative outcome of any situation that must be openly and freely shared to benefit all. Anyone can openly say, 'I had a learning moment, here's what happened, and here's how it will be better tomorrow.' Or 'I had a learning moment and here's what happened, here's the great result I got, and here's what I want to share.' No one should be afraid of reprisals from their managers for making innocent mistakes. If you take the fear of the result out, you create a culture that's more open to learning."

If fear of mistakes were prevalent in the company in the early fifties, the original inventors might have abandoned the product after WD-39. Lucky for us all, they had the courage, and lack of fear, to take their learnings and create WD-40.

CHAPTER 11

STEP #8: FERRET OUT SKEPTICS AND NONBELIEVERS EARLY

> If you asked me when I joined what I intended to do,
> or what I was going to do, I would have said I absolutely
> have no intention of changing out my senior team.
> —FRANÇOIS LOCOH-DONOU, CEO, F5 NETWORKS

Of all the steps in successfully renovating your culture, this is the hardest one.

Intuitively, most understand the necessity. To be successful, make sure naysayers, skeptics, blockers, nonbelievers, doubters, and pessimists are out of the way. Make way for the proponents, advocates, supporters, executers, achievers—that's how a culture change will get done. As Jim Collins famously wrote in *Good to Great*, focus on "First

Who, Then What." Get the right people on the bus before figuring out where to drive the bus.

That sounds like solid advice, but it's not the way real life usually works.

In any company, there are people who appear to be the right people, but they secretly thwart the best-laid plans. We encounter people like this all the time, those saboteurs that sometimes openly—but many times discreetly—derail internal initiatives. There are many reasons for their behaviors. Often, they feel threatened. Their power base is being eroded, their authority usurped, their scope diminished. Other times, it's purely ego-driven; maybe the idea wasn't theirs and they need it to be. Sometimes they just intellectually disagree or disagree on principle with the new direction but may or may not be candid about their disagreement.

In my career, I've encountered dozens of these people, maybe more. It can be very frustrating. The hardest ones to deal with for me were always those who practiced the art of "the sun always shines up." They were fantastic corporate citizens to my face. Saying all the right things. In alignment with our vision. Promising to carry out the strategy the right way. But in reality, they were an absolute typhoon to other people lower in the organization. Berating people, subjugating the purpose/vision/mission of the company, seeking control at the expense of others and at the expense of the corporate good. This personality type exists at various levels in most organizations. The key is to move those people away from their ability to do damage as quickly as possible, which often means removing them from the organization.

Successful CEOs ferret those sentiments out early and make the necessary adjustments. And that starts at the top. Almost 40 percent of organizations that have had a successful culture renovation replaced senior leaders who were not willing, or able, to embrace and model the desired culture. They needed to reassign these executives to other positions or encourage them to pursue other opportunities. This is absolutely critical. Thirty-eight percent of organizations told us that their companies tolerated the behavior of leaders who resisted the change and their opposition was a primary inhibitor to success.

Legion of Superheroes

Satya Nadella certainly has made changes at Microsoft, replacing almost all key executives since taking the company's CEO title from Steve Ballmer in 2014. Just a few years in, only Amy Hood, chief financial officer, Kurt DelBene, EVP of corporate strategy (after a brief hiatus that bridged the Ballmer-to-Nadella transition), and Brad Smith, president, remain from the previous regime's leadership team. In *Hit Refresh*, Nadella talked about the changes and about the people that he needed to transition out:

> They were all talented people, but the senior leadership team needed to become a cohesive team that shared a common worldview. For anything monumental to happen—great software, innovative hardware, or even a sustainable institution— there needs to be one great mind or a set of agreeing minds. I don't mean yes-men and yes-women. Debate and argument are essential. Improving upon other's ideas is crucial. I wanted people to speak up. "Oh, here's a customer segmentation study I've done." Or, "Here's a pricing approach that contradicts that idea." It's great to have a good old-fashioned college debate. But there also has to be high-quality agreement. We need a senior leadership team (SLT) that would lean into each other's problems, promote dialogue, and be effective. We needed everyone to view the SLT as his or her first team, not just another meeting they attended. We needed to be aligned on mission, strategy, and culture. I like to think of the SLT as a sort of Legion of Superheroes, with each leader coming to the table with a unique superpower to contribute for the common good.

While Nadella did not go as far to say that the previous SLT had been somewhat dysfunctional, with few of the top executives putting the common good first, that was the implication of his remarks to some insiders. There were probably a few too many yes-men and -women as well.

So, changes needed to be made. Upon becoming CEO, Nadella was very purposeful in creating an SLT that he thought would propel his vision for the future culture of Microsoft. Nadella was also transparent on what he expected from the SLT: an all-in commitment to change the culture of the company. Shortly after his appointment, in a memo to all that announced some initial changes, he wrote:

> One of my consistent themes has been a point I made in my original mail—we all need to do our best work, have broad impact and find real meaning in the work we do. Coming together as teams fuels this on a day-to-day basis. And having the Senior Leadership Team (SLT) set both pace and example means a lot to me. I have discussed this point in various forms with the SLT and have asked for their "all in" commitment as we embark on the next chapter for the company. We need to drive clarity, alignment and intensity across all our work.[1]

With that e-mail he announced that Skype executive Tony Bates, who had been a candidate for Microsoft CEO, was leaving along with Tami Reller, the executive vice president of marketing. That began a series of departures including Windows chief Terry Myerson, Nokia leader Stephen Elop (also once a CEO candidate), business solutions executive Kirill Tatarinov, HR chief Lisa Brummel, and eventually artificial intelligence and research head Harry Shum, among others.

With all those departures, it would be easy to assume that the amount of experience and institutional knowledge walking out the door would create a significant gap. But that wasn't the case. Eight of the fourteen people Satya brought on to the SLT had been at the company for at least two decades. Change at the top doesn't mean an organization needs to suffer from a lack of internal expertise if it has ready successors on the bench, as Nadella clearly thought the company had.

There was one role, however, that Nadella paid very careful attention to as he thought about renovating the culture: the position of chief people officer.

The Power of the Chief People Officer

When he became CEO, Nadella inherited a very experienced HR chief in Lisa Brummel, who had been at Microsoft since 1989. Brummel didn't start out in HR. She held a variety of roles in management and marketing in several divisions, including Microsoft's hardware, consumer, and productivity business, before she was plucked to run HR by Ballmer in 2005 when the company was at a recognized low.

Brummel's years at the HR helm were sometimes criticized because of the stack-ranking policy she oversaw, a process she defended by saying it "seemed to be right for the time" when the program was phased out.[2] And she was likely correct. There may have been times when it was right; the employee base fluctuated significantly during her tenure. Under Brummel the workforce more than doubled, from 61,000 employees to 128,000, but there were also tough times. She oversaw two large-scale layoffs, the first because of the 2008 recession, and the second due to the failed acquisition of Nokia's handset business.

Nadella clearly understood the impact an effective chief people officer can have when changing a culture and, like Ballmer, went outside the world of HR to find Brummel's successor.

Kathleen Hogan was not the most obvious choice for this role. She had been successfully running Microsoft Services, the largest single Microsoft organization with more than 21,000 employees worldwide. Prior to joining Microsoft in 2003, Hogan was a partner at McKinsey & Co. and previously had been a development manager at Oracle. She earned her bachelor's degree in applied mathematics and economics, magna cum laude, from Harvard and an MBA from Stanford.

"Kathleen is an accomplished, well-respected and well-rounded leader who obsesses over our customers and is motivated by people's passion for how technology can change the world," Nadella said in the press release announcing her appointment. "She is the right person to continue pushing our cultural transformation forward, and she will ensure Microsoft remains the best, most inclusive place to work."

"When Satya first approached me about leading HR," Hogan recalled, "I remember coming in and asking, 'What's my scorecard?' . . . and Satya said, 'The one thing I want you to do is help me transform the culture.' So even back then, he was crystal clear that that was really going to be important . . . the culture that I want to be eternal. Our strategy is going to evolve, but that's [culture] going to be really important to us."[3]

Nadella has often referred to Hogan as his partner in Microsoft's culture journey, and it's clear he is one of her biggest fans. Having the right people leader can make or break a culture renovation, something Nadella seemed to understand from the start. Equally, Hogan has consistently made it clear that having the right CEO and a senior team that is supportive of a culture change is critical to success.

"The first—and most important step—is to engage the CEO and the senior leadership team," Hogan said "Our appointment of Satya Nadella as CEO was a significant milestone for the company, and his role in culture change has been instrumental. Having a CEO and senior leaders who champion and embody culture change helps set the tone and provides a path for employees to follow."[4]

But Hogan was also clear that her HR team has had a great deal to do with the successful renovation.

"It has been significant. From envisioning to coaching, defining, guiding, and leading change management," Hogan recalled. "We worked alongside our company leaders with dedicated resources. All the while, we have kept both customers' and employees' best interests top of mind and evolved as we listened and learned. It has been incredibly gratifying work for HR to partner with the business, and while it hasn't always been easy, we've found that the insights from the HR teams have been invaluable and have helped ensure our efforts remain authentic to how the change is manifesting itself internally and externally. It's an ongoing effort, and we continue to learn and evolve as we go."[5]

Hogan had enough experience at Microsoft to recognize that building on the company's storied past was going to be the best way to renovate Microsoft under Nadella.

"I don't necessarily look at it as 'old' Microsoft vs. 'new' Microsoft. We have such a rich history, and it's really about building on and honoring where we've been as we move into the next phase for our company. Ultimately, for us the primary shift includes embracing a growth mindset. As we've translated that into our company norms, we're moving from a place where employees felt a need to be the single source of knowledge, to a culture of collaboration where employees find more value in working together to best leverage diverse knowledge. This has also included the evolution of our performance system, which today places a premium on collaboration and contributing to the success of others. We're also moving towards a mindset that embraces risk and failure. A shared understanding that risk, failure, and experimentation are the ways to learn and innovate and that not every idea may work every time."

With their collective internal experience, understanding who could best represent a renovated culture was likely very intuitive for Hogan and Nadella. In general, CEOs who are promoted from within probably have a better idea of who the skeptics and nonbelievers are and what leadership changes need to be made. CEOs coming in from the outside don't necessarily have that luxury.

Not the Intention

François Locoh-Donou was one of those CEOs coming in from the outside. When he left his former company and took over as CEO at F5 in January 2017, he inherited a leadership team of nine people. It wasn't immediately obvious which of these leaders might not be right for the future of the company.

"Eight of nine of the executives that were there when I arrived have since left the company," said Locoh-Donou to me when I specifically asked about the changes he made. "So, we ended up doing pretty much a wholesale replacement of the executive team. This was not my plan. If you asked me when I joined what I intended to do, or what I was going to do, I would have said I absolutely have no intention of changing out my senior team."

That is often not the intent of the new CEO coming in. While many understand they will need to evaluate the team for future fit, few would project they would remove the majority. This was certainly Locoh-Donou's thinking.

"Of the leadership team that was in place when I arrived, when I looked at each of their competencies in their domain, they were very competent. People don't make it to the top executive role if they aren't competent and don't have the ability to deliver results. They had built F5 as we know it. But I can think of a few of that original group where the person was competent, but they weren't really in favor of the change in culture we wanted to build, and therefore we made the decision to part ways. As CEO, you have to make a lot of decisions early on, decisions that likely delay gratification. But the earlier you make those decisions, the sooner the gratification will come. My advice to anyone trying to change culture is first, make the hard decision—take a hard look at your team and make sure you have a leadership team that represents the culture you want and will energize the future culture.

"Those were the decisions I made early on. And yes, it was delayed gratification and results. But, in the end, it was worth it and is now paying huge dividends."

Like Nadella, Locoh-Donou relied on his head of HR to help guide the culture change.

"A critical element to changing our culture is that Ana White joined the team as our chief HR officer early on. It turned out to be a masterstroke to make the decision to bring Ana on as CHRO because Ana helped me through some of those pretty tough decisions regarding my team, and what we'd need to truly renovate our culture. We wanted a leadership team that first would model the right behaviors—and that starts with me. It involves humility, being generous, and having each other's back. The new leaders we brought in were chosen to operate as a team and work with each other, versus previous siloed behavior. And once your leadership team is operating in unison and working for the good of the company rather than only being concerned about their particular group, that's very, very contagious throughout the organization. So, the choices that we made were sometimes very tough but, in the end, we have a leadership team today that I think is quite extraordinary, and that has made a huge difference.

"The role of HR has been so critical in this process, particularly Ana. I have learned that Ana is a very, very generous and courageous person. And as a result, she does a lot of things that are never on the job description. This ranges from constantly encouraging every one of her team members and cheering them on, and frankly encouraging and cheering on me as her boss," Locoh-Donou admits. "Ana is probably the first person that will be on call at midnight, or on an early Friday e-mail, sometimes helping retain someone who is thinking of leaving that we don't want to leave. The talent side is so critical. She has phenomenal energy in recruiting top talent, and just trying to help people out in the organization. One example that stays with me: we had to lay off a few people, and one of our employees, a young man that was being let go, was trying to find a new job in F5 but was having trouble. Ana had a full weekend of kid activities, but she offered to this guy to come to her son's lacrosse game so that she could walk around the field with him to weigh his options.

"I cannot stress enough the impact that Ana has had by her individual, personal actions, which, by the way, is also contagious because she makes everyone around her, including me, better and want to do more and to be as generous as her. So, I think we were lucky to have an exceptional leader in HR. But the bigger part of it is how Ana and her leadership team—she's retained and recruited a great team—how they translate their ideas and creativity into programs that have made a difference. Whether it's codifying and clarifying our BeF5 leadership principles, redefining performance management, calibrating our leaders, planning successions, and being more disciplined on talent management practices, as well as diversity and inclusion. This is not the old personnel department that will help you with performance reviews. They are a source of new energy in the company. Of creativity. Of new ways of doing things. All of these things have contributed to moving forward with cultural changes across the organization that make us a better company."

As Locoh-Donou gushed about the impact White has made on the company while she listened, I could sense her blushing at the compliments.

"Wow. That was awesome to hear, François," she chuckled. "Thank you so much. But I have to say, despite all the praise, François has been the beacon of the culture change. He exudes it every single day. When renovating, obviously you want to keep what's amazing about the culture, but it's so important to really ensure that all leaders, from the CEO's directs on down, exemplify that change. Because if they don't, it becomes a bit of a joke and mere words on a PowerPoint, versus things that people can look at and see that their leaders care about and are doing."

Strategic HR

Culture change happens more seamlessly when a CEO and CHRO are in lockstep, as clearly Microsoft's and F5's teams were when changing their cultures. Today, more CEOs than at any point in history realize the importance of the CHRO, not only for the health of the culture, but for bottom-line business impact.

David Brandon, chairman of Domino's, has seen the impact a good CHRO can make on an organization many times.

"First and foremost, if the HR lead in the company doesn't report directly to the CEO, he or she should find another company to work for. To the extent the HR function is delegated—for example, HR reports into the chief administrative officer, or CFO, or the general counsel—then HR is not viewed as a priority to the CEO. In my opinion, that in and of itself sets the stage for a problem."

"The HR leader must be involved in virtually every discussion that takes place around the leadership team table as it relates to the strategy and operations of the company," Brandon continued. "Strategies don't get executed without the human capital in place to make them happen. If the HR leader is not deeply engaged in the planning process every step of the way, then that HR function is being left out on an island, separated from the ongoing strategy planning and the day-to-day operations of the business. And that, in my opinion, is a recipe for disaster."

"Boards seek a sense of the strengths and weaknesses of the culture . . . what issues are percolating," said Jamie Gorelick, a board member at Amazon and VeriSign. "Board members want to know what the leadership of the company can do to foster a stronger culture—to address shortcomings and underscore strengths. Providing a real outlet for people is the most important way to affect your culture. Employees know the community in which they operate. So, I think the single most important thing that an HR executive can do is make sure that information is flowing freely, that within the chain of command it is welcomed, that there are avenues outside the chain of command that are robust and real, and that there is zero fear that someone who raises an issue or makes a suggestion will suffer any untoward consequence."

Gorelick highlights a dichotomy that exists in most companies, particularly large public organizations: while the CHRO reports to the CEO, he or she has to address the board frequently on fiduciary and governance matters that may not put senior management in the best light. In particular, the CHRO discusses and advises on executive compensation issues regarding the CEO and other executives with the board. In essence, the CHRO is in the precarious position of influencing what the compensation package should be for his or her boss, a phenomenon that plays out almost nowhere else in an organization.

While the compensation relationship is unique to the CHRO and the board, the same level of corporate responsibility does apply to a couple of other roles on the senior team, which Irene Chang Britt, a board member at Dunkin' Brands, Brighthouse Financial, and Tailored Brands, pointed out.

"CHROs should be able to tuck away their own personal interest, their interest in protecting their boss, their status as an employee and be able to rise above that," she advised. "I expect the same of great CFOs and general counsels as well. I think that triumvirate has to be dispassionate about their own standing as well as the standing of their boss. In the matters of HR, finance, and legal, sometimes the best course for the company is different than what their direct boss will want. And as a board member, I expect those three leaders to rise above the demands of them being an employee of the company."

It's not unusual for the best companies in the world to have an industry-acknowledged top HR executive in the C-suite. And increasingly, many high-performance organizations showcase the CEO-CHRO relationship—something that rarely was done in the past. I'm always heartened to see a senior team where it's the CHRO who is widely considered internally as the right-hand person, or at least one of the top three inner circle members.

"Wise CEOs know they must draw from a wide variety of resources to help them lead their companies toward a bright future," said WD-40's Ridge. "Powerful influence comes from all around: books and boards of directors, other leaders we meet at conferences, consultants on occasion, the talent from throughout our entire organization of individual contributors and our inner circle of C's—financial, marketing, public affairs, all those 'chiefs' who promise delivery of the highest-level advice.

"But there is one C who stands apart from the rest. The chief HR officer. CEOs who are blessed with a CHRO whom they can trust utterly, and with whom respect is a freely flowing, two-way dynamic, have the advantage of working with a true partner in the service of a shared vision. Often that vision is one that only the two of them can fully comprehend. And, as a team of two, they move the company forward toward an ineffable, people-driven reality that the numbers professionals will be able to quantify only later. It's a sparkling loyal partnership and a creative chemistry that I wish for every CEO and for every CHRO to experience in their careers. If they could only find each other."

CHROs are critical partners these days in crises as well. The first several months of the COVID-19 pandemic proved that. Many CHROs found themselves directing key aspects of the corporation's strategy, under conditions for which there was little to no scenario planning. The organizational agility of companies was tested during this time like no other time in history, and CEOs came to appreciate the CHROs that stayed calm, decisive, and agile.

In fact, *The Economist* wrote that "when the financial crisis rocked the business world in 2007–09, boardrooms turned to corporate finance chiefs. A good CFO could save a company; a bad one might bury it. The covid-19 pandemic presents a different challenge—and highlights the role of another corporate function, often unfairly dismissed as soft. Never before have more firms needed a hard-headed HR boss."[6]

In January 2020, as the word "coronavirus" entered the lexicon, Diane Gherson, CHRO of IBM at the time, thought the biggest challenge she would face would be how to protect employees as they attended industry trade shows and conferences. "My chief medical officer and I reviewed the precautions from the experts about how to screen people who were going to these events and why there needed to be a no-handshake policy," she said. "It all feels very quaint now, and so long ago."[7]

As the virus spread worldwide, it was clear that business as they knew it would need to be altered. Gherson led the team that quickly created a work-from-home transition for IBM's 350,000 employees. Eventually, about 95 percent of IBM's employees were working remotely, which was not a simple endeavor. Hundreds of complex data centers had to be operated from a distance, and leaders were ramped up quickly to understand how to manage remotely in this new reality.

Like many CHROs, Gherson was equally front and center in planning for an eventual return to the workplace. Gherson strategized with the CEO and other senior leaders on questions they never contemplated before: Who comes into the buildings? Do we require masks? How many people are allowed in an elevator at one time? How does the company configure floor plans to keep people far enough apart from each other so they feel safe?

"We're in 175 countries, and we have a lot of buildings, so this isn't an easy thing to do," said Gherson.[8]

The early days of the pandemic elevated the CHRO as a central strategist during the worst crisis most companies ever faced. Not only were they having daily sessions with the CEO and other senior leaders; they were also counted on to keep anxious and worried employees informed about policies and resources—medical and financial—to help them stay healthy, calm, and productive.

The pandemic also provided a lens, of sorts, on leadership. I heard from several CHROs on this issue, and many were a little surprised by leaders' actions. Some of the best leaders remained calm, engendered trust, communicated often and effectively, and were creative when faced with situations they had never encountered or even contemplated. Others less so. "This pandemic has taught me everything I need to know about some leaders in my company," one CHRO confessed to me via video chat one day, just a few months after COVID-19 hit worldwide. "I don't need to do any leadership assessments; it's pretty clear who is going to help and who is going to be a roadblock."

It's Not Just the Leaders

While the right leadership is critical to culture renovation, and blockers at the leadership level are important to remove, culture change efforts can get thwarted at other levels in the company as well. It's not uncommon to have certain departments, an acquired company, or even geographies as opponents to culture change. These can sometimes stop change efforts in their tracks unless they are dealt with swiftly and decisively.

"It's important to always keep in mind, it is not just the leaders," cautions Babson's Rob Cross. "Work we have done in a bunch of scenarios shows that when you put just one de-energizer on a team the overall ratings drop dramatically. Or if you put an energizer on a de-energized team their results drop threefold. Clearly, the leader is a part of this. But it is also the day-to-day experiences built into the interactions that most significantly shape the person's perception. This can be huge when trying to change a culture."

In his highly acclaimed book *The No Asshole Rule: Building a Civilized Workplace and Surviving One That Isn't*, Stanford professor Bob Sutton wrote about the importance of not tolerating de-energizers in the culture, no matter how brilliant they are. The book was based on a popular essay Sutton wrote for the *Harvard Business Review*. Ironically, Harvard Business School Press wouldn't publish the book because Sutton insisted on having the word "asshole" in the title,[9] so he got it published elsewhere. The book sold over 115,000 copies anyway and won the Quill Award for best business book in 2007.

Sutton offers two simple tests for deciding if someone fits the bill:

> **Test One:** After talking to the alleged asshole, does the "target" feel oppressed, humiliated, de-energized, or belittled by the person? In particular, does the target feel worse about him- or herself?

> **Test Two:** Does the alleged asshole aim his or her venom at people who are *less powerful* rather than at those people who are more powerful?

In the book, Sutton identifies the following "dirty dozen" techniques that assholes use:

- Personal insults
- Invading one's "personal territory"
- Uninvited physical contact
- Threats and intimidation, both verbal and nonverbal
- "Sarcastic jokes" and "teasing" used as insult delivery systems
- Withering e-mail flames
- Status slaps intended to humiliate their victims
- Public shaming or "status degradation" rituals
- Rude interruptions
- Two-faced attacks

- Dirty looks
- Treating people as if they are invisible

Sutton acknowledges that almost everyone is guilty of some of these traits at some point in time, but a certified asshole displays a persistent pattern and usually has a history of episodes that end with multiple people feeling belittled, disrespected, and de-energized. Psychologists separate states (fleeting feelings, thoughts, and actions) from traits (enduring personality characteristics) by looking for consistency across places and times.[10]

It's the consistently de-energizing people that ultimately slow down or take down cultures. Ferret them out as early in the renovation as possible.

CHAPTER 12

STEP #9: PAINT A VISION FOR THE FUTURE

> They'll keep defending their history until you acknowledge the history. As a leader, you've got to acknowledge the history, but also acknowledge that what got us here may not necessarily get us to where we want to go. You've got to paint a picture of the future that others can see themselves in. And the only way they're going to see themselves in that picture is if they helped create it.
>
> —PAT WADORS, CHIEF PEOPLE OFFICER, PROCORE

It's hard to beat a great story. In our research, stories are a common component of any healthy culture, especially when renovating. In fact, 73 percent of successful culture change efforts relied on stories.

Great leaders usually tell great stories, and in high-performing organizations, employees can usually recite stories about the company that embody its spirit and soul. Stories about the past can help set the tone for the culture you want in the future. Some companies have used this to great advantage and—let's be real—in the history of the world, stories about the past are often embellished and shaped to convey the message the storyteller wants the reader to envision. It's no different with good companies; they fashion stories to convey an image of the past that best portrays the image they want of the future.

One of my favorite uses of storytelling to shape culture comes from Qualcomm, the leader in wireless chip design for mobile phones and other devices, and one of the largest employers in the San Diego area.

Qualcomm was founded in 1985 and led by Irwin Jacobs who, based on Qualcomm's success, would later become a billionaire and one of San Diego's wealthiest citizens and most prominent philanthropists. The company started as a contract research and development center largely for government and defense projects. Based on a satellite communications system for trucking companies, Qualcomm grew from 8 employees in 1986 to 620 employees by 1991 when the company went public. But that was a relatively quiet start to what the company would ultimately become.

The company's ascendancy really began after the IPO when the 3G standard was adopted utilizing Qualcomm's CDMA patents, a hotly debated issue at the time since the standard required companies to license the patents from Qualcomm.[1] But as a result, Qualcomm became one of the hottest stocks in the 1990s and through the 2000s due to its worldwide dominance in chip design for mobile devices.

While Qualcomm's success has been envied and challenged over the years, there's one descriptor that remained constant: innovation. The company boasts some of the top engineers in the world designing chips that almost anyone reading this book has used. With over 140,000 patents to its name, Qualcomm helped create the smartphone as we know it today.

At the height of its growth in 2005, the company underwent some changes. After a nearly 8,000 percent appreciation in stock price since the IPO, including a 41 percent gain in the past year, Irwin, 71, decided it was a good time to step down as CEO and hand the reins to his son, Paul, who had worked at the company for 15 years and was a member of the executive team. While Irwin stayed involved and continued in his role as chairman, Paul set out to make his mark in his first stint as CEO, and to get out from under his father's very large shadow. An engineer by training like his father, Paul recognized that continued innovation and execution were critical to future success.

The company's chip design business was exploding as the cell phone had been married to the Internet just a few years earlier, showing off what a Qualcomm-designed chip could really do. On the verge of Apple's introduction of the iPhone, the company was hiring like mad. While revamping the onboarding process of new employees to the culture of Qualcomm, several members of the HR department recognized how important it was to get new employees aligned with the values of innovation and execution. They also recognized the criticality of retaining those first-year employees, who are often considered some of the most expensive to lose given the cost of recruiting and training them. They asked themselves a simple question:

How can we indoctrinate new hires to the innovative spirit of the company quickly, and get them immersed in the Qualcomm culture?

What they came up with is so beautifully effective and ridiculously cheap, I'm shocked more companies don't do the same thing.

The team built a program titled *52 Weeks*, which consisted of one story e-mailed each week to new employees that captured momentous points in time in the company's history. Told from the employee perspective, the stories provided insights about the company. Those insights included good (and some bad) business decisions made along the way, technology milestones, some background on certain leaders, and the genesis of key products. To make them more personal, the stories were visually represented with pictures from the past. The stories also had emotion to them, documenting humorous episodes as well as tougher times (like divesting a business and layoffs) that the company went through.

In creating the stories, the members of the team took time to choose the ones they wanted to share based on a few criteria:

▶ Does the story fit into one of the company's values, such as execution or innovation?

▶ Does it share an organizational strategy or information about the culture that would be of interest to employees?

▶ Is it a teachable moment with a lesson learned?

▶ Is it memorable?[2]

Mostly, the team looked for stories that would reinforce the future that management envisioned. From day one all new hires at Qualcomm were signed up for *52 Weeks* and, for the next year, received a new story each week. This consistent drip of organizational history immersed new employees into the culture and cemented the cultural tenets that Paul Jacobs wanted his CEO reign to be about.

An interesting thing happened, however, that the HR team didn't anticipate after they rolled this out as part of a revamped orientation program. They started getting registration requests from existing employees to receive the stories. Eventually, thousands of Qualcomm employees were receiving the same weekly e-mails as the new hires—providing them stories that reinforced the best aspects of the culture they experienced every day.

Never Waste a Good Story

This simple and inexpensive practice showcases the power of organizational storytelling in shaping culture, a practice that frankly too few companies really take advantage of. Research has proved what we instinctively already know: storytelling can have an amazing and long-lasting impact. For example, some studies have shown that:

▶ Stories are 22 times more memorable than facts and figures alone.[3]

▶ Our neural activity increases five times when listening to a story.[4]

▶ Storytelling lights up the sensory cortex in the brain, allowing the listener to feel, hear, taste, and even smell the story.[5]

The corporate world is filled with famous stories. From companies that began in a garage like Hewlett-Packard, Apple, or Google, or originated in a college dorm room like Dell, Facebook, or even Microsoft, most iconic companies have a story about when they were founded that they strategically leverage with the workforce and their customer base. For example:

▶ FedEx began when Fred Smith turned in an economics paper at Yale outlining an overnight delivery service for smaller items and unused airport time. Reportedly Smith's professor didn't like the paper, but Smith persevered to prove him wrong.

▶ Amazon was started when Jeff Bezos decided to quit his Wall Street job to explore an idea he had for an online bookstore, an idea he honed while driving cross-country with his wife and later in his Seattle-area garage (it's clear garages don't get enough credit in corporate history). Bezos named the company by looking through the dictionary. He settled on "Amazon" because it was a place that was exotic and different, just as he had envisioned for his new company.[6] Earlier names of Cadabra (a lawyer confused it with "Cadaver") and Relentless. com (too sinister) were aborted. Relentless.com still redirects to Amazon.

▶ Gatorade was created in 1965 by a team of scientists at the University of Florida following a request from the Florida Gators football team to help replace fluids lost during physical exertion.[7] The team credited Gatorade as having contributed to its first Orange Bowl win in 1967, and the company took off from there. It secured a licensing arrangement with the NFL two years later; the Quaker Oats Company purchased the brand in 1983 for $220 million; and in 2001, PepsiCo acquired the company for $13 billion. To this day, the University of Florida receives tens of millions in royalties.

▶ Trader Joe's founder, Joe Coulombe, owned a small group of convenience stores, but worried they were too similar to the 7-Eleven chain in his California area.[8] To differentiate, Joe changed to a South Seas motif after traveling around the Caribbean and noticing Americans went home with newfound tastes for foods they couldn't get in regular grocery stores. The first Trader Joe's market opened in 1967 in Pasadena (and is still open), and the chain now has hundreds of stores across the United States.

▶ Yankee Candle was started by a 16-year-old named Michael Kittredge in 1969. He had no money to buy his mom a Christmas gift, so he made a scented candle from melted crayons. A neighbor saw the candle and offered to buy it, and Kittredge began selling his candles to the neighborhood, which spawned a small business that eventually grew into a behemoth. The company was last sold for close to $2 billion, with revenues of around a billion.[9] All for a product that was created by the Romans in 500 BC and has arguably not seen much innovation since that time.

The last story is personal to me, since Yankee Candle blossomed just three miles from my childhood home in South Deerfield, Massachusetts. I watched its flagship store grow from a modest little tourist stop to what eventually became a 90,000-square-foot facility that I jokingly refer to as the "Disney World of Candles." Attracting over 3 million unique visitors per year,[10] it is the second-largest tourist attraction in the state of Massachusetts, second only to the Freedom Trail in Boston (which takes the visitor on a tour of where America began, such as Paul Revere's house, Old Ironsides, and the sites of the Boston Massacre and Boston Tea Party). The flagship store is home to 200,000 candles, an indoor snowstorm, a museum, and a Christmas display that rivals any in the country.

People travel to Yankee Candle mostly because they hear stories about it from others. The point is this: whether it's your external or internal brand, it's hard to think of any successful company that doesn't have an interesting foundational story. Employees love unique stories about their employer—they want to be part of something bigger and to be inspired—and smart companies shape those stories to create the company they want to be long term.

When telling a company story, boil it down to three simple concepts:

1. **The Origin.** What was the source of the original passion, and/or what events prompted the company to get started?
2. **The Customer.** What problem was solved by a new or unique solution?
3. **The Future.** What is the purpose, and how will the company change the world?

The last step is an important one in culture renovation. As mentioned earlier, while not every company will change the world, companies that successfully changed their culture focused the message on the future, not the past. In fact, our research, as depicted in Figure 12.1, showed interesting negative correlations to culture renovation success for any company that said it was changing its culture because of:

▶ Poor business performance (companies that were unsuccessful at changing culture were five times more likely than successful organizations to cite this as a reason for changing)
▶ Pressure from the board and/or investors
▶ Low employee engagement

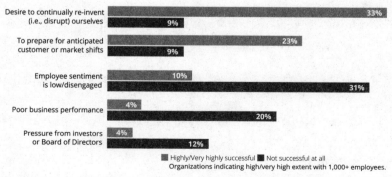

FIGURE 12.1   Drivers of the Cultural Initiative
Source: i4cp

Companies that were successful at changing culture were almost four times more likely to reference "A desire to continually reinvent ourselves" as a primary catalyst for change, along with "To prepare for anticipated customer or market shifts." Proactive versus reactive reasoning is a hallmark of high-performance organizations.

Two Different Approaches

When trying to effect change, language and positioning matter quite a bit. Consider these two different approaches from new CEOs.

In April 2009, Yahoo! hired famed Silicon Valley CEO Carol Bartz to take the company to a better future. She immediately began her tenure by pointing out past mistakes and perceived weaknesses. In her first all-company meeting shortly after taking the helm, she "threatened any employees who leaked information to the press with a one-way ticket to a faraway place, by way of her heels, however stiletto'd," according to the *Observer*.[11] In her first conference call with investors, she said, "We have good engineers but have to hire more and get them focused on the right stuff," signaling to the engineering staff they had been focused on the wrong stuff all along in her opinion.[12] She went on to say, "We sort of had a one product management person for every three engineers. So, we had a lot of people running around telling engineers what to do but nobody is f***ing doing anything."[13]

Unsurprisingly, the employees didn't appreciate hearing they weren't doing anything before her arrival and never warmed up to Bartz. She was fired two and a half years later. The blame game continued on her way out, with Bartz saying, "These people f***ed me over. The board was so spooked by being cast as the worst board in the country. Now they're trying to show that they're not the doofuses that they are."[14]

Satya Nadella's inauguration as CEO of Microsoft was quite different than what employees and investors experienced with Bartz. In Nadella's initial letter to the employee base at Microsoft, he wrote,

"There was no better company to join if I wanted to make a difference. This is the very same inspiration that continues to drive me today."[15] He went on to say, "Our industry does not respect tradition—it only respects innovation. This is a critical time for the industry and for Microsoft. Make no mistake, we are headed for greater places . . . as we start a new phase of our journey together."

He concluded by writing, "Many companies aspire to change the world. But very few have all the elements required: talent, resources, and perseverance. Microsoft has proven that it has all three in abundance. And as the new CEO, I can't ask for a better foundation. Let's build on this foundation together."

The differences in the two approaches are striking. While Bartz was lauded initially for her "no pulled punches" approach, she focused squarely on the past in describing why the culture needed to change. She pointed out all the things Yahoo! had done wrong and what needed to be fixed. Nadella's letter was markedly different—it was all future-focused. While he acknowledged the need for a culture renovation, he used phrases such as "we are headed for greater places" and "our journey together" along with words like "forward," "ahead," and "opportunity." While not ignoring the past, he never dwelled on it or succumbed to public shaming. Instead, he painted a vision for a future and a journey on which he invited the existing workforce to join him.

Nadella continued the forward-looking visions in his first earnings call as well, saying, "What you can expect of Microsoft is courage in the face of reality. We will approach our future with a challenger mindset. We will be bold in our innovation. We will be accountable to our customers, partners and shareholders."[16]

It's always surprising to me when CEOs say something on an earnings call to analysts and shareholders that they wouldn't necessarily say to the workforce. The formal communication to the team doesn't stop with internal e-mails or town halls; the workforce is listening to all communication, and it's important to be consistent in the internal and external messaging at all times, but especially when trying to effect culture change.

Another example comes from Boeing, a company that has had consistent culture challenges for many years. Former CEO James McNerney showed how just one slip of the tongue can infuriate employees when he addressed analysts on a 2014 earnings call. According to the *Seattle Times*, McNerney was talking about his plans to stay on at the company after he turned 65, the company's official age for executives to retire, when he said:

"The heart will still be beating, the employees will still be cowering, I'll be working hard."[17]

This enraged the all-important unions at Boeing. One union said his statement represented "anti-personnel management," and another circulated a poster that showed a man crouched behind his desk with the caption, "If I'm away from my desk, then I must be cowering somewhere." McNerney later sent a companywide email that said, "I should have used different words, and I apologize for them."

McNerney stepped down as CEO less than a year later.

This incident was just one of many the Boeing culture has weathered. McNerney was originally brought into the company in July 2005 to restore the company's reputation after two major military procurement scandals and a sex scandal involving his predecessor. Most felt his tenure was less than successful. In looking at his career, the *Seattle Times* wrote that "McNerney has alienated engineers and machinists—and even some executives—in the Pacific Northwest with what they see as his coldblooded approach to moving work and forcing union concessions."

"A lot of employees feel top management doesn't value them, treats them as expendable," said Leon Grunberg, a University of Puget Sound professor of sociology, who surveyed more than 3,000 company engineers and machinists for his book *Emerging from Turbulence: Boeing and Stories of the American Workplace Today*. McNerney created an atmosphere of "lowered trust, anger and disgruntlement," he wrote, and "pretty much put the final nail in the coffin of the old heritage Boeing."[18]

According to that same *Seattle Times* article mentioned earlier, an anonymous former Boeing executive felt McNerney, who never worked in aviation, lacked any passion for the company. "The sense I always got from him in meetings is that it could have been any business." Another former executive who also asked for anonymity concurred: "I don't think anyone gets really close to him. He doesn't let emotions get in the way of him making decisions he thinks are best for the corporation. It's all about the business. He's pretty dispassionate."

When Dennis Muilenburg replaced McNerney in 2015, the largest union at Boeing (the Machinists) was less than impressed and issued a brief statement that also underscored the bitterness of its relationship with McNerney.

"CEOs come and CEOs go," said the two-sentence note from District 751 president Jon Holden. "We welcome Boeing's announcement that Dennis Muilenburg is taking over as CEO, and encourage him to invest in the workforce and recognize the value of each and every employee at the Boeing Co."[19]

However, Muilenburg's hiring did not seem to improve Boeing's culture. In fact, the cultural and business issues only compounded during his tenure, with tragic outcomes.

Labeling it a "culture of concealment," a 2020 report by the US House of Representatives claimed Boeing's culture was a significant contributor to two crashes of Boeing 737 Max jets within months of each other that killed 346 people in late 2018 and early 2019. Aviation authorities worldwide grounded the Boeing 737 Max passenger airliner after investigators determined that a new automated flight control, the Maneuvering Characteristics Augmentation System (MCAS), malfunctioned on both flights, sending each plane into repeated nosedives. Boeing had omitted the system from crew manuals and training.[20]

Muilenburg was fired just before Christmas 2019, prior to the report coming out. His almost four-year stint didn't renovate the culture, but there are many who feel Boeing's culture of concealment started well before Muilenburg took the job. The date often pointed to was May 2001, when the company decided that corporate headquarters should be anywhere but the Seattle area, where most of the planes were produced. In a dramatic unveiling, Boeing anointed

Chicago as the new place where top management would sit—roughly 500 people in all—a solid 1,700 miles away from the engineers.

The distance was deliberate. "When the headquarters is located in proximity to a principal business—as ours was in Seattle—the corporate center is inevitably drawn into day-to-day business operations," Boeing's CEO explained at the time. Fast-forward almost 20 years to the 737 Max disaster. Many believe it occurred *because* management was too separate from engineering.[21]

"You had this weird combination of a distant building with a few hundred people in it and a non-engineer with no technical skills whatsoever at the helm," said aerospace analyst Richard Aboulafia.[22] But it was more than a lack of engineering skills at the top, Aboulafia continued: "It was the ability to comfortably interact with an engineer who in turn feels comfortable telling you their reservations, versus calling a manager [more than] 1,500 miles away who you know has a reputation for wanting to take your pension away. It's a very different dynamic. As a recipe for disempowering engineers in particular, you couldn't come up with a better format."

The merry-go-round of CEOs was a consistent theme at Boeing, and when Muilenburg was let go in late 2019, it was chairman Dennis Calhoun who took over. After the 737 Max crashes and the House's report, it was clear to Calhoun—like everyone else—that the culture needed to be revamped. His first chance to address that publicly came in—what else?—his first earnings call with analysts and investors in late January 2020. Ronald Epstein from Bank of America asked him, "How do you change the culture as a big organization?"[23]

Calhoun sighed. "Boy, is that a big question," he replied. Calhoun discussed Boeing's culture problems, particularly as reflected in some e-mails and texts from a small group of engineers that were called out in the House's report. "The system didn't apparently listen or watch for things like that, and it didn't react appropriately. And I have to do everything in my power to make sure going forward that it does," said Calhoun. "Listening starts with leadership and it starts with me. And I think we need to do more of it. And then slowly, steadily, you change culture. People want to believe in that, and they will."

It sounded like Calhoun might have some *Culture Renovation* religion and would listen to the workforce and paint a go-forward vision for the future. Instead, Calhoun went the route that most CEOs of culture change failures follow—he couldn't resist ripping into Muilenburg's previous leadership just a few weeks later and focused his messages squarely on the past.

"It's more than I imagined it would be, honestly," Calhoun whined to the *New York Times* regarding the turnaround efforts. "And it speaks to the weaknesses of our leadership. I'll never be able to judge what motivated Dennis, whether it was a stock price that was going to continue to go up and up, or whether it was just beating the other guy to the next rate increase. If anybody ran over the rainbow for the pot of gold on stock, it would have been him."[24]

Master Craftsman

In nearly all highly successful culture change efforts (89 percent), the CEO made a commitment to the future vision by dedicating the necessary resources and time toward the renovation. This included both organizational resources and the CEO's own personal resources—most importantly, time, attention, and action. At organizations that report a highly successful culture change, this often translates to a regular cadence of communication events, such as CEO-led all-company (town hall) meetings to discuss the vision for the future. Good CEOs typically lead meetings about change in different company locations and with a variety of functional levels. They also meet with senior-level cross-organization teams to transparently share feedback gathered from different regions, units, and so on.

Pat Wadors of Procore shared with me one day how, in a previous role, the company's CEO regularly brought up anecdotal stories about the why and what of the change when visiting customers, spending time with employees at various sites, or just walking around the office. "Eventually, it becomes part of your mantra," said Wadors. "It's woven in. Whether [the CEO] was having a fireside chat with our sales or engineering teams, our ongoing transformation is what he wove in every single time."

"The premise for acknowledging your roots, your history, is really based on the emotional science around grieving," Wadors explains. "You can't move forward from grief unless you acknowledge what you had to do to get to the next chapter. And the stories that you tell yourself, and the impact that person or that thing had on you and your life—you've got to be able to celebrate it, understand what it is, and then put it to bed to get to the next chapter. And those people that don't give that nod have a really hard time transitioning. And have a hard time accepting a new reality."

"It's the same with culture change, because often employees feel that if new leaders come in and just paint a new picture, they feel it's disrespectful," Wadors told me. "Like, you're standing on the shoulders of other great people. You wouldn't have this privilege if it weren't for what we did in the past. They'll keep defending their history until you acknowledge the history. As a leader, you've got to acknowledge the history, but also acknowledge that what got us here may not necessarily get us to where we want to go. You've got to paint a picture of the future that others can see themselves in. And the only way they're going to see themselves in that picture is if they helped create it."

Helping guide the workforce toward that vision is often more art than science.

"Really great craftsmen do that well," observed Wadors. "They bring people through a facilitation, and they have some of the guardrails already in place, so people get to paint within the lines. There are lines drawn, but the facilitator doesn't make those lines so obvious to others. So, they feel like they have more freedom than they probably do. But it's like almost a presumptive close. We know we have to evolve our culture. We know that some things are really great. What do we want to keep, and what do we want to evolve? But you've typically already told them, and with certain things, great craftsmen won't allow a debate; they just naturally segue and say, of course we're going to keep this because of these reasons. And then he tees up those things he knows we have to evolve. That's a master craftsman."

The Power of Symbols

Stories are often accompanied by symbols as constant reminders to the workforce—a visual shorthand that immediately conveys the organization's values and behaviors and creates an emotional reaction to purpose. In effective culture change, symbols are often present and almost always are universally understood. Sometimes those symbols are indirect and esoteric, but often they are very literal. For example, earlier I referenced Microsoft's growth mindset posters in conference rooms, which was a not-so-subtle reinforcer of the attitude Nadella and his team wanted to impart in any meeting that occurred there. Other companies have used symbols in the same way.

When Horacio Rozanski stepped into the CEO role at Booz Allen Hamilton in January 2015, he wanted to renovate the culture. The company created a new purpose statement and refreshed the values. To ensure the initiative would succeed, the roughly 150 senior-most leaders had opportunities to help shape the values; they came up with five that were distinct and intended to evoke an emotional attachment and personal commitment to the future culture:

- ► Unflinching courage
- ► Collective ingenuity
- ► Passionate service
- ► Ferocious integrity
- ► Champion's heart

They went a step further than simply talking about these values, or even writing them down. The values were set in stone—literally. When an employee demonstrated one of these specific values in practice, the employee was awarded a stone with the value engraved in it, and a story was shared about how the employee demonstrated the value. The employee became the custodian of that stone, keeping it as a treasured reminder of his or her commitment to the firm's purpose and values. The ability to display a stone has become a symbol of pride, and some employees make it a goal to "collect all five."

Having a symbol that represents achievement is important to people, whether it's a rock or something that others might deem silly. It's the meaning attached to the symbol that matters.

Bensussen Deutsch & Associates (BDA) is regarded as one of the best merchandise agencies in the world. The agency works with many Fortune 500 companies via branded merchandise campaigns, although it is most often recognized for its work with major sports teams and leagues such as the MLB, NFL, NBA, NHL, Premier League, and PGA Tour. Through these contracts, the company works with almost all professional sports teams and their sponsors with fan activation programs. The agency may be best known for driving the popularity of sports bobbleheads.

BDA is also run by one of my best friends, Jay Deutsch. Jay founded the company with his childhood friend Eric Bensussen when the two were in high school. Over 35 years later, the company is still going strong.

"When you think about two business partners sticking together for as long as Eric and I have, it creates a unique culture that absolutely starts with the word 'family,'" Jay told me over cigars one day. "And it's not just a word. You know, our number one core value is team and family. And we didn't write that down until we had already had the company for 15 years. And today we live by it. It's our credo. It's what our own employees talk about when we talk about BDA team and family."

I can personally attest to this, having keynoted a couple of BDA's leadership team off-sites. When we've talked about cultural traits, "team" and "family" are words quickly uttered by the group. Some may think those words only work with small companies—and at 800+ employees, BDA is one of the smaller companies I interviewed for this book—but it's a descriptor a CEO of any company, no matter the size, would want employees to use as the number one attribute of their company culture.

"No matter how small or big any company is, they would love to have the characteristics that we have," said Jay. "When times are good or times are bad, you can count on this company to stand behind you.

And, you know, whether that's somebody going through a tough time in their personal life, a death in the family, or any difficult situation, they can count on our team and family to have their backs completely."

Deutsch is realistic, however, that he needs to pay attention to the culture as the company continues to grow.

"Team and family are characteristics I don't ever want to lose. The bigger companies get, the easier it is to lose those traits. And even at our size, I can see why they get lost because, when you're talking about employing over 800 people around the globe, it's not easy to sustain. It's so hard to instill that sense in somebody who's new, or who was hired on the other side of the world, compared to people who have been with you for 20+ years, working in the headquarters, especially when they've personally lived through the growth and the trajectory. How do you instill that same sense of team and family in somebody who's only been with us for three months, or even three years?"

"One thing that I love that we do to instill it and show that every-body matters as a family is expand the traditional sales trip to include people in the company that aren't in sales," continued Deutsch. "We refer to it as our owner's trip, and while we certainly reward the top salespeople and other top performers in the company, from day one we've included others who aren't in direct revenue-producing roles. Last year we brought 110 people on this trip, and we create reasons to include more people. As an example, all family members celebrat-ing their tenth anniversary with BDA, and every five-year anniversary after that, get to bring a guest with them on the trip, and this is from the front desk person to the warehouse person. It becomes a 'family vacation' and celebrated for all the contributions they have made, and they have been just as critical to driving our company's growth. I truly enjoy hanging with my peeps!"

While the trip is one type of symbol the company uses to instill the family and team aspect of culture, BDA is also famous for adopt-ing a Disney character to symbolize another important trait.

"Howard Behar [the former president] of Starbucks taught me a great little quip that I've remembered forever," explains Deutsch. "He said the 20 percent that love you will always love you, trust you, and follow you. Another 20 percent will not trust you and are always going to be resistant to change. Your real focus *must be* to tune into and lead the 60 percent in the middle of these two groups. And if you can get that momentum going and get the 80 percent working together, the other 20 percent will either follow by inertia or you'll have them fall off and you'll replace them. But to get that 60 percent in the middle to move, you've got to be bold. And you've got to truly believe in what you say and have conviction. This conviction leads to a big word for me, authenticity. This will allow you to lead with what you believe in even when it may not be your standard conventional stuff."

"A good example is our unofficial mascot, Tigger," Deutsch explains, invoking the character from the Winnie-the-Pooh series. "Tigger was adopted by me almost 20 years ago after 9/11, when the economy took a major hit. It was the first real recession that we had seen as a company. And as a leader, I handled it wrong. I held onto people too long because I didn't want to let any family members down. When the world was laying off, I was still holding on. It created serious angst in our halls, and even worse, serious challenges in the business. Predictably we had to eventually cut costs—but it was a full year later, and far later than we should have acted.

"I hurt the company because of that, but I owned it. At that time, I stood up before all my remaining employees and said, 'Listen, my bad, I really screwed up, made a mistake, and I am sorry. Now we can either say, well, that's the end of BDA, or we can band together, tough it out, and make this work. I am determined to get us through this, but I cannot do it alone.' I needed everyone to focus on what was needed to be done to make this work to come out stronger on the other side, and thus rally people by saying 'Who's with me?'

"That was the late summer of 2002. My wife and I just had our first child, a little girl, so there was a ton of Winnie-the-Pooh stuff in our house. In looking at the characters I realized either you're going to be an Eeyore and say, 'We're never going make it,' or you're going to be a Tigger and you're going to say, 'Let's go team! We can do this!' Now I completely know that Tigger is not the smartest cat in the forest, but what he lacks in intelligence he more than makes up for with this incredible positive 'can-do attitude,' . . . a Tigger *spirit*. And that attitude is, if Piglet's lost, we're gonna go find him! If somebody is down, I'm going to cheer him up! That Tigger spirit got us through a dark time in 2002–2003, and today that infectious Tigger attitude has driven our incredible growth, and happy to say is alive and well today at BDA."

Deutsch acknowledges that it took an authentic Tigger spirit to continue promoting the concept of Tigger.

"Sometimes—as the leader—to get change to happen you must practice humility, and this can be mixed in with a little silliness. I am *all in* on a Tigger, even when there's people in the company, and there still are a few today, who go, oh no, here he goes on the Tigger thing again. There are many leaders who would have stopped because of the criticism. But this was the 20 percent that never are going to adopt Tigger and always be the contrarians. But almost 20 years later, I continue to live and proliferate Tigger to rally our 80 percent plus that want that positivity in their lives. I have the majority fired up right now to say: *'I want to be a Tigger! I want to be a Tigger in my life! I want to be a Tigger at work! I want to be viewed as a Tigger by people around me! And you know what? I'm actually more successful when I buy into this Tigger thing, because if I can inspire and motivate a room to do something, then we actually accomplished what people thought could not be done!'* This fires me up! It has been a powerful cycle that feeds itself.

"The leaders who get their people thinking like Tiggers see their people believe and succeed in this environment, and then they've got their next leaders coming behind them, and it's very infectious and contagious. Sometimes you just gotta be courageous and bold about something silly. But if you authentically believe in the right message, and the message resonates and works, it will absolutely make your culture a huge competitive advantage. This is where we are at with our Tigger spirit."

As a result, it's not hard to figure out who has the Tigger spirit at BDA.

"Disney must be very happy with how many Tiggers we've purchased over the years as awards to people who exemplify our spirit.

The biggest award they can receive from Eric and me is an actual stuffed Tigger. We attach a personalized thank you note. And for our top employee of the year, they get a three-foot-tall Tigger. I have Tiggers in my office, in my home office, and when I go on video to the workforce, he's there. Sounds a little weird, right? I mean, you think 'This is a CEO of a half a billion-dollar company pulling up a stuffed Tigger?' Sure Tigger can be dismissed as a simple prop, but the prop to me is a very real way of life, way of doing business, and an attitude that if you adopt it, I don't think it takes you down a bad path.

"I think a Tigger spirit will lead you to success. I dare you to give it a try!"

As a friend of Jay, I can say without a sliver of a doubt, he is the biggest Tigger you will ever meet. That spirit, and the vision he's painted for the company, is why the company continues to be a success today and will be for many years to come.

CHAPTER 13

STEP #10: CONSCIOUSLY COLLABORATE

> Our best efforts are collaborative, and the
> Patagonia culture rewards the ensemble player while
> it barely tolerates those who need the limelight.
> —YVON CHOUINARD, FOUNDER, PATAGONIA

While most successful renovations paint an enticing vision for the future, they also rely on strong internal collaboration to propagate it across their employee networks. But in many poor-performing companies, collaboration morphs into a cultural norm that is detrimental to change efforts.

"When it comes to culture, I have seen three dysfunctional archetypes in my work on collaborative networks," said Babson's Rob Cross.

"First is an *overly participative culture*; one of over-consensus where connectivity is through the roof because everyone believes they need to be consulted on decisions. That sort of culture usually doesn't work. It overwhelms organizations, placing too much focus on consensus building. The inevitable result is collaborative overload.

"The second archetype is the *hierarchical culture*. There, the focus is skewed toward leaders. Organizations may have created open spaces to encourage connection, or actively promoted the idea of collaboration. However, almost every interaction comes back to the leaders. In our work, we've seen this implicit and embedded in hierarchical networks. Because of this structure, collaboration in those organizations is often slow, unagile, and bureaucratic.

"The third archetypical culture is *one of fear*. We have mapped the idea of fear in collaborative networks for some time. What we find is that people hold back ideas because they are intimidated by others. In those fear-driven networks, collaboration can't reach its full potential because individuals don't feel they can fully and safely contribute all that they might otherwise offer."

Cross uses these collaboration scenarios to showcase the power that strong internal networks have on culture.

"These three archetypes offer illustrations that confirm cultures and networks are intimately intertwined," Cross continues. "Culture defines who interacts with whom and how and is reinforced by the networks that are in place. In cultures that maximize collaboration and performance, energy is high, and a sense of purpose is pervasive. People tend to think that work itself is the basis of purpose, but it isn't. We've found that both energy and purpose are built on network interactions. The people you interact with give you a sense of impact, that what you do matters. In turn, that effective interaction gives you a sense of energy and purpose in your work. Ultimately, it drives engagement, lowers turnover, and reduces talent risk."

Cross partnered with my team on a series of research reports we conducted on the topic of organizational collaboration. Our research was very clear: high-performance organizations don't just let collaboration "happen." Instead, they are very intentional about how collaboration occurs, they actively manage it, and they reward for it.

Culture renovation benefits immensely from effective workforce collaboration, but effective collaboration starts with leaders. Leaders at high-performance companies are three and a half times more likely than those at low performers to structure work in ways that take advantage of the power of collaboration. For example, they purposefully select collaborative group members based on the expertise of the individuals or relevancy to the project at hand rather than their relationship with the person. They are also more likely to encourage collaboration across all employee and leadership levels to break down information silos and to help individuals build more effective personal networks across the enterprise. This is especially beneficial and important in organizations made up of highly complex systems (operating units in multiple countries, distinct businesses with similar customer groups or suppliers, etc.) where personal connections and information exchange are essential.

In fact, a next practice revealed in our research (as outlined earlier, we define "next practice" as a practice that is highly correlated to market performance but is not yet widely used) is having leaders actively help others build effective networks. High-performance organizations implement this practice eight times more than lower-performing companies. And the benefit is clear: employees who establish broad and helpful networks tend to be more productive and tend to stay much longer at a company.

One company that is serious about collaboration is Patagonia, one of the most revered cultures in existence.

Patagonia: The Provost of Purpose

Consider these statistics. Over 60 percent of consumers want companies to stand up for the issues they are passionate about. Another 66 percent think transparency is one of a brand's most attractive qualities.[1] Eighty-six percent of millennials (those born between 1981 and 1996) would consider taking a pay cut to work at a company whose mission and values align with their own.[2]

As our social consciousness has risen, consumers have been paying attention to the brands they frequent and want to be associated with, and employees are doing the same. While more and more companies are touting their efforts in sustainability, diversity, transparency, and pay equity, most would benefit by studying more closely what "taking a stand" really means. They could learn a great deal from a little company from Southern California with an odd name—Patagonia.

While Patagonia is renowned for its excellent outdoor gear, iconic vests, and trendy backpacks, its best creation may be the company culture. The culture was a natural outgrowth of the company's original commitment to purpose and, over time, has earned Patagonia a deep loyalty from its customers and employees that is unmatched by almost any other organization.

Founded by outdoor enthusiast Yvon Chouinard in 1973, the 2,500-person company is based in Ventura, California, a stone's throw from some of the best surfing the state has to offer. Its logo, however, is not California at all—it is the outline of Mount Fitz Roy, which is at the border between Chile and Argentina, in the region of Patagonia. And while he is an avid surfer, the logo is a tribute to Chouinard's true love: mountain climbing.

That love inspired Chouinard to start the company based on a primary new product: climbing pitons. Traditionally, a piton is a piece of metal that climbers hammer into the side of the mountain. But when you do that, you destroy the mountain a little bit, which bothered Chouinard. To resolve this concern, he invented a removable piton, which became popular with other climbers who shared his concern. These were so popular that Chouinard opened a blacksmith's shop in Ventura to make the pitons—and that became the basis for the company.

When he launched Patagonia, it would have been hard for the casual observer to see that Chouinard was anything more than a free-spirited adventurist and opportunist. As history has shown, he became an incredibly successful businessman by doing things a bit differently, staying true to himself, and pioneering how important a strong purpose is to building an iconic brand.

For 45 years the company's mission was "Build the best product, cause no unnecessary harm, use business to inspire and implement solutions to the environmental crisis." This mission personified

Chouinard, and over the years Patagonia has always been a leader in environmental activism, public land preservation, and sustainability. While many companies talk about these issues, Patagonia went to lengths most companies wouldn't even dream of, such as taking the Trump administration to court over its public lands policy and giving back $10 million in tax cuts to grassroots environmental organizations (on top of the 1 percent of annual sales that it already donates). The 45-year-old mission suited the company well.

Chouinard, however, like CEOs of many companies with strong cultures, doesn't rest on his laurels. To reinforce the company's purpose more boldly (and simply), in late 2018 the company unveiled a new mission:

"Patagonia is in business to save our home planet."[3]

"We're losing the planet because of climate change, that's the elephant in the room," Chouinard explained to *Fast Company* at the time of the new statement's rollout. "I decided to make a very simple statement, because in reality, if we want to save the planet, every single company in the world has to do the same thing. And I thought, well, let's be the first."

Chouinard's goal was to apply the company's resources where they could have the most impact. Patagonia came up with three key answers: agriculture, politics, and protected lands. While agriculture and protected lands might seem in line with the company's previous mission, "politics" stands out like a sore thumb. Most companies try to avoid political proclamations at all costs, let alone stating that utilizing their political influence is a main corporate focus.

When you are a successful private company that's 50 years old and still led by your charismatic founder, you have the freedom to do things that most public companies don't have.

Ahead of the 2018 midterm election, Patagonia became one of the first consumer brands ever to make the endorsement of a specific candidate part of its brand marketing. The company endorsed two candidates, Representative Jacky Rosen in Nevada (who later became a senator for the state) and Senator Jon Tester in Montana, both Democrats, for their stances on protecting public lands. It promoted the candidates on the website, across social channels, and in customer e-mails. Both won their elections. Chouinard was thrilled.

"Jon Tester barely won in Montana. I've had people in Montana tell me he probably wouldn't have done it if we hadn't helped," he said. "That makes me feel pretty good! We have this political power, a few million customers who are really behind what we're doing. So why not use it to do some good?"[4]

In 2020, without any advanced publicity, Patagonia produced a pair of shorts that sported a tag inside which said, "Vote the Assholes Out." According to the company, Chouinard has been using the phrase for the last few years to refer to politicians from any party who deny or disregard the climate crisis. The shorts sold out immediately.

If consumers and employees are serious about wanting brands to take a strong stand, Patagonia is the poster child.

The renewed purpose carries just as much weight internally as it does externally. Chouinard reportedly gave the HR department, run by a friend of mine—Dean Carter—some new marching orders in the process of rolling out the new statement. "Whenever we have a job opening, all things being equal, hire the person who's committed to saving the planet, no matter what the job is," he said. "And that's made a huge difference in the people coming into the company."

When it comes to human capital, Patagonia boasts statistics and benefits that are way beyond the norm and are probably incomprehensible to many companies:

- ▶ Turnover at an incredible 4 percent (versus an industry average more than triple that figure)[5]
- ▶ A 9/80 work schedule that gives employees a three-day weekend every other week
- ▶ Paying to send nannies on business trips to support work-life integration
- ▶ Hosting childcare at its facilities (a big reason why the company boasts a near 100 percent retention rate among working mothers)

- ▶ Free yoga
- ▶ Nearby access to hiking trails
- ▶ Paying bail (and their spouse's bail), along with legal fees and corresponding time away from work, for employees who are jailed for peaceful environmental protests

It's hard to envision that last perk existing at any other organization. When asked why the company put that in place, Carter told a crowd at a conference, "We want them to be who they are."[6]

Patagonia just does culture differently. On the company's website, the entire section on culture is a three-paragraph excerpt from Chouinard's excellent book *Let My People Go Surfing*. It says:

> If you care about having a company where employees treat work as play and regard themselves as ultimate customers for the products they produce, then you have to be careful whom you hire, treat them right, and train them to treat other people right. Otherwise you may come to work one day and find it isn't a place you want to be anymore.
>
> Patagonia doesn't usually advertise in the *Wall Street Journal*, attend job fairs, or hire corporate headhunters to find new employees. We prefer instead to seek out people through an informal network of friends, colleagues, and business associates. We don't want someone who can just do a job; we want the best person for the job. Yet we don't look for "stars" seeking special treatment and perks. Our best efforts are collaborative, and the Patagonia culture rewards the ensemble player while it barely tolerates those who need the limelight.
>
> We also seek, as I mentioned above, core Patagonia product users, people who love to spend as much time as possible in the mountains or the wild. We are, after all, an outdoor company. We would not staff our trade show booth with a bunch of out-of-shape guys wearing white shirts,

ties, and suspenders any more than a doctor would let his receptionist smoke in the office. We can hardly continue to make the best outdoor clothing if we become primarily an "indoor" culture. So we seek out "dirtbags" who feel more at home in a base camp or on the river than they do in the office. All the better if they have excellent qualifications for whatever job we hire them for, but we'll often take a risk on an itinerant rock climber that we wouldn't on a run-of-the-mill MBA. Finding a dyed-in-the-wool businessperson to take up climbing or river running is a lot more difficult than teaching a person with a ready passion for the outdoors how to do a job.

Underscoring the notion that "Our best efforts are collaborative," at Patagonia the culture takes a conscious approach to collaboration—and it's an important part of the company's success.

"The more a group understands their purpose—why they're coming together, what they're doing to collaborate on a business issue—the better the outcome," said Carter. "Collaboration has been a part of our vision and mission, and a key value for the company for so long that when people make decisions, they do so within teams. Lone decision-making simply doesn't happen."

Carter said that employees take collaboration seriously. Whether it's a store team working together to support a companywide financial goal, or a group of employee volunteers helping rehabilitate injured sea lions or restoring endangered wetlands—Patagonia is about the power of collaboration.

"Our people are proud when we hit our business objectives," said Carter. "The motivation to collaborate is great when it means that we're able to create top-quality products, support the communities where we live and work, and give millions to save the environment. Everyone across the company chips in to achieve goals, and they see the far-reaching results their teamwork produces."

It's not a surprise that companies that collaborate, like Patagonia, have had great success. i4cp's research shows that high-performance organizations are more likely to leverage collaboration to achieve desired business outcomes and more likely to base collaboration on specific business needs or goals. They typically don't leave collaboration to chance. About 80 percent of high-performance organizations make a practice of clearly defining and reinforcing the importance of collaboration in development programs, and they are much more likely to include collaboration as a performance goal for individual employees, leaders, and teams.

Booz Allen Hamilton is one of those high performers that are very intentional with their collaboration efforts.

"One of our values is what we call collective ingenuity. It's about bringing people together and harnessing the power of different teams and diversity to make sure we're solving problems in the best possible ways we can," said Aimee George Leary, Booz's talent strategy officer. "That's what our operating model is all about, and it's done through networking and collaboration inside our organization."

But reinforcing this requires a multiprong approach.

"There is no single silver bullet. We have used multiple channels to work on this," said Leary. "We've dedicated spaces; we've held events to bring people together. We've created people programs, like training. We have implemented tools and technologies to support collaboration, and we've established and highlighted incentives for people. We've had to have multiple touchpoints and stay at it."

Practices Booz Allen Hamilton has implemented include coaching on how to pitch ideas and how to share and collaborate to build new solutions. The company has also created "solver spaces" where people present a challenge and the company brings a group together to work on solving the problem. Collaboration is also a measure included in the performance review process and in recognizing excellence. The company has created an annual award to recognize employees for collaborating, solving problems, and driving service outcomes through working collectively across the organization.

Collaborative Overload

One downfall of collaboration is a phenomenon called "collaborative overload." Cross brought this to worldwide attention with a *Harvard Business Review* cover story in 2016. Cross's research found most knowledge workers spend 85 percent or more of their time each week on e-mail, in meetings, and on the phone, placing an enormous (and invisible) cost on organizations and people.

Collaborative overload was already an issue in many organizations, but the COVID-19 pandemic demonstrated just how large the problem had become. Suddenly, there was a new legion of home workers being inundated with collaborative requests. While technology enabled working outside the office, it had its downside, as afflictions like "Zoom fatigue" entered our business lexicon.

Collaborative overload isn't just a technology issue, however. It often affects a company's most productive people. The old adage of *if you want something done, ask a busy person to do it* certainly plays out every day in most organizations.

"As people become known for being both capable and willing to help, they are drawn into projects and roles of growing importance," says Cross. "Their giving mindset and desire to help others quickly enhances their performance and reputation."

Unfortunately, this also makes them the go-to person for all others who need help, making them more likely to fall subject to collaborative overload, burnout, disengagement, and even turnover. Today, technological access means those busy people are more accessible than ever, which makes it very easy to burn out the top performers. About half of all companies take no action at all to identify where collaborative overload exists or may be building.

"Historically, to identify overload issues, we have done our people survey, which was more of a climate or engagement assessment," said Leary. "But we're shifting gears to focus on culture and the behaviors within a culture that enable collaboration and innovation. We want to ensure that the behaviors in our organization support our values, our purpose, and exemplify the attributes found in collaborative and constructive environments."

Patagonia uses surveys to provide employees with a way to communicate issues and problems with the collaborative process. Carter said the company has worked to refine the survey process to gain greater insight into these challenges.

"There's a pendulum effect with collaboration. It can swing from too much collaboration that can cause work to stall, to the other extreme of not enough collaboration, which can affect the quality of decisions." Carter and his team redesigned survey response options so employees can more accurately pinpoint the effectiveness of collaboration along a continuum. "We found we needed a scale that reflected that pendulum idea to enable us to understand if people think we need to move this way or that. It's a nuanced question. Effective collaboration is about understanding the sweet spot for your organization."

Another common by-product of overload is the creation of unnecessary bottlenecks that slow down execution. To circumvent this, top companies allow employees to shift work—without going through a formal chain of command—to those with the expertise to accomplish it. Another approach is to give employees permission to say no (or at least a partial no) by negotiating and agreeing to a percentage of the time or task requested—which in some instances will encourage a rethink of the request. It can also involve shifting the work to another individual who is facing fewer collaborative demands and stress or could benefit from the development associated with the execution of that task. Organizations should also encourage employees to make introductions to other colleagues when the request doesn't draw on their own unique expertise—a practice that has the added benefit of broadening the requester's network and potentially opening future collaborative opportunities.

One of the easiest ways to combat overload, however, is to create an environment where employees feel they can safely report being at risk of overload from too many collaborative requests. Top companies tend to encourage individuals to report their own collaboration problems to their leader or manager, without fear of retribution. Despite this, most organizations don't know which employees are at greatest risk of overload.

"There's no collaborative overload officer, so there is no single person accountable for identifying and then addressing collaborative overload in the organization," said Cross. "I can't think of a single company that has such a role; in fact, for most organizations their first reaction is to argue that they don't have an overload problem but rather think they don't have enough people collaborating."

Measurement and analysis of collaboration are key if companies want to get out in front of the unwanted attrition and costly bottlenecks that overload creates.

"All leaders react to whatever measurements are put in front of us, such as financial metrics, sales data, process flows, and so on," said Cross. "But without doing a robust organizational network analysis, it is hard to get a sense of the collaborative costs. The problem of collaborative overload is huge—the volume and diversity of collaborative demands placed on employees today has exploded—but is largely invisible, and so it isn't taken seriously. Leaders are at best reactive when a significant issue arises and causes pain on a team or for an individual, but aside from those cases relatively few organizations are taking proactive steps."

CHAPTER 14

STEP #11: ESTABLISH A CO-CREATION MINDSET

Sell. Don't tell.

—BRET SNYDER, CEO, W.L. GORE & ASSOCIATES

I've met thousands of HR executives over the years. One of the most unusual I ever came across is Kenny Moore.

Kenny is the former head of HR for KeySpan Energy, a utility that delivered gas to millions of customers in New York and New England and had 12,000 employees in the early 2000s. KeySpan was purchased in 2007 by National Grid for $7.3 billion in cash,[1] at the time creating the second largest utility in the United States. Over a dozen years earlier, KeySpan CEO Bob Catell had picked Kenny to run HR for the entire company.

Kenny was an atypical choice. He had no previous HR experience. In fact, he had no previous business experience. That's because, for a significant part of his life, Kenny was a monk.

"At an early age, I felt called to the priesthood," said Moore.[2] "Trouble was, I was such a poor student, the Archdiocese of New York wouldn't accept me. Finally, a strict monastic order in New Jersey said they would give me a chance."[3]

One of six children, Moore was raised in Queens and acted on his calling at the age of 19. He eventually was ordained a priest. But at the age of 34, he gave it up after he became troubled that the church wasn't changing fast enough. "I thought if I stayed, I would become embittered or disheartened. So I left," Moore explained.

Through some people he knew, Catell hired Kenny at the Brooklyn Union Gas Company, the predecessor to KeySpan, even though Kenny had no relevant job experience. He wasn't hired immediately to head up HR, just to be a contributor in the department.

"It was an experiment," said Catell. "I don't think either one of us knew how it was going to work out. It was something new, something different." Kenny's lack of business experience didn't bother Catell. "It wasn't really his business acumen that I was looking for. It was his ability to connect with the human side of people that I was really looking for."

The job suited Kenny. "I knew nothing about business, but I realized I could help people. We were training them in a [performance appraisal] system that required having difficult conversations. Priests know how to do that. After a year and a half, I was promoted."[4]

The CEO and the former monk got along famously. However, after a decade together, the culture of the company was in jeopardy due to mergers and market deregulation. The energy business was being disrupted, and if the 100-year-old gas utility was going to survive, Catell and Moore knew they would have to renovate the culture. The company was transitioning from Brooklyn Gas to a new name—KeySpan—and to signify the change to the employees, Moore advised doing something radical. He argued that change doesn't start with a beginning, but with an ending.

"Why don't we do a corporate funeral?" Moore asked Catell.

"I thought he was crazy," recalls Catell. "It took me a little while to grab hold of that."

Moore was serious. And so he staged a funeral. Four hundred KeySpan executives, most unaware of what they were walking into, were invited to the mock service. Moore described the scene in a couple of articles.

"In one corner, I put two tombstones from our Halloween display and a funeral urn. I wore my priestly stole and played a tape of Gregorian chants. 'Dearly beloved,' I said, 'we are gathered here today to bid a fond farewell to the Brooklyn Union Gas of old.' Then I asked people to write what was over for the company on index cards and put them in the urn."

Initially, everyone was a tad stunned. The CFO asked if he was in the right meeting.

"Faces are looking at me like, what the hell's going on? Then one of the managers leaves. I just waited. The tension mounts. Then one union employee says, 'You mean like lifetime employment?' I said, 'That's right. That's over for us.' I wrote it on the card and dropped it in. Somebody says, 'Lack of competition. We used to have no competition as a monopoly. I think we're going to have competition.' Right. Wrote that on it and put it in. After a while people started catching on. I wrote some more cards and I put them in the funeral urn and I said, okay, we're going to now lay this to rest with dignity. I took out some water and blessed it. I blessed the crowd. I felt like the pope."

This was only the first step in Moore's mock funeral.

"In the next corner was a steamer trunk for the things we needed to keep on our journey," Moore continued. "We are not leaving everything behind. There are actually some things we have to take with us that have been critical to our success as a company. We wrote things like *great people* and *dedication to the community* on cards and threw them in. Finally, I had a stork from our Valentine's display to symbolize our birth as KeySpan. I made everyone draw what the future of the company might look like with crayons on poster paper. By then, everyone was participating.

"When it was over, the CFO said to me, 'You have some set of balls. Nobody but you could have gotten away with this.' But I didn't feel like I had been very brave. People are dying to be connected, invited, involved. They don't like having things shoved down their throats in a formulaic way. They show energy and commitment when they can be players and influence an initiative's outcome."

Unbeknown to the attendees, the co-creation movement had begun.

"We used those 400 or so people in the room to be, I guess, sort of apostles to go out and talk to the rest of the employees about the need for this change," said Catell.[5]

Over the years Moore did more than just stage mock funerals. He was a confidant of Catell's, relaying to him what he was hearing from the workforce.

"I spend most of my time dealing with employees. Two-thirds of our employees are union. I also had the ability to say, Here's how it's being interpreted on the street. Here's what the employees think about this, and it would probably be worthwhile for you to get off this executive floor and meet face to face with these people."[6]

Equally, Moore had the trust of the workforce and could relay to the workers what he was hearing in the C-suite.

"For years, I worked on employee surveys, and I noticed three trends. Nobody trusts. Nobody believes in top management. And people are too stressed to care. In the monastery, we called that a crisis of faith, hope, and charity. So corporate America not only has financial problems, it has spiritual problems. Maybe that's the realm I work in. A wise leader realizes that if you can engage not just employees' physical energy but their emotional, mental, and spiritual energy as well, you've got something powerful."[7]

Author and management guru Tom Peters once challenged Moore on this dual role, asking him if he worried that employees were afraid he was "ratting them out" to the CEO.

"It's possible," admitted Moore, "but what I think is probably more compelling is the fact that people have a chance to see me day in and day out and watch how I respond and how I use the information, and did I use it in a way that got people in trouble, or did I use it in a way that helped move the business forward?"

Moore adds one more unique advantage he held. "You don't expect to be lied to by a priest."

A Co-creation Mindset

Catell and Moore went on to write a book together titled *The CEO and the Monk* that documented their unique relationship. Clearly, Moore understood not only the concept of culture renovation when changing a culture, but also the power that co-creation has in successfully carrying out a new beginning.

Though almost all successful culture change efforts begin top-down, it is critical to also get the buy-in of the workforce by creating a bottom-up (and middle-out) contribution mechanism. That entails enlisting and empowering key influencers at almost every level of the organization to be involved in actively building the renovation—a practice that sustains momentum for the initiative and creates positive energy and supporters throughout the organization. It was a common refrain from CEOs and others who oversaw a culture change: make sure the employee base doesn't see this as a top-down edict, but rather something that everyone had a say in developing.

One way to encourage a co-creation mindset, as mentioned earlier in the book, is through a hackathon, which Ford experimented with in 2018. Ford's hackathon research started in late January of that year, but it could not find a company that had hacked its corporate culture the way Ford envisioned doing (since most are used for software development), though it did locate a few companies that had used hackathons for nontechnical topics. None was an exact match.[8]

"We knew that culture and strategy go hand-in-hand, so as our business evolves, so must our culture," said Julie Lodge-Jarrett, the former head of talent at Ford. "We also knew that there are a lot of levers we can pull to impact culture . . . changing our people policies and processes, honing our assessment tools, furthering employee sentiment analysis, creating explicit leadership competencies, etc. And while all of these are important, the one lever we prioritized above all others was creating new and different employee experiences. One exciting way we've done this is by inviting people to #hackFORDculture.[9]

"This wasn't a typical hackathon, where people collaborate and code. Instead, it was an opportunity for a diverse group of interested employees from all experience levels and functions, to come together and define their vision of Ford's culture and generate ideas to bring that to life."

The team at Ford held a two-day event where employees worked in randomly selected teams to generate ideas to either fortify elements of the culture they loved or fix elements that weren't serving the company well. Although it started at headquarters in Dearborn, Michigan, the hackathon then went on the road and was conducted at Ford sites in China, Germany, Argentina, and Mexico. The objective was threefold:

1. Give employees a chance to share their stories and become part of the movement.
2. Generate diverse and global ideas to help transform Ford's culture.
3. Teach and practice tools that inspire innovation and curiosity.

As a result of the culture hackathons, several ideas generated in each region were put into place. But according to Ford, just as rewarding was the level of engagement displayed by participating employees and the birth of a co-creation mentality. In each region, the organizing team was able to engage with employees and empower them to serve as agents of culture change. Survey data collected at the beginning and conclusion of the global events found the percentages of employees who felt they could change company culture increased between 20 and 40 percent.

No Consultants Necessary

One important aspect of Ford's efforts that might get overlooked by organizations looking to model its efforts is that Ford did this internally, without the aid of consultants. External consultants are commonly brought in to assist, lead, or manage a culture change. However, i4cp's research found that there is no positive statistical relationship between using consultants and market performance, and only a slightly positive correlation to culture change success. Though consultants can bring a valuable external perspective, too often they don't truly understand the unique DNA of the organization they're trying to help and, as a result, sometimes offer ideas or models that ultimately won't work in their client's unique cultural construct. Many companies that have successfully renovated their cultures did so without the aid of external consultants.

But they often learn that lesson the hard way. W.L. Gore and Associates was one of those companies.

You know W.L. Gore as the maker of Gore-Tex and other technical apparel. But Gore also makes specialty industrial products and implantable medical devices—essentially products derived from fluoropolymers—which are known for being highly resistant to solvents, acids, and bases (the best-known fluoropolymer is Teflon).[10] The company, based in Newark, Delaware, bills itself as a "global materials science company" that solves complex technical challenges in demanding environments—from outer space to the world's highest peaks to the inner workings of the human body.

The company was founded in 1958 in the basement of Bill and Vieve Gore's home, and the vision was that it would provide opportunities for growth and development and encourage intelligent experimentation and risk taking, while also leveraging shared ownership for workers. Gore set up the environment and circumstances needed to enable employees (called associates) to drive the kind of innovative work that would not only deliver business success, but also contribute to the greater good and make positive differences in the world. As a result, Gore has been the subject of many business books over the years due to its unique operating style and philosophies.

Today Gore has over 10,000 employees, has well over $3 billion in revenue, and is one of the 200-largest private companies in the United States. Gore has been granted more than 5,500 patents world-wide in a wide range of fields, and it has offices in more than 25 countries, with manufacturing operations in the United States, Germany, United Kingdom, China, and Japan.

Despite its size and growth, Gore is still a family-run business. One of those family members is Bret Snyder, the grandson of Bill and Vieve Gore, who has been the chairman of Gore since 2016 and a member of the board since 2011. Snyder was named President and CEO of the company in the fall of 2020. Bret described to me one day the pitfalls of bringing in consultants when trying to change culture.

"We tried to put it in harmonized computer systems a while ago, and business processes to go along with those systems. While we are generally known for a lattice-type structure with a lot of freedom, in essence this really was moving from a decentralized structure to a more centralized one," Snyder explained.

"It's important to understand that we generally have a 'sell, don't tell' type of culture. When we want to make change happen, we sell the merits internally rather than mandate it. But in this system migration process we inadvertently switched to a tell. And it was a failure," recalls Snyder. "That was obvious in our culture survey scores. We have the same questions year after year, and they took a nosedive. We had been on the Great Place to Work top 100 list ever since it was started back in the early eighties, one of only three or four companies to claim that, and for the first year we fell off the list . . . out of the top 100."

While there were multiple reasons for this, Snyder looks back on it and realizes there was an overreliance on external advice and also a top-down approach to culture change.

"One of the big issues, in our efforts to get outside expertise on how to be more efficient, is we brought on way too many consultants. Our consultant spend was tens of millions. And then we hired a whole bunch of very senior external people to 'show us the way.' So, the message we implied to our associates was Gore's culture needed to change, and their experience may not be helpful. And to fix it, we are going to do what everybody else is doing. And that was a confidence-sapping move on our part. The external people, through no fault of their own, came in with big roles and were there to make changes, because that's what they'd been asked to do when they were hired.

"At Gore, you have this organization where everybody's grown up locally and been internally developed, made a lot of decisions on their own, and used their own judgment over the years. And suddenly they're being told to do things by well-meaning outsiders. Combine it with many consultants who were pushing their solutions . . . well, let's just say it really turned people pretty sour.

"At one point I asked, how did we get here? I think leadership was honestly trying to rectify what they saw as inefficiencies in the culture in our organization and trying to really get us ready for the digital world. We had good intentions, but all the consultants said there's no reason we need to have multiple processes, multiple systems. Sure, it makes sense on paper, but when you aren't immersed in a culture, it can really backfire.

"So, we went back to doing much more internally. We reduced the consultants, pushed them into a smaller role, and got back to our cultural roots. That doesn't mean we aren't benefiting from some of the external hires we've brought in, but there's a big difference between bringing them in at the middle of the organization versus right into a key leadership role without careful onboarding. We have really pared back on bringing in high-level external people even though we still do it occasionally. But we had to do a huge culture reset."

Gore always seemed to understand the co-creation mindset but needed to get back to its old roots and enlist influencers and energizers among the leaders.

"To really change the culture, we had to get the associates involved. We simplified the messages and went back to our founding principles, but we did it in a very labor-intensive way for the leadership team. We did seven meetings in over a six-month period with 100 to 200 people in each meeting. These were two-day meetings where we flew everybody to a location where we operated, and we did an in-depth cultural kind of retraining. People were, I think, impressed by the investment. Impressed that we cared. Impressed that the leadership team traveled to a region and met face-to-face with folks. Impressed that it was a lot more than just nice words on a PowerPoint. It had a feeling of getting back to the Gore that people know where we follow a few basic principles but leave a lot to individual judgment. That gesture meant a lot."

When renovating, focus groups can be a powerful way to launch a co-creation mindset internally. That notion at Gore is as old as the company.

"We like to test changes with focus groups and pilots to anticipate objections and challenges," Snyder revealed. "I would recommend not going big on something that is a big change without having tested it. I'll give you an example. My granddad would do something like changing the way we do compensation. And he would have said something like, 'You know, we have tried it in a plant. Somebody in a plant said, hey, I think we should do a different way.' And he would say, 'OK, you go ahead and do that that way. And tell me how it goes.' And let's say it goes well. And it seems promising. He might then say, 'I'd put a memo out to everybody and say, you know, there's this other business that has tried this way of working and has gotten some pretty interesting results that seem very positive for everybody working there. And it's been satisfactory for growing the business. And it might be worth considering.' And he would do a selling job from there, pointing out it would have been tried somewhere first and he would then be encouraging others to adopt it."

"Sell, don't tell. That's the best way to sum it up."

CHAPTER 15

STEP #12: PROVIDE TRAINING ON THE DESIRED BEHAVIORS

> An organization's ability to learn and translate
> that learning into action rapidly is the
> ultimate competitive advantage.
> —JACK WELCH, FORMER CHAIRMAN, GE

Companies that successfully renovated their cultures did so in part by training their leaders (at all levels) on the desired behaviors and how to model those in their daily routines. Perhaps no company in history did this as swiftly and dramatically as Starbucks in 2018.

On April 12, 2018, Rashon Nelson and Donte Robinson were waiting at a table at a Starbucks situated in the tony Rittenhouse Square neighborhood of Philadelphia. The two men, both age 23 and best friends since the fourth grade, were there to meet Andrew Yaffe, the middle-aged founder and president of his own company, AY Industries, to discuss a real estate deal they had been working on for months. Nelson and Robinson originally were supposed to meet Yaffe at a Starbucks across town. But the plan changed, and they agreed to meet at the Rittenhouse Square location where they had met several times before.[1]

Unfortunately, Yaffe was late. And that's when the trouble began.

Nelson and Robinson, both black, didn't order anything while they waited. Nelson asked to use the restroom and was refused by the manager, a white female, because he wasn't a paying customer (a policy of Starbucks at the time). After Nelson sat back down, the manager asked the two men to leave the Starbucks, but they explained they were just waiting for a business meeting.

A few minutes later, the two hardly noticed when the police walked into the coffee shop, until the officers started walking in their direction. "That's when we knew she called the police on us," Nelson said.

After the two officers arrived, there were several minutes of conversation, where the officers reportedly asked the men to leave. They were eventually joined by a police supervisor along with more officers and were told they would be arrested if they didn't comply. Yaffe, who is white, finally arrived at the Starbucks in the middle of this conversation, surprised to see the officers confronting Nelson and Robinson and hearing of the pending arrest. Yaffe immediately confronted the officers.

"What did they get called for, because there were two black guys sitting here, meeting me? What did they do?" Other patrons told the police and Yaffe that the men did nothing wrong. Yaffe told the police that he and his friends would just leave and go somewhere else, but that idea was dismissed.

"They're not free to leave," one of the officers replied. "We're done with that."

Nelson and Robinson, who had never been arrested before, were calmly handcuffed and charged with "defiant trespassing." They were released about nine hours later, at 2 a.m., after the Starbucks employees and the district attorney's office declined to press charges.

Unfortunately, this scene plays out all the time in retail establishments across America, and too often ends in violent confrontations.

The death of George Floyd is one of many examples we see regularly across the United States; black men and women are singled out, and too often they end up dead. Luckily, in this situation, that was not the case, but the incident caused an uproar across the country.

Like many others, this scene became famous because it was captured on video by Philadelphia-based author Melissa DePino, who is white, as were most of the other patrons. DePino posted it immediately to Twitter and called out the racial implications by captioning the video with "All the other white ppl are wondering why it's never happened to us when we do the same thing." The video quickly went viral—it was viewed 10 million times in just a couple of days—and sparked outrage about the blatant racial discrimination nationwide.

Likely you heard about the story and maybe even watched the video. There was a second video of the incident made at the same time from a different angle. From my perspective, it was one of the tamest arrests I've ever seen. Nelson and Robinson were completely composed (polite even), and the only slightly raised voices come from Yaffe and the other patrons, but even those are relatively restrained. The two were calmly and quietly walked out of the store in handcuffs, heads held high.

"When you know that you did nothing wrong, how do you really react to it?" Nelson said. "You can either be ignorant or you can show some type of sophistication and act like you have class. That was the choice we had."[2]

Over the ensuing weekend, attention and anger over the video grew, prompting a protest at the Rittenhouse Square Starbucks and calls for a national boycott. The mayor, Jim Kenney, who is white, said what happened at the Starbucks "appears to exemplify what racial discrimination looks like in 2018." The police commissioner, Richard Ross, who is black, said in a Facebook post that the arresting officers "did absolutely nothing wrong," and added that Nelson and Robinson were disrespectful to the officers (the commissioner later apologized for his remarks and admitted he had "failed miserably").

The Starbucks Response

Starbucks issued a statement early that Saturday that read: "We apologize to the two individuals and our customers and are disappointed this led to an arrest. We take these matters seriously and clearly have more work to do when it comes to how we handle incidents in our stores. We are reviewing our policies and will continue to engage with the community and the police department to try and ensure these types of situations never happen in any of our stores."

Several felt that the statement was lackluster and didn't truly address the situation. After the volume on the backlash kept increasing, Starbucks CEO Kevin Johnson came out with a much stronger and more specific response later that same day. On Sunday, Johnson told customers he "will fix this" via a video message on the official Starbucks website. "This is not who we are, and not who we are going to be," he asserted. Johnson then flew to the East Coast to better address the situation.

The next day, in an interview with the *Philadelphia Inquirer* and *Daily News*, he called the incident "reprehensible," vowing to work with store managers and employees to address any "unconscious bias" across the coffee chain.[3] He made similar statements in an interview that same Monday on *Good Morning America*, and he also asked to meet with Nelson and Robinson, saying, "I'd like to have a dialogue with them so that I can ensure that we have opportunity to really understand the situation and show some compassion and empathy for the experience they went through."[4]

Johnson also confirmed that the manager who called the police is no longer working at that store and had left the company by mutual agreement. In his *Good Morning America* appearance, Johnson refused to say whether she had been disciplined, explaining, "I know it's easy for me to say and point blame to one person in this incident [but] my responsibility is to look more broadly . . . to ensure this never happens again."[5]

Johnson met with Nelson and Robinson in Philadelphia that day. He also met with Mayor Jim Kenney and other city leaders.

Throughout that same day, protesters gathered inside and outside the Rittenhouse Square store chanting, "Starbucks coffee is anti-black." One protester said, "We're going to occupy space, we're going to make it very uncomfortable until they make changes and until specifically, they meet the demands we set forth." Another said, "We don't want this Starbucks to make any money today. That's our goal."

The next day, Tuesday, April 17, Johnson issued a stunning announcement. The company said it will be closing its more than 8,000 company-owned stores in the United States on the afternoon of May 29 to conduct racial bias education geared toward preventing discrimination. The training will be provided to nearly 175,000 partners (employees) across the country and will become part of the onboarding process for new partners.

"I've spent the last few days in Philadelphia with my leadership team listening to the community, learning what we did wrong and the steps we need to take to fix it," said Johnson. "While this is not limited to Starbucks, we're committed to being a part of the solution. Closing our stores for racial bias training is just one step in a journey that requires dedication from every level of our company and partnerships in our local communities."

The statement went on to say that partners will go through a training program designed to address implicit bias, promote conscious inclusion, prevent discrimination, and ensure everyone inside a Starbucks store feels safe and welcome. The curriculum would be developed with guidance from several national and local experts, and once completed, Starbucks would make the education materials available to other companies for use with their employees and leadership. The morning following the store closure announcement, the man most associated with the company, co-founder and executive chairman Howard Schultz, went on *CBS This Morning*, co-hosted by Gayle King.

"I'm embarrassed, ashamed," Schultz told King. "I think what occurred was reprehensible at every single level. I think I take it very personally as everyone in our company does and we're committed to making it right. The announcement we made yesterday about closing our stores, 8,000 stores closed, to do significant training with our people is just the beginning of what we will do to transform the way we do business and educate our people on unconscious bias," Schultz said. "It will cost millions of dollars, but I've always viewed this and things like this as not an expense, but an investment in our people and our company. And we're better than this. There's no doubt in my mind that the reason that they (police) were called was because they were African American. That's not who Starbucks is."

From the day of the incident to the announcement of the closing of stores for bias training was a mere five days. Many hailed the Starbucks response as swift, direct, admirable, and textbook crisis management. Others called it lip service, insufficient, and a PR stunt.

A couple of weeks later Robinson and Nelson agreed to a settlement with Starbucks for an undisclosed sum and an offer of free college tuition to complete bachelor's degrees through an online program with Arizona State University that was created four years ago for Starbucks employees. In a separate deal, they got a symbolic $1 each from the City of Philadelphia as well as a promise from officials to establish a $200,000 public high school program for young entrepreneurs.

"We thought long and hard about it, and we feel like this is the best way to see that change that we want to see," Robinson told the Associated Press.

Johnson also was so impressed with Robinson and Nelson, he offered to personally mentor them. In mid-May Starbucks announced that anyone who walks into its cafés is considered a customer. "Any person who enters our spaces, including patios, cafes and restrooms, regardless of whether they make a purchase, is considered a customer," Johnson said in an e-mail to employees.

On May 29, Starbucks did something few other companies have ever even considered doing: it shut down its entire business to conduct unconscious bias training. The training started with employees watching a short film by Stanley Nelson, an award-winning documentarian, called *You're Welcome*. That was followed by a video of Schultz and Johnson on the importance of providing inclusivity in "the third place," or the idea that Starbucks provides a third location where people gather between home and work. Rapper Common also addressed the employees via video. Employees then separated into small self-guided groups to talk about racial bias and how race impacts them, with toolkits to work from. Managers went through the exact same training as baristas, as did the executive team prior to the 29th. The entire training took four hours.

"We realize that four hours of training is not going to solve racial inequity, but we have to start the conversation," said Schultz.[6] Comments from employees ran the gamut of "I've already known this" to "It definitely made a lot of people in my job who work with me understand better."

Whether the training is enough misses the main benefit. Starbucks clearly made a statement about who it is as a company, and the behaviors it expects—from its leaders to the frontline employees. It also made it clear if these values aren't for you, then the company is likely not a good fit.

Personally, it pained me to listen to any criticism of how Starbucks handled this incident. In under five days it accomplished more than almost any organization would have done in a similar situation—in fact, most companies would have probably taken five days merely bringing the right people together to try to decide how to mitigate their brand and legal risk. As we are reminded far too often, the topic of racial discrimination is highly sensitive and emotional, with many different viewpoints. Unfortunately, discrimination never seems to diminish in society. The fact that Starbucks devoted so much time and was willing to forgo so much revenue toward addressing it says quite a bit about its values. Other companies have taken notice and followed suit.

A Homecoming

The handling of this unforeseen incident prepared Starbucks for other unexpected events that would soon follow: the 2020 pandemic and George Floyd's death.

Like many retailers at the onset of the COVID-19 crisis, Starbucks closed most stores worldwide due to mandates and safety concerns. It began with 2,000 store closures in China in January, and ultimately most others around the world, including all cafés in the United States and Canada in mid-March. In the beginning of May, Starbucks reopened those North American stores and brought back personnel to a very different environment of social distancing, new ordering procedures, and enhanced sanitation, among other changes.

But before it reopened, it reacclimated returning partners to that new environment through two days of training classes that drew on their experience from two years earlier.

"We called the program Homecoming: Connecting to Our Purpose Together," explained Molly Hill, vice president of global talent and the overseer of the initiative. "We learned a lot from the bias training we conducted in the wake of the Philadelphia incident. What most people don't know is that we've shifted most of our training to that same format over the last two years and have been delivering these offerings focused on what it means to create the third place every seven to eight weeks since the close of our stores two years ago. Based on the way we closed our stores initially, we conduct training that is all about having trust in the learner to have the right conversations and ensuring our leaders are learners alongside their partners."

The conversation-focused program is one of the keys to Starbuck's swift execution.

"What that means is it doesn't rely on a facilitator, doesn't rely on formal online learning, and doesn't rely on the store manager to actually be an expert on these topics," Hill explained further. "In order to reopen our stores, we used the existing format in our Homecoming training that allowed learners to carry the conversation. The one difference versus before was not requiring partners to gather around an iPad to watch videos. Instead we made a modification that relied more on audio so that people could be separated by socially acceptable distances.

"The two days were separated by their focus," Hill told me. "Day one's focus was called To Be Together. It emphasized empathy, allowed partners to share their stories, their fears, their experiences. Day two was more operational in nature, and focused on understanding new store formats, safety procedures, and health check procedures. And just like we did after the Philadelphia incident, we were allowed to conduct the training in a closed café format to give partners the space and the time they need to be comfortable in that environment."

After George Floyd's death, in the wake of the ensuing social unrest, Starbucks was also well suited to continue the dialogue while other companies were left scrambling to put something together.

"We had broadened the series quite a bit, making it very much focused on bias and inclusion, but are coming back to the topic of race and racial injustice in particular. We're not changing the format; we are just touching on topics, again, that we already touched on in the past, and coming back around to things like microaggression. But always with new speakers and new content."

Since Starbucks has been a clear leader in bias training, many other organizations have reached out to learn from the company. However, many of them simply aren't comfortable with the format.

"I'm surprised sometimes by how many organizations are still so incredibly fearful of the open dialogue, and then not having a system in place just in case the conversation goes awry," said Hill. "We used to have counselors on site and have a call-in number just in case people are upset by the conversation or needed help or a store manager needed help. But on 5/29 when we originally shut down the stores, we ended up getting five phone calls, and they were all technology related. We didn't get a single phone call from someone that needed support. But I think organizations are still concerned about legal risk which still has a lot of HR professionals freaked out about entering into this conversation.

"Overall, we have a heavy emphasis on behaviors, and the 'green thread' which is the partner journey in our organization and includes everyone, from those wearing the green apron to non-retail employees."

Training on behaviors is an important part of any culture change effort. When doing so, it's important to understand the behaviors needed to support the right type of culture. For example, take these four culture types and some of the critical leadership behaviors that support them:

Agile Culture

- Identify and break down structural silos.
- Develop and move talent to address changing business needs.
- Create a safe and inclusive environment.
- Establish the why of the work and nurture a shared sense of purpose.
- Set goals and ensure teams are clear on priorities.
- Encourage intelligent risk taking.
- Help others establish productive connections across the enterprise.
- Build relationships with external stakeholders.

Collaborative Culture

- Establish a transparent and trusting environment that provides psychological safety for all team members.
- Establish collaborative teams that represent diverse and relevant perspectives and experiences.
- Help others build network connections that benefit the individual and the organization.
- Encourage collaboration that breaks down formal chains of command and connects silos.
- Hire for collaboration skills.
- Measure and reward based on team contribution.
- Make decision-making authority and processes among teams clear.
- Measure collaboration flow through a formal network analysis.

Innovative Culture

- Sponsor highly creative and innovative individuals for visible or challenging opportunities.
- Support the development of innovative ideas that have potential to further organizational goals.
- Create or sponsor systems that reward creativity and innovation.
- Create an environment in which best practices are freely shared among teams throughout the organization.
- Demonstrate awareness of cross-cultural diversity with a propensity and ability to see patterns across countries and markets.
- Demonstrate ability to see scenarios and patterns across systems and identify future possibility and risk.

Inclusive Culture

- Promote the open acceptance of different points of view on the part of all team members.
- Display a nonjudgmental attitude that is open to differing viewpoints.
- Demonstrate awareness of variances in global business customs and cultural practices.
- Establish productive relationships with people from other cultures, countries, races, and backgrounds.
- Provide education on bias and the value of diversity and inclusion.
- Challenge exclusionary institutional practices and policies within the organization.

While multiple culture types exist, understanding the behaviors that support those types helps organizations focus on the most appropriate training content.

Leaders as Teachers

One of the most effective ways for companies to teach the desired behaviors, especially for leaders, is to have leaders do the teaching. The concept of "leaders as teachers" was popularized by Jack Welch during his tenure as CEO of General Electric. Jack spent a great deal of time teaching at the company's legendary leadership center in Crotonville, New York, the oldest corporate university in the United States, and required his direct reports to do the same.

I've visited Crotonville several times, and it's impressive—a 59-acre campus an hour north of New York City. The college campus feel, the hotel, the classrooms, technology, and convening spaces all make it a special experience. Since it was initially opened in 1956, GE's commitment to learning continued to increase and became a hallmark of the company under Welch. One of Welch's most famous quotes is, "An organization's ability to learn and translate that learning into action rapidly is the ultimate competitive advantage." It's clear Welch was committed to that philosophy. Some labeled him the great inquirer, as he had an insatiable thirst for knowledge. "Jack asked more questions than anyone I've ever known, and it wasn't to show off his own intellect or importance. His aim was to sponge up as much information as he could," wrote Claudio Fernández-Aráoz for *Harvard Business Review* upon Welch's passing.

That thirst for knowledge translated to a commitment to teaching under the philosophy that you'll never understand a subject better than when you are forced to teach it.

In a study i4cp conducted of 1,361 learning and business professionals in conjunction with the Association for Talent Development, we found that companies that leveraged leaders in their learning process tended to be high-performance organizations. However, it's a small percentage of companies that have formal programs in place (17 percent), although high-performance companies were more apt to have established these versus low-performance companies, which were twice as likely to have no program at all. Those same top performers were two to three times more likely to leverage C-level and senior level executives (vice president and above) as teachers in these programs.

That same study found benefits in multiple areas. In learning organizations, workforces were more engaged, and the classes exposed employees to leaders they otherwise wouldn't have access to. Equally, however, leaders found the programs enhanced their self-awareness, created more talent appreciation through interaction with employees they might not have encountered otherwise, and broadened their understanding of information and different opinions within the company.

One of the biggest findings, however, is that 53 percent of all organizations felt these programs aided in organizational culture change. This number was even higher (68 percent) for larger, high-performance organizations.

While leaders as teachers is one of the most effective ways to reinforce behaviors, it's clear that successful culture change relies on overall leadership training across the organization. A full two-thirds of companies that have successfully changed their culture provided training on the desired behaviors for leaders at all levels so that they could model these behaviors in their daily routines.

Enlisting leaders as teachers to conduct training may be the best method for modeling I've come across.

A BLUEPRINT TO RENOVATE CULTURE

PHASE THREE

MAINTAIN

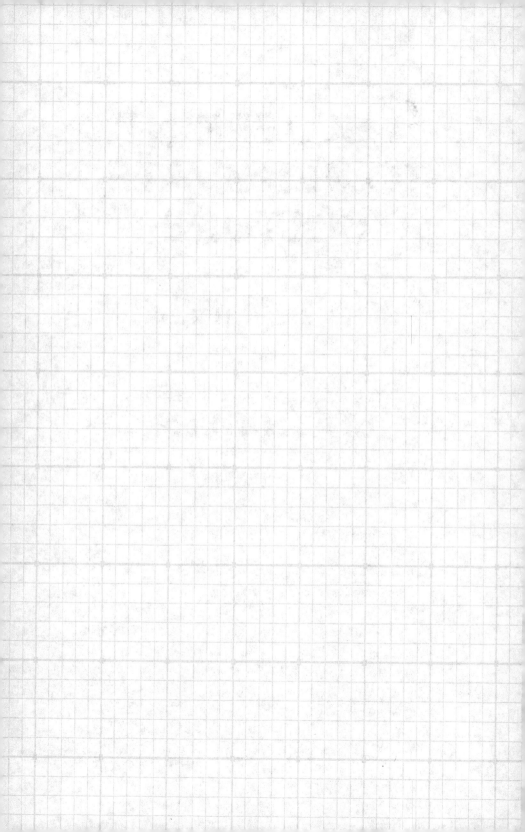

CHAPTER 16

STEP #13:
MAKE ONBOARDING ABOUT RELATIONSHIPS VERSUS RED TAPE

> Onboarding that many people, to have them
> understand Toyota, that will be a challenge . . .
> but we're up for the challenge.
> —JIM LENTZ, CEO, TOYOTA NORTH AMERICA

Picture this scenario.

It's day one for a new employee. She's anxious before she even arrives. What do you wear on the first day to fit in, but acknowledge it's your first day? Not wanting to be late, she leaves early and arrives at the campus where she encounters her first problem of the day: no one told her where employees should park. Wasting precious time, she drives aimlessly around the crowded campus, finally succumbing to the clock and just paying to park. The next problem: the garage she chose was across campus, forcing a long brisk walk. Now she's late. A great start, she thinks.

When she breathlessly arrives at the address she was given, the receptionist doesn't have her name on the list, and she can't reach her new boss, or anyone else, on the phone. Confusion reigns. After several strangers sort it out, she's finally let through security and hurriedly escorted to "orientation" in a conference room filled with other anxious newbies. Even though she's the last to arrive, she tries to look confident. She fills out some forms, receives a company ID badge (but her building key card isn't ready, maybe tomorrow). She watches a video from the CEO and some other nameless executives and a semi-documentary on the history of the company and its values and mission. There probably was some other important company information that she tuned out because it sounded like so much corporate-speak she's already heard a hundred times in her career. Upon conclusion of the orientation, she and the other newbies are congratulated by a couple of people who don't seem to have anything to do with her new department.

Next, she is escorted to her desk. It's covered in dust, and the remnants of the previous inhabitant can be found in every drawer. She is supposed to meet her new boss, but now it becomes clear why he was missing—he's at a conference halfway across the country. She is given her new laptop, but it's not set up yet. IT can't be found to help. Leaving it behind, she meets some new coworkers in the general area of her dusty desk. More surface-level congratulations and small talk ensues, and to fill the rest of her morning HR stops by and asks her to fill out some additional paperwork with information she swears she has provided three times already. Soon enough it's lunchtime, but she's on her own. Everyone looks too busy to ask where she should even go.

She wanders around campus, wondering if she made the right choice. Meanwhile, someone is checking off that her onboarding is "complete." She is feeling quite incomplete. And alone, overwhelmed, and insecure. Welcome to your new career.

You might think that scenario is embellished, but it isn't. It's a compilation of just a few real-life experiences of new employees I have spoken with. I've heard the joke several times that the best day of an employee's life is when he or she gets offered the job, and the worst day is the first day on the job. There's a lot of truth to this—most of us can think back to a first day on the job, and most of us would not label it one of our best days. That often extends to the first week, month, quarter. It's easy to see why new hire attrition is so high in organizations; estimates range from 20 percent[1] to much higher.[2] And as most know, losing new hires at any point in the first year is not only frustrating but expensive (from 50 percent of salary for an entry-level role to 200 percent for an executive[3]).

That recognition is why there's been much more emphasis on improving the onboarding experience at organizations around the world over the last few years. And there is definitely room for improvement. In our research, 90 percent of organizations have an onboarding process, but only 44 percent indicated that their process achieved the outcomes they wanted. Feedback from the workforce is worse. Only 12 percent of employees think their company did a good job onboarding.[4]

If you want to maintain that culture renovation you worked so hard to put in place, you can start by improving your onboarding process.

Most companies' onboarding programs start the day the employee starts, but you might be surprised to learn that's too late. If communication and outreach doesn't occur between when the candidate accepted the offer and the start date, that introduces significant opportunity for second-guessing by the new hire. In fact, "ghosting" is a more popular term these days to describe candidates who simply don't show up on day one. This is an incredibly infuriating yet now more frequent occurrence in companies, and a big reason for it is lack of communication leading up to the start date.

An onboarding process that starts before "day one" can help ease concerns that candidates may be experiencing. A big part of this can be getting some of that annoying paperwork out of the way early on and getting a new employee established technologically. This helps new hires hit the ground running when they do start, instead of being bogged down for their first few days filling out benefits forms or waiting to get set up on the network. Another is to start getting them connected to key people in the company instead of waiting until the official start date.

While most companies would benefit from altering their perception of when the onboarding process starts, they should also examine the length of the process. In the example above, it was a half day. Although that is pretty typical, it is much too short. While over a quarter of organizations we've studied say their onboarding process doesn't exist or is less than a day, another 42 percent say it is less than one month.[5] Even if it is a full month, this is also too short.

Onboarding should be an ongoing process, ideally over the employee's first year with the company. Think "journey" versus a one-time event.

But the most overlooked aspect of onboarding has proved to be the most critical: helping the new hire establish a network of trusted subject-matter experts who will contribute to that person's career success.

Focus on the Network

Sometimes referred to as "newcomer socialization," i4cp's research found that only 20 percent of companies feel that helping new hires establish an internal network is currently an objective of onboarding. Most organizations never even consider introducing network building into the process. Research has repeatedly shown that relationships matter a great deal in determining whether a new hire will thrive or flame out quickly. Through the right relationships, new hires often get the information, advice, and support they need to speed their indoctrination into the organization. Often this improves productivity and early successes—which in turn builds an internal reputation and leads to bigger and more visible assignments and a lengthier tenure.

It also helps indoctrinate the new hire into the culture of the organization, especially if it's a newly renovated culture.

While helping new employees understand the culture quickly assists in their assimilation, it's the quality and effectiveness of their internal relationships that often separates productive employees from the unproductive. And it's the relationships formed with managers, internal experts, peers, mentors, and even other new hires that allow new employees not only to have a sense of inclusion, but to understand the cultural expectations.

Research also shows that there are significant differences, however, in how these networks are used. The concept of "pull" versus "push" becomes important in determining the success and longevity of a new employee. While intuitively it makes sense that a new employee who reaches out internally to a significant number of people in an effort to contribute would help (the "push"), that isn't the critical ingredient.

Instead, being *sought out by others* is the magic elixir. Rather than promote or push expertise within the organization, the most successful newcomers started by finding opportunities to help others in ways that established the newcomer's reputation and legitimacy as a useful resource. This caused the newcomer to be "pulled" into new opportunities, a major determiner of feeling included and a contributor to the organization's success.

This is an important nuance. Push often is defined as people reaching out to others in the organization and trying to demonstrate their expertise and worth; however, in many cases it actually creates mistrust, especially if new people rely too heavily on their prior experience in another organization. More successful new hires will take an "ask" approach versus a "tell" strategy and set up exploratory meetings to discuss potential areas of mutual value with senior executives, experts, and other critical contacts internally.

Leaders should be the key enablers in helping to make this happen. High-performance organizations are filled with leaders who purposefully help their teams build strong, collaborative networks. Our research found those top companies were eight times more likely to have leaders who regularly did this versus lower-performing organizations. Additionally, teaching leaders and individual contributors how to build effective networks is included in development programs of high-performance organizations at a rate that is triple that of lower performers.

However, the axiom of "It's who you know" certainly applies. While the absolute size of someone's network is not a great predictor of success, who the person is connected with is. Specifically, people who had a shorter time-to-productivity cycle, and were more likely to stay at the company, were adept at identifying and engaging people who were well connected. These relationships significantly benefited the new hires by giving them indirect access to information and expertise across the organization. And perhaps just as important, these relationships gave credibility to the new employee, as they in essence borrowed the credibility of more established and connected members.

Leaders in any organization should consider these questions:

▶ Do leaders intentionally create personal networks for their direct reports? This is helpful in creating bridges between disparate (yet increasingly reliant) functions or business units and dismantling knowledge silos that impede productivity and innovation.

▶ Do leaders understand that the ability to execute work efficiently and effectively in today's highly matrixed environment grows out of the connections people create? Seeding relationships and driving influence through their networks promotes the ability collaborative leaders need to efficiently advance projects and achieve results.

▶ Do leaders enable trust and energy to create a "pull" environment? Successful leaders know that creating awareness of expertise and reputation, while also injecting energy into interactions, ultimately attracts better information, opportunities, and talent.

Don't Limit Onboarding to New Employees

While indoctrinating new hires into the culture as quickly as possible certainly is important to effective renovation, so too is applying the same concepts to other new team members who may arrive via acquisition, or even as expatriates (expats), internal transfers, or "boomerangs." Our research found 9 in 10 organizations indicated their employee onboarding efforts focus solely on new hires, and this is a missed opportunity with other population sets.

Expats are a great example. While multinational companies invest a lot of time and effort in preparing employees for overseas or stretch assignments, they often neglect the needs of returning employees. I've personally witnessed this several times. Expats return after years abroad, only to find little thought has been given to their return. In fact, we found 52 percent of companies have no strategies in place to support their people moving into new roles, which is especially risky with expats. The attrition rates for expats within two years of repatriation are often much higher than an organization's normal percentages.

Expanding onboarding can also be an important step when organizations have a major change like an office relocation, as Toyota did with its North American headquarters in 2017.

"Most everyone, when they think of Toyota (N.A.), they think of a single company in the U.S., and we are really not," said Jim Lentz, CEO of Toyota North America back in 2014, explaining the reason for the move. "We are a group of affiliated companies working together."[6]

Under an initiative dubbed "One Toyota," the company announced its plan to relocate to Plano, Texas (just north of Dallas), the same year after the company decided to consolidate three separate hubs in Torrance, California (the former headquarters), northern Kentucky, and Michigan. The $1 billion move began officially in May of 2017.

"Each of these entities had their own legal departments, IT departments, and communications," Lentz said. "I want to make sure we have a high-performing team, and that they wanted to work together and will work together."[7]

Toyota admits it originally estimated that the company would lose 75 percent of its employees in the move, which would have triggered massive hiring and retraining. As a benchmark, when Nissan moved its North American headquarters from California to a suburb of Nashville in 2006, reportedly fewer than half of its employees made the move. Lentz said that figure was something Toyota hoped to improve upon, but leaders knew it wouldn't be easy.

"We knew we had to work very hard to try to keep as many people as we could," he said.

Ultimately, out of 4,200 employees who were asked, about 2,800 agreed to move (around two-thirds), with the majority coming from the former headquarters in California. This extremely high percentage was aided by a well-thought-out process—akin to a massive onboarding of existing employees—guided by the Toyota Way twin pillars of *Respect for People* and *Continuous Improvement*. This provided the foundation for a commitment to being transparent and supporting team members with timely information and communications.

To enable this success, it was critical to develop a convincing case that would help employees with their decision, make them feel valued regardless of what they decided to do, and keep them engaged throughout their personal transition. Toyota was committed to frequent communication and transparency and even guaranteed that jobs would be kept at the same level and pay. The aim was for employees to always feel that they came first and that their decision, whatever it might be, would be respected.

The company put several things in place to make this transition easier. It started with dedicated staff that worked across the organization and strategized each piece of the complicated move. Representatives from HR, IT, Risk, and Communications were part of the team, as were members of each internal business group—which allowed for customization within those groups. Leaders were prepared to counsel with the workforce and were provided leader alerts, talking points, and FAQs. They participated in quarterly in-person meetings and virtual leader briefings. Lentz was visible throughout to share his vision and provide inspiration and enthusiasm for the move.

To make information on the move ubiquitous, the company created a dedicated website with tools, tips, and resources in the form of video vignettes, reading lists, coping skills, activities, and self-assessments. The site also contained retention package data, information and resources on the new location, construction updates, and more. Internal support groups, like the existing business affinity groups, were also offered as connection points. These resources complemented the relocation benefits the company offered, which were based on industry benchmarks to help employees through the decision-making and transition processes. Through feedback during the process, some benefits were increased, such as spousal benefits and career counseling.

Despite those resources, one component might have been the most effective: all team members were given an all-expenses-paid three-day trip to visit Plano and the surrounding area to explore neighborhoods, schools, and other community offerings.

"The best money we spent was sponsoring a trip for team members and a spouse or significant other, just to come and see," Chris Nielsen, Toyota North America, executive vice president, said. "Some of the perceptions they had, perhaps, of tumbleweeds rolling down the main street were pretty quickly put aside."[8]

As the process ensued, the Toyota team created road shows to help connect team members who had already moved with those still deciding to provide insights on neighborhoods, spousal concerns, the weather, schools, and other concerns.

For those who decided not to make the move, the company provided an off-boarding program, which began with a road map to help them understand what they could expect and what actions they would need to take as they began to plan their departure. Program offerings included items such as benefit overviews, résumé writing, and interview skill–building sessions, as well as outplacement services. This level of support didn't go unnoticed and made all employees feel comfortable that the company was working in their best interest.

For those who did make the move, when they arrived in Plano, they were treated to a brand-new 100-acre corporate campus, which was constructed in record time. I've toured the new headquarters a couple of times, and it is beautiful. Borrowing from Toyota's Japanese roots, it boasts a Japanese garden, a large internal courtyard, a fitness center with a two-story climbing wall, 11 different places for employees to have breakfast or lunch surrounded by plenty of open space, and an on-site convenience store. In addition, there are thousands of square feet of workspace designed for collaboration.

Lentz is clearly very happy with not only the physical campus, but also the location.

"I think life is a little bit easier for people here, and as a result, I think the work-life balance is much better," Lentz said. "I think people, as a result, have a lot more energy being here. If you live in Southern California, and you're driving two or two-and-a-half hours each way, you're leaving at 5 a.m. and you're getting home at 8 or 9— that kind of wears on you."

Lentz's only regret?

"We should have done it 10 years earlier."[9]

Inspiration via Onboarding

Despite the success in retaining employees, Toyota understood it would still have to hire to fill numerous vacated roles. Ultimately, the company hired about 1,200 workers, most coming from the Dallas–Fort Worth area, and it hired many very quickly as the move occurred. That meant rapid onboarding as well. And in the company's words, "It was imperative that those new team members be quickly and effectively infused from the start with the company culture and DNA," which was no small feat since Toyota is a traditional, conservative company with a deeply established culture.[10]

Toyota's goal with onboarding new hires was to "inspire" them from their first day on the job. This initiative was termed the "team member experience," a comprehensive matrix of elements impacting team members, as well as opportunities available to them, designed to enhance the overall employee experience from day one.

"Employee experience" is a broad term that is used a great deal in organizations—in fact, it's probably overused. It's meant to capture everything the employee encounters and feels at the organization. This generally starts with the initial candidate experience prehire, and encompasses onboarding, learning and development opportunities, total rewards, the job itself, mobility and other career opportunities, the social aspects of the workplace, all the way to the experience at the end of employment. Much like "customer experience," employee experience examines all aspects of work life to determine where improvements can be made, programs enhanced, and synergies found. Ultimately the employee experience influences the brand of the organization, from both an employer and customer perspective.

Toyota's onboarding initiative is very conscious of getting the team member experience off to the right start. According to Toyota, the organic nature of the culture instilled during onboarding is observable as new hires routinely get together on an ongoing basis, especially on their three-month, six-month, and one-year anniversary milestones. New employees proactively foster those relationships and often will broaden the invitations to other team members and even other cohort groups.

While "inspire" may seem like a lofty goal, Toyota measures inspiration as a key performance indicator for onboarding program effectiveness by simply asking new hires, "Do you feel inspired?" Related questions help validate those responses, such as, "Did you feel a confirmation of your decision to join Toyota?" This data, along with personal interviews and follow-ups, helps Toyota continuously improve the program.

In years past, Toyota team members described onboarding as "formal," "rigid," "a snooze fest," "boring lectures," "overwhelming," "long days," "HR stuff," "necessary evil," and "a thousand pages of paperwork." Now, the team receives descriptors such as "excited," "greeting was amazing," "my decision was the right decision," "it was a great decision," "refreshing," "formed friendships and made me feel like I was a part of the team already," "energized," "inspired," "stays with you from day one," "feel the passion," and "exceeded all my expectations."

To date, the onboarding program has attained an inspiration score of more than 9 (out of 10) and has helped reduce turnover to approximately 6 percent.

Most importantly, it has helped maintain a culture that extends through generations.

CHAPTER 17

STEP #14: PROMOTE THOSE WHO BEST REPRESENT THE NEW

> Culture change is really hard. But if you stay true
> to who you are with an eye toward the capabilities
> and behaviors you want for the future, you can maintain
> and grow what you set out to build.
> —CHRISTINE DEPUTY, CHRO, EVP HUMAN RESOURCES,
> NORDSTROM

To maintain what's been built and prevent regression to the old normal, it's important that the workforce understands that behaviors that support the renovated culture will get rewarded. The most effective way to exhibit this is by showcasing the career advancement of individuals who best "represent the new." Ideally these individuals have the traits and attributes that embody the future direction, are champions of the new culture, and have significant potential to continue to expand the efforts that were initiated during the build phase.

However, similar to the conundrum of not knowing who the influencers and energizers are in the company without conducting an organizational network analysis, a large percentage of companies don't have a good (or even an adequate) understanding of the talent they have internally. Years ago (2011), I published a book—along with Pat Galagan—titled *The Executive Guide to Integrated Talent Management.* The book discussed how various talent practices need to be integrated for organizations to have a true handle on the capabilities of their workforce. In the first chapter, Pat and I wrote:

- ▶ How does organizational talent become a capability?
- ▶ Why do so many otherwise exemplary companies continue to acquire, develop, and deploy their talent with isolated practices that, if put together and coordinated, could become so much more effective?
- ▶ Why do so many leaders proclaim that people are their most important asset but then not manage this asset from a unified perspective?

Those same questions continue to plague most organizations today. Part of the issue is simply understanding what integrated talent management is to begin with. To educate people on the concept, I often use this example:

> Most talent acquisition teams do a great job of understanding the strengths and capabilities of a job applicant, as well as any skill deficiencies or other weaknesses that might be uncovered during the hiring process. They gather this data through a variety of methods, sometimes through surveys and complex assessment technology and other times the old-fashioned way via interviews. And when we hire that individual, where does all that valuable information go? Typically, straight out the window, never to be viewed again.

Smart companies, with an integrated talent management approach, don't let that happen. The data they collect during the hiring process feeds directly to the learning and development system and team so they can help incoming employees work on their skill deficiencies. It ideally also informs the performance management process so the manager can have a more complete picture of the incoming employees, and is utilized as part of succession management so the organization can be more strategic in future workforce planning. And I'm sure we can come up with many other areas in which this data could be utilized to better manage and develop the workforce.

To this day, I'm still amazed that many organizations don't have this automated and integrated.

By not integrating, by not sharing talent data and not having a central repository of skills, organizations are moving much slower than they could be moving—than they *need* to be moving. They are hiring externally when the best candidate might be right under their nose. They are missing opportunities to move talent into areas that best suit their skill sets. They are staffing projects with people who happen to be in the right spot on an org chart or are within eyeshot versus people with the best capabilities. And they are tolerating less than ideal talent in critical and pivotal roles throughout the organization.

Here's a good and simple test. Let's say your organization is opening a new office in Saudi Arabia. Or if you have one already, let's pretend you're expanding. You have an urgent need to staff talent there—time is of the essence. Are you able to quickly determine who in your organization knows how to speak Najdi, Hejazi, or Gulf Arabic? Or can you identify people with the background, experience, or skills that are needed there?

The primary reason you don't know is because it was never cataloged when employees were initially hired. Or if it was, there is no central repository where you can look it up. It also surprises me how often we conveniently ignore all the skills and capabilities people brought with the people to the organization when they aren't needed for the role we hired them into. It's almost like we prefer thinking of an employee in the narrow confines of the current role versus taking an approach of wanting to know all the capabilities our workforce currently possesses.

I've heard from many heads of HR who say, "LinkedIn knows more about my employees than I do."

A Talent Ecosystem

Companies are slowly realizing that perhaps they are using antiquated methods to manage and deploy talent, to source great people, and to develop and grow top performers throughout their organizations.

Part of the problem is most of us have been programmed to think about talent in the framework of a hierarchy, which may be the most ineffective way to conceptualize the workforce. If you ask many CEOs to list the people in the most critical and pivotal roles, they'll usually think in terms of the org chart and list those at the top. That's almost always wrong. Some of the most valuable people in key roles are buried below the upper echelon (think about the relationship manager to the largest customer, for example. These critical employees are often missed by senior leaders). Many times, there is no thought of succession to these roles, and the risk to the organization has if the person leaves is underestimated until it's too late.

Managing succession is something high-performance companies consistently do better than low-performing organizations, according to i4cp's research as well as many others. Over 50 percent of high performers place a high priority on succession (versus 29 percent of low performers), and high performers are much more likely to have a formal process in place. While too few companies overall do this well, top companies are also more likely to identify high-potential employees internally, agree on ready-now or "ready-enough" candidates for promotion, retain leaders and top talent by showing them a clear succession path, and not only focus on a pool of successors versus one-for-one succession, but also have a diverse pool of succession candidates.

A lack of understanding of the talent the organization possesses slows down the best succession management processes and hinders the company's ability to plan for the future or backfill quickly. When a role does unexpectedly open, often companies are too quick to search externally because the hiring process is often much (much!) easier. "Poaching" talent internally is often frowned upon in many organizations, and we make hiring managers jump through multiple hoops if they want to bring an internal employee into their group or department.

From the employee's perspective, it's the same phenomenon. Often, it's far easier to find a new job externally than internally. Outside opportunities don't come with the bureaucracy or rules of engagement that require managers to sign off in order for an employee to interview or explore other opportunities internally. There is no stigma attached to looking at roles externally that many employees carry when it's revealed they are doing so internally ("I'm a dead man walking" is a comment I've heard from several friends when it was discovered they applied for another role internally). And employees aren't locked into a salary band externally that often still applies internally. They can "free" themselves of any labels that have been applied to their role, rank, compensation, etc., that often hinder internal movement.

This does not go unnoticed by savvy leaders and HR talent in top organizations. Some are doing something about it and have begun utilizing a "talent ecosystem" model that allows them to locate talent from a variety of sources, both internal to the company and external, and helps to match the best skills to the most important opportunities. To visualize how this system can work, Figure 17.1 shows a Talent Ecosystem Integration Model i4cp created (with help from the Walt Disney Company) that outlines some of those sources and ways to think about talent.

In our research, three and a half times more high-performance organizations than low-performance companies establish a talent ecosystem to share, rent, and borrow talent. That ecosystem typically centers on the capabilities of the individual versus the internal "labels" of employment status, current role, job level, compensation band, or whatever reputation the employee's current team, group, or department might have. A few of the areas that make up a talent ecosystem include:

▶ **Internal talent marketplace.** Applying the concept of the "gig economy" internally, some companies have started to share talent across silos by matching skills and capabilities to work.

▶ **External talent marketplace.** In addition to understanding the capabilities of available freelancers to dynamically staff projects, some companies purposely swap talent with customers, distributors, suppliers, and other partners external to the company.

▶ **Overlooked talent pools.** Progressive organizations make use of workers with physical and intellectual disabilities to augment their talent needs, along with other talented groups such as military veterans, individuals with childcare responsibilities, ex-convicts, and even ex-employees.

One of the reasons a talent ecosystem can be so powerful is because jobs, and the needs of the business, change so quickly. Some

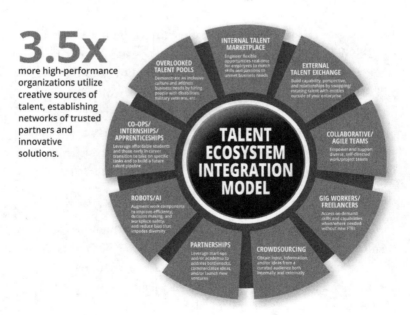

FIGURE 17.1 Talent Ecosystem Integration Model
Source: i4cp

of the most in-demand jobs today didn't even exist just a few years ago, which is quickly making the concept of a "job description" an artifact of the past. The talent ecosystem is designed to help with this and to be flexible to shifts in the business environment and the labor market. When sudden world events dramatically shift labor supply and demand, having an open system of talent sharing can dramatically impact an entire business.

People + Work Connect

There are few world events that impacted the view of talent sharing as much as the COVID-19 pandemic. Perhaps the best example of this was how four leaders in the HR industry—in fact, four of the top CHROs by any measure—banded together to solve a unique challenge that arose at the beginning of the pandemic in the United States: some companies needed to quickly off-board thousands of employees, while at the same time others were desperately trying to hire an equivalent amount. For example, large hospitality chains like Marriott announced they were furloughing tens of thousands of employees in mid-March, while simultaneously companies like Amazon and Walmart, which saw consumer demand skyrocket, were hiring hundreds of thousands.

During a meeting at Accenture in late March, the four CHROs—Ellyn Shook of Accenture, Lisa Bettinger-Buckingham of Lincoln Financial, Pat Wadors of Procore, and Christy Pambianchi of Verizon—decided to put their years of expertise and insight together and find a solution to this unique challenge (it also helped that the four have been friends for years). What they created, with the aid of Accenture's software developers, was a business-to-business platform to match those organizations displacing employees with those that were hiring.

"This crisis has created massive job loss, and people need help finding work," said Wadors. "By connecting companies that are hiring with a talented and available workforce, technology is truly acting in service of people. Working together, we can quickly make a meaningful impact on the people who need it most."

The online tool, simply titled People + Work Connect, was launched in days. It is an analytics-driven platform that pools non-confidential and aggregated workforce information by categories, such as location and experience, and gives organizations that have open positions a view into workforces available to fill those jobs, while enabling organizations that are laying off or furloughing employees a mechanism to help them find new roles. There is no cost to use the platform (Accenture developed it for free and runs it for free), and the group has pledged it will remain free as long as there is a need. It is global and open to all industries but is not available to individuals or staffing agencies.

"When the four of us decided to pick this ball up and run with it, the first thing we did was create a set of principles that would help us understand if we were making the right decisions because we knew we were going to work fast," Shook told an i4cp forum in mid-April, just days after launch. "We were going to take a 'progress is greater than perfection' mindset. Our goal was speed at massive scale. So, we started with a set of principles:

1. **Be inclusive.** It's a B2B (business-to-business) platform and anyone can get on this platform if they have 100 jobs or 100 people they have laid off or furloughed. It doesn't matter if they are our competitors—it's inclusive.
2. **We wanted to make sure it was cross-industry.**
3. **Get a Minimal Loveable Product out.** Everyone can overengineer a solution. We had a crisis we were trying to address, so we said we were going to get out a basic platform that addresses the needs quickly."

It's easy to think, "Didn't this type of marketplace for talent exist already?" While there are job boards and other sites that provide help during times of layoff, this site is different in that it is a platform for businesses to work directly and confidentially with each other. Connections are made CHRO to CHRO. The platform is designed for senior HR leaders, and only those leaders can be "providers" and "buyers" of talent.

The speed at which the platform allows laid-off or furloughed workers to be hired is likely unprecedented. Part of the reason is that a retailer can look at a group of employees from a hotel chain and say, "They generally have the capabilities, and have been trained in the skills, which we need right now." Another reason is trust in those organizations; while a hiring company may typically require background checks, in this situation it can waive that requirement if it trusts the company laying off or furloughing workers has already done the checking. Other unusual arrangements, such as the furloughing company continuing to provide benefits while the hiring company picks up wages, have also been brokered.

"Life is filled with many moments that matter, including some that are tougher than others. People remember who shows up during those tough times to help them through," said Buckingham. "A small group of CHROs came together because we share a passion for making sure that we—and the companies we represent—are remembered for addressing this tough moment with compassion and a sense of responsibility that transcends the business we do every day."

What's fascinating about this story is that had these companies attempted to create something similar outside the pandemic, it would have taken months to come to agreement. Business models would have been argued and negotiated, cost sharing would have been debated, and in the end the lawyers probably would have nixed the entire idea citing numerous employment law problems. Instead, the urgency of the situation created a solution almost immediately— a solution that some are predicting might be a harbinger of things to come in how talent is shared between organizations.

"While the current pandemic has been the impetus for People + Work Connect, we expect this type of collaboration to become the norm going forward," said Pambianchi. "Now is the time to build a more resilient workforce—for today and tomorrow."[1]

Hidden Talent

The norm that Pambianchi envisions points to a future where organizations can easily swap talent as a normal course of business instead of in swift reaction to a pandemic. What that will require, however, is a better understanding and cataloging of the capabilities of the workforce. Much like the statistics on the back of a baseball card, this databased approach will allow for simpler sharing of talent to meet critical needs.

Internally, talent sharing is happening in certain organizations in a variety of effective and creative ways.

Disney Consumer Products and Interactive Media (DCPI) is leveraging hidden talent in the organization through its DCPI Gigs program. Launched in November 2017, the initiative enables Disney employees to pursue their personal passions—fitness, photography, music, and much more. And while many organizations encourage workers to volunteer in their communities and independently of work, DCPI Gigs enables its people to explore their creative interests as part of their jobs.

Disney employees have curated music for the company's annual meeting, recorded voice-overs for Disney productions, created artwork for Disney events, and helped to devise DCPI's employee health and fitness strategy. To promote such opportunities, DCPI has created a dedicated internal gigs website and has been filling 60 percent of the posted gigs internally, meaning that the organization has not had to seek out (or pay) external talent or other contracted resources to fill these roles. DCPI employees have welcomed the opportunity to put their lesser-used talents to work.

"I've found freedom outside the constraints of my day-to-day job to do what I love while contributing to new work," said one designer and gig participant. A Disney employee who posted openings for Disney's "Jedi Challenges Voice-over" gig says that seeking internal volunteers for these jobs pays off from a business perspective as well. "Getting help from people who chose to be there—rather than being recruited or convinced—makes a huge difference to the quality of the work."

Employees are not paid beyond their normal job duties to take on these gigs, which are open to all DCPI employees, including those in temporary or contract positions. Nevertheless, the enthusiasm about the program is spreading, and the company recognizes that it opens new ways of thinking about how work can be accomplished.

Leveraging internal talent to perform gig assignments is a win-win situation for both the employee and company and contributes to the organizational culture. Employees get to exercise their skills and capabilities in new ways, and the organization sees how employees can contribute outside their assigned role.

To maintain the momentum of a culture renovation, it's critical that organizations reward those who exhibit the right behaviors. At the same time, it's important to hire new employees who will be a cultural add. It's always a conundrum, however, what the right mix should be between promoting from within and hiring externally. One company that has discussed that a great deal is Nordstrom.

A Digital Progression

Ask people in the retail industry the first words that come to their mind when they think of Nordstrom, and they'll immediately tell you "customer service." A US luxury department store chain, Nordstrom was founded by John W. Nordstrom in 1901 as a shoe store and evolved into a full-line retailer with departments for clothing, footwear, handbags, jewelry, accessories, cosmetics, fragrances, and other items.[2] Many of its full-line stores have in-house cafés, restaurants, or espresso bars. With corporate headquarters in Seattle, Nordstrom (a public company) operates over 350 stores in 40 states.

I sat down with chief operating officer Ken Worzel, who, after almost a decade with the company, was promoted to the newly created position in the fall of 2019. The appointment makes Worzel the highest-ranking executive in the company not named Nordstrom. While Worzel didn't grow up with the company, he was a consultant for a dozen years to Nordstrom and was asked to join the team several times over the years before doing so officially in 2010.[3] With Nordstrom's CHRO Christine Deputy, who joined in 2015, we talked about a range of topics. What caught my ear was how they've maintained the core of their culture, even as it changes in concert with the constantly morphing retail industry.

"Obviously, we are known for our customer orientation and have been for years," Worzel told me. "We will never go away from that, but the methods evolve a bit, and we've had to get people used to some change. For a retail business, we have low attrition, and have many people in the workforce that have been with us for years and years. During that time, the retail world has of course undergone tremendous change. Normally we empowered our people at the store level to do what's right from a customer service perspective because they know the local clientele and their community . . . that strategy has always worked for us and is part of the secret sauce of our customer service reputation. But in a digital world, there is a need to be consistent across all stores, and some of the in-store methods don't always apply.

"That's changed a little how we hire and promote. We used to promote mostly from within—and still do that to a great extent—but in a world that is being constantly disrupted, and as the industry moves to digital, we intentionally have been adding outside hires to offer a different perspective," said Worzel. "Admittedly some of our 30-year veterans needed to accept our new reality where change and disruption is happening at tremendous speed. Some people will ask, 'When will things calm down?' What they really want to know is when will it be like the old days and have the change stop."

"It's going to be a roller coaster for the foreseeable future, and that roller coaster isn't for everyone," Worzel continued. "Just like at the amusement park where 60 or 70 percent of people when the ride is finished want to jump right back on, there's 30 or 40 percent who say that's enough. And that's fine—no judgment—but our industry can be a roller coaster these days, and it makes sense for some but it's not for everyone. Disruption is here forever."

As Nordstrom has moved from bricks and mortar into the digital arena, it has been careful to not lose the "pixie dust" that makes it so beloved with its customer base. "I've been involved with two companies that had the pixie dust—Starbucks and Nordstrom—and we are adamant that as we become digital, we can't lose the pixie dust," said Deputy.

Nordstrom, like most major retailers, has been undergoing a digital transformation—really a progression—for years. The company's most visible digital innovation is ironically best viewed in the physical location of its Manhattan "flagship" store, opened in 2019, which is made up of seven floors and 320,000 square feet in the base of the new Central Park Tower, the tallest residential building in the world. Seven years in the making, the store is just south of Central Park at the intersection of 57th Street and Broadway and is the company's first full in-line store in New York, which was already the company's largest market for online sales.[4] The store represents the largest single-project investment in Nordstrom history and is one of the first new stores of its size to open in Manhattan since the 1920s.

The store is a blend of the convenience of online shopping with the hard-to-duplicate aspects of the in-store experience and represents the direction Nordstrom and other retailers are heading. At its core, the store provides the ability to buy online but then pick up and try on clothing in the store, a practice that has experienced year-over-year growth of more than 40 percent across the industry.[5] Half of Nordstrom's digital sales growth has come from in-store order pickup, and it is the company's most profitable transaction.

Nordstrom is also placing its Trunk Club, an online retail company purchased in 2014, in the flagship store, thereby blending the two experiences (other stores will follow). However, that's not the only technological innovation the new Manhattan store has offered. For example:

▶ Dressing rooms have a touchscreen that allows customers to call for on-demand alteration services.
▶ An augmented reality experience called Lipstick Finder lets people "try on" 400 lipstick colors. And the "Beauty Stylist Virtual Mirror" does the same for makeup trend looks.

▶ The "Fragrance Finder" is an interactive quiz designed to help customers find a particular scent—just press a button and smell the scent.

▶ Wayfinder maps and phone charging stations are spread throughout the store.

"Investments in digital capabilities, along with assets of people, product, and place, enable us to serve customers on their terms," Erik Nordstrom, CEO, said on an earnings call. While the company has invested close to $1 billion in technology-related initiatives,[6] it's equally investing in the people needed for a digital future.

"From an overall culture change, one of the things that I was tasked to do was to think about how do you evolve the organization from a very store-centric model to a much more combined digital experience, and at the same time to be true and hold on to the DNA of what has made us great," said Deputy. "We've had to do a lot of work over the past couple of years to think about what's the talent we need in order to deliver that experience."

"From a promotion standpoint, people were mostly getting tapped on the shoulder to move up," Deputy added, "not because you were like me, but because your results were amazing and you delivered amazing experiences for your customers and you created and built team members who were getting promoted. But if you were new to the company and you didn't know that, you could be perceiving that this is about relationships, not about merit."

"We generally have a recognition culture," Worzel explained further. "Stores are recognizing their people at the start of the day, and it's a sales culture. But with so many long-term employees, the thing we have to be careful of when promoting people internally is favoritism. In fact, we talk about a 'favoritism index' that we need to measure for and be careful of when advancing our people in their careers."

"Culture change is really hard," Deputy added. "But if you stay true to who you are with an eye toward the capabilities and behaviors you want for the future, you can maintain and grow what you set out to build."

CHAPTER 18

STEP #15: CHANGE PERFORMANCE MANAGEMENT PRACTICES

*It's all crap. Everybody hates it—the employees,
the managers doing the ranking, everybody. But nobody
has ever had the guts, the chutzpah, to blow it all up.*

—LARRY MYERS, FORMER CHRO, T-MOBILE

In my role running a prominent HR research firm, I've entertained thousands of conversations on a wide variety of people-related topics. Most HR topics, despite what some business executives might think, are pretty common across industries and organizations. Because we study the people practices of high-performance organizations, I get this question from time to time from business executives: "What's the most consistent trait of top companies that you've found in your research?"

My answer: "They all think they're unique."

I joke about this because there is an element of truth to it. At i4cp, we're fortunate to work with many well-known, well-respected organizations worldwide, and specifically with their HR teams. Many people I meet in organizations do think their issues are distinct to their company, while in fact many others deal with the same exact issues. The benefit of working across thousands of organizations is that it's easy to see this—it's much harder to spot when you are inside one of those organizations.

One issue that is clearly ubiquitous—and a favorite of HR professionals—is how to manage performance. No matter the industry, the issues are often extremely similar. As a result, when my team and I converse with all levels of people in HR, many want to discuss their performance management system.

And I'm here to confess for the first time publicly that there's no topic I personally hate discussing more than performance management.

That's because, much like the topics of advertising, movie reviews, or politics, everyone has an opinion on performance management. And often that opinion is purely a personal observation, lacking any data. And it's almost always a negative one.

I can't think of any people I've ever encountered who told me they love performance management and talk about a bulletproof system or process that has worked perfectly. The conversation is always about how their performance management approach is broken, is old-school, and needs to be overhauled.

There is no HR process that's been overhauled more than performance management.

To be clear, I'm a firm believer that performance management is critically important. Done right, it reinforces culture and can make an organization incredibly efficient, transparent, and successful. But done wrong, it can be the Achilles' heel of a company, with the potential to seriously weaken an otherwise strong business. (Microsoft's forced-ranking system outlined earlier in the book is a great example.) Too often the return on investment is dubious. The time and money spent on performance management is not always offset by improved business results. In countless organizations, the application is uneven, and in many ways, the traditional approach to managing performance has failed to keep up with the changing business environment.

Despite these shortcomings, performance management remains a consistent practice employed by almost all companies.

Performance Management Origins

In case you need a refresher, performance management is generally when a manager provides feedback to an employee on his or her work performance. The way the manager gathers that feedback can vary from data-driven, objective measures to subjective assessments that may involve a variety of people—often referred to as 360-degree or multi-rater assessment when it involves feedback from subordinates, colleagues, and supervisors, as well as a self-evaluation by the employee.

Too often though, subjective feedback primarily emanates from just one source: the manager's direct observation. While goals and objectives are often set and performance is measured at a point in time (traditionally annually), many companies have transitioned to a process of ongoing feedback and omit "rating" the employee's performance on a scale, although rating employees is a practice that is still widely in use today in companies with more formal performance management processes. Last, while compensation is tied to the performance process in most organizations, there are some companies that have separated performance reviews from compensation decisions.

While performance management, as we mostly think about it today in the context of the workforce, is only a few decades old, humans have been judging the performance of other humans for centuries (some historians cite examples "as early as 221 AD, when Wei Dynasty emperors rated their family members' performance"). In the workplace, others have pointed to "the 1800s, when Robert Owen had 'silent monitors' observing the performance of his cotton mill workers in Scotland."[1] Or the early 1900s, when Walter D. Scott of WD Scott & Co. in Sydney—one of the largest consultancy firms in

Australia—invented performance appraisals (referred to as a "man to man comparison" scale) as early as World War I. In fact, during World War I, the US military had a "merit rating" system to identify poor performers for discharge or transfer.[2] And Elton Mayo, the Australian researcher involved in the Hawthorne experiments mentioned earlier in the book, is often cited as an early influencer of performance management. Mayo's work helped change the treatment of employees in the 1940s by encouraging managers to start acting more like leaders instead of taskmasters.

But most point to 1954 as a major turning point when Peter Drucker introduced the concept of management by objectives (MBO) in a book titled *The Practice of Management*. MBOs encouraged the use of individual goals for employees (rather than overarching corporate goals) and allowed managers to take work one step at a time to allow for a calmer yet productive work environment. It also allowed workers to see their individual accomplishments, which reinforced a sense of achievement.

Ideally, when employees have been involved with setting goals, they are more likely to fulfill their responsibilities. An important part of MBO is the measurement and comparison of employees' actual performances versus their objectives, and for this, Drucker created a simple five-step process:[3]

1. Review organizational goal.
2. Set worker objective.
3. Monitor progress.
4. Evaluate.
5. Give reward.

George Odiorne, one of Drucker's students at New York University, developed the idea further in his book *Management Decisions by Objectives*, published in the mid-1960s.[4] Odiorne eventually became a famous business school professor and dean, a consultant, a corporate manager, and the author of 300 articles and 26 books—but is best known for championing MBO throughout business. MBO was popularized by companies like Hewlett-Packard, which claimed it led to the company's success.

Coincidentally, Odiorne was also one of the founders of i4cp's predecessor organization, which was launched in the sixties, and he was a personal mentor to my i4cp co-founder, Jay Jamrog. Jay describes how he met Odiorne and his relationship over the years with the famous professor and author:

> I first met George as a first-year student in the MBA program at the University of Massachusetts in 1983. I had left my corporate job to pursue my degree, and George taught a mandatory class in Management Theory. We had approximately 70 students in my class, but with others often crashing the class, it was standing room only. I quickly understood why. George was a great presenter with fantastic stories, and one of those guys who didn't need notes or overheads to capture our attention. As he went through the various management theories by Maslow, Herzberg, and others, I kept thinking I wished I had known about this when I was working in the real world.
>
> About halfway through the semester, he introduced Management-by-Objectives (MBO). He was finally talking about something that I had experience with, but I wasn't too excited about the subject. I hated MBO. When I was working, every year I would sit down with my boss and agree on my goals for the next 12 months, but when it came time for my annual performance review, I never seemed to have completed them. That was because, unfortunately for me, I had developed a reputation for putting out fires and turning around poorly performing business units. I was always being assigned to different projects in the company which took me away from the goals my boss and I had originally established.
>
> At the end of his MBO lecture, I approached George and said "Dr. Odiorne, until today I have really enjoyed

learning about the many management theories you've presented, but I have to say this thing called MBO really doesn't work in the real world." He stared at me, I'm sure incredulous at my naïvety, and calmly said, "Come to my office later and we can discuss it more."

I went to his office later that day. He immediately pulled about six articles on MBO from little cubbyholes all over his office and said again calmly, "Read these and come back tomorrow." As I skimmed over the articles walking from his office, I realized they all were written by him and had all been published in prestigious management journals. A panicked wave of realization came over me. I had immediate thoughts of transferring to a different school.

By the next day I decided transferring was probably a bad idea and met with George in his office again. I sheepishly apologized for not realizing his influence on the concept of MBO, but then mustered up the courage to describe my objection to the annual performance review being based on MBO goals in relation to my work experience. He explained how a good boss should have handled the situation, and we ended up having a great conversation about performance management that continued for the next decade. It eventually included Peter Drucker who was George's mentor.

A couple days later he asked me if I wanted to be one of his research assistants for a not-for-profit institute, the Human Resource Research Center, which he founded with Rensis Likert (creator of the Likert scale) when he was at the University of Michigan. He and a couple of his colleagues at HRRC were doing consulting for several companies around the concept of Strategic Workforce Planning. The process of SWP included something called Environmental Scanning and they needed someone to take on that project. The research project included about 5 trends, and I was assigned the task of researching them and forecasting out the implications for each trend over the next 5, 10, and 20 years.

The next year (1984) I presented my findings on these trends to a small conference that George and his colleagues held at the Hotel Northampton in Western Massachusetts. I must have been a hit because after the conference several of the attendees asked George if we could do the same work for them. George and I developed a plan for an expanded version on the project, and six companies contracted us, a group which included heavyweights such as GE, IBM, and Digital Equipment. George and I were now in business together.

In 1985, George was offered and endowed a Chair at Eckerd College and moved to St. Petersburg, Florida. In the following year, 1986, I graduated and joined him in Florida. In that year I officially changed the name of the institute from HRRC to the Human Resource Institute (HRI). We held our first conference and had about 35 participants with George and Peter presenting. With George's help and contacts in the industry, we began to grow and gain industry recognition.

George was truly a great mentor. George was always in great demand on the speaking circuit, and he would occasionally drag me along to present with him. Unfortunately, I usually followed him on stage, and I was always a letdown for the audience. I eventually asked him about being a better presenter, and he gave me three pieces of wisdom: (1) remember you are the expert not them; (2) keep doing it, you will get better; and (3) don't worry, they're only going to remember 10 percent of what you said anyway.

I learned a lot from George and am proud he was a good friend for several years of my life.

Odiorne passed away in 1992, but his impact on management, human resources, performance management, and my co-founder Jay is still felt to this day.

Performance Management Applied

While Odiorne's work had a heavy influence, the process of managing employee performance took another major turn when Jack Welch took over the helm of GE in 1981. Jack was a huge believer in the concept of forced ranking because he loved the transparency—employees always knew where they stood. "If you are a leader and you are a manager, shame on you if people don't know where they stand," Jack would say often. "You have a moral obligation leading people's lives, talking about their future and . . . telling them where they stand."[5] Welch obsessed over people in the company. He said that as CEO, "I have only two jobs: allocating capital and evaluating people." He claimed that he spent more time on the people part than on everything else, and he didn't always know the CFOs of GE's incredibly diverse businesses, but he always knew the HR chiefs.[6]

Originally created by the US Army before entering World War II, the system of forced ranking (also referred to as forced distribution) was designed to identify officer candidates. Instead, Jack and GE used it to "thin the herd" and take out the poorest performers. The system—often nicknamed "rank and yank"—forced managers and the company to rank employees and place them in three categories: the top 15 percent, the middle 75 percent, and the bottom 10 percent. The system's main purpose was to force managers to make tough decisions and remove that bottom 10 percent of the workforce, which GE did regularly. Welch earned the nickname "Neutron Jack" for the tens of thousands fired during his tenure, but it also helped to earn him widespread acclaim and fame—Fortune named him the "manager of the century" in 1999.

While forced ranking might seem barbaric to some, it is not without its merits. It can be a very effective tool to slim down a company, and at the time it was implemented it made sense for GE. When Jack was named CEO, the company was too bloated, and his methods helped GE become the most valuable company in the world. Of course, most companies aren't bloated today, but in the 2000s you would have thought that was the case—largely as a result of GE's fondness for forced ranking it was estimated that 60 percent of Fortune 500 firms used this method for managing performance.[7]

That enthusiasm started to wane in the decade that followed. A 2011 study conducted by my company found that the number of total companies using forced ranking fell from 49 percent in 2009 to 14 percent in 2011, but our analysts had a strong belief that some of those companies (reacting to negative press) simply changed the name while retaining the same practice.[8] The practice did eventually fall out of favor though, as many prominent companies abandoned forced ranking—such as Microsoft and eventually even GE—when they realized it created too much internal competition and inhibited teamwork.

Other trends influenced performance management along the way as well. By 1990, self-appraisals came into vogue, as well as 360-degree (multi-rater) feedback. By 1996, one study estimated that 90 percent of Fortune 500 firms had some form of multi-rater feedback, and other studies also indicated that its use in large corporations was extremely high.[9] Another methodology, the balanced scorecard, created by Robert Kaplan and David Norton, debuted in the 1990s. The balanced scorecard is a strategy performance management tool that can be used by managers to keep track of the execution of activities by the workforce. It typically focuses on strategy and a set of financial and nonfinancial objectives to measure (originally divided into four "perspectives": financial, customer, internal process, and learning and growth).[10] The "nine-box" is another tool that appeared in this era. It uses a grid for measuring employees based on their performance and their potential (the x and y axes of the nine-box grid). Typically, this is a tool used for high-potential employees in the process of succession planning and mobility.

Over the decades, however, assigning a numeric rating to employees on their performance is a practice that has endured. The mechanics of the rating scale, however, are often debated. While a rating scale of 5 is common (5 usually being the best, 1 being the worst) companies were concerned there were too many 3s—which led them to think managers were opting for neutral grades because they felt it was often safer than being negative. To combat this, several companies went to a 4-point scale to eliminate the neutral option; others decided a 3-point scale was simpler and better; and several went the other direction and created a 10-point scale. Some organizations don't use numbers at all and instead utilize descriptors ("meets expectations," "exceeds expectations," etc.).

Whatever the scale, our research has consistently shown that there is no linkage between the type of scale used and organizational or performance management success. Having a rating scale (or not) doesn't make a difference by itself, nor does technology used in the process. What does make a difference is the frequency and usefulness of feedback, clearly defining the business purpose of the performance process and aligning it with the culture and values of the organization.

In short, despite many articles written by consultants and firms trolling for engagements, there is no magic bullet when it comes to the "right" performance management system. It is very dependent on the individual company and its culture.

The Future of Performance Management

The latest trend is to abolish ratings altogether, a move that started in the late 2000s and early 2010s as organizations began to question the need for a rigid, formal performance structure that was equally dreaded by employees and managers alike. Companies such as Adobe, Deloitte, Accenture, Gap, Juniper, Microsoft, GE, Kelly Services, REI, T-Mobile, and many others were quite vocal about how they replaced the tradition of annual review and ranking with a process of ongoing managerial feedback and coaching. They cited not only the internal discontent, but also the enormous time and expense (Deloitte estimated that creating the ratings consumed close to 2 million hours a year . . . and 58 percent of its executives believed that Deloitte's approach drove neither employee engagement nor high performance).[11]

Other companies concurred. "It's all crap," said former T-Mobile head of HR Larry Myers, when describing why T-Mobile transitioned away. "Everybody hates it—the employees, the managers doing the ranking, everybody. But nobody has ever had the guts, the chutzpah, to blow it all up."

T-Mobile had the guts to blow it all up, and did away with formal, written, scored annual reviews, employee ratings, and pay linked to ratings. It replaced the system with a process called SYNC (Supercharge Your Next Conversation). SYNCs are informal, frequent, two-way conversations between an employee and manager. While the common criticism against managerial-led performance management discussions is "Managers don't do it," T-Mobile set out to rectify that.

Once managers get into the conversation, they are generally fine in having a constructive conversation with their direct reports. The main problem is that starting the conversation can often be awkward. To help, T-Mobile created a place mat with "conversation starters" for the manager. One side of the place mat had day-to-day check-in questions under the headings of "Clear Expectations" and "Ongoing Feedback," while the other side had more long-term conversation starters under headings of "Development," "Recognition," and "Compensation."

This discussion guide allowed managers to navigate the new world of meaningful conversations, not rote reviews. And it put decisions related to compensation on a different track and different time of year. "Traditionally, people would just leaf through their performance review to see what the number is at the end," said Myers. "With [this new process], they really pay attention to what they and their manager are talking about."

One aspect of T-Mobile's story that I love is a meeting I witnessed several years ago when a talent management executive from the company shared SYNC with several peers. Soon after, an executive at Warner Brothers adopted the same idea but created the conversation starters in the form of playing cards for both managers and subordinates, under the theory that it's not always the manager's job to start the conversation. Ford also loved the concept and created a smartphone app based on the idea, something T-Mobile did later as well.

While there has been a trend of moving the performance process to ongoing, regular managerial discussions, many remain critical of abandoning the formal rating process. One of the top concerns revolves around the legal aspect. Specifically, what are you supposed to do about proving a lack of bias in a termination?

One of the main problems in ratings-driven environments is that poor performers often are not rated poorly. Many HR heads and legal counsel have told me that performance ratings are often of no help to the company when there is a disputed termination because the manager wasn't honest in the ratings assessment.

"In-house lawyers love no ratings," confirms Julie Holbein, director of global talent management at Cardinal Health. "If an employee is let go after years of receiving a numerical rating of 3 out of 5, even if written comments along with the rating took note of performance issues, the 3—as an above-average rating—is what's going to get the attention," making it harder to defend against charges that the termination was discriminatory, she said.[12]

Another criticism is that while companies have been vocal externally about going "ratingless," internally some kept a hidden rating system. Often referred to as "shadow" accounting or ratings, a private pecking order of merit has helped some managers quantify an employee's bonus and merit increase without showing the employee a numeric rating or ranking. "If you differentiate on bonus payouts, in effect you have a rating system," is the common refrain.

The concept of calculating compensation without reference to ratings is often difficult to accept among the business leaders that I speak with regularly. A study conducted in 2016 by a partner of ours, Gerry Ledford, a senior research scientist at the Center for Effective Organizations (part of USC's Marshall School of Business), concluded there are multiple ways managers determine variable compensation in a company that has eliminated ratings.[13] The study, conducted in partnership with WorldatWork, showed:

► Eighty percent of organizations say that managers make decisions on their own within budget constraints about how to allocate rewards.

▶ Reward allocation is determined in calibration sessions involving a large pool of employees in 42 percent of organizations.

▶ Rewards are allocated according to a specific distribution at 24 percent.

▶ Twenty-two percent of organizations use "shadow" performance ratings for allocating rewards; these ratings are not communicated to employees.

▶ Management in 20 percent of organizations ranks employees from first to last (stacked ranking); it varies whether this ranking is communicated to employees.

"The percentages indicate that many companies use multiple approaches," explained Ledford.

Subsequent research we conducted with Ledford (and Benjamin Schneider) in 2018 showed that companies with a culture of performance feedback are more effective at performance management and are financially healthier.[14] An analysis of financial results for a subsample of 57 publicly traded US companies showed that companies in the top third on our measure of companies that excelled at a culture of performance feedback—compared with those in the bottom third—doubled net profit margin, return on investment, return on assets, and return on equity.

Creating this culture internally establishes an environment where managers feel compelled to deliver quality performance feedback to employees. Companies that have done this say they coached managers on the types of communication and behaviors necessary to give ongoing feedback to employees. Specifically, they provided:

▶ Training on how to do it effectively
▶ Modeling by senior executives in how they do it for their subordinates
▶ Rewards and recognition for doing it well
▶ Monitoring to make sure it gets done

   ► Manager selection and promotion based on performance feedback competencies

When these practices are in place, managers know that the organization values high-quality performance conversations. Positive organizational results generally follow.

Companies are often reviewing and changing their performance management programs. In a recent study we conducted, fully two-thirds (67 percent) of 272 companies indicated they were at least rethinking their existing performance management practices. But when a company is renovating its culture, changing performance management takes on new meaning—it's a signal to the workforce that we aren't doing things the way we used to and we are going to measure the performance and compensation of our workforce differently in alignment with our new direction. Our research found that 55 percent of organizations that successfully renovated their culture reported making changes to their performance management practices as part of the overall change initiative.

The moral of the story: when deploying and maintaining your renovated culture, ensure that how you measure performance aligns with the behaviors you want to enforce in the post-renovation world.

CHAPTER 19

STEP #16: LEVERAGE EMPLOYEE AFFINITY GROUPS

> You can have the best training in the world, but if
> you don't have an environment where someone
> can talk about what it's like to come to work and
> have these feelings in your head, the benefits to any
> of those [diversity] programs are muted.
> —TIM RYAN, US CHAIR, PWC

I began writing this chapter at the same time the protests broke out in response to the horrific death of George Floyd in Minneapolis. Both violent and peaceful demonstrations erupted, eventually involving hundreds of US cities and many others around the world, protesting police brutality against African Americans, and more broadly systemic racism. The day after the initial riots in Minneapolis, I sent an e-mail to my employees. I went back in history and mentioned the similarity to the Los Angeles riots that started after a trial jury acquitted four officers of the Los Angeles Police Department for using excessive force in the arrest and beating of Rodney King, which had been videotaped and widely viewed in TV broadcasts. I asked, "Haven't we learned anything in the three decades since?" knowing full well the answer to my question.

My comparison was far too shortsighted.

"We haven't seen a spasm of riots like this since the assassination of Martin Luther King, Jr. in 1968," said historian Douglas Brinkley. "There were more deadly and expensive riots in the 1960s, like Newark, Detroit, and Watts—but there is no comparison to the toxic combination of George Floyd's murder, Covid-19, and economic depression. 2020 is an election year and our entire democratic process is bursting at the seams."[1]

It was gruesome irony that the riots broke out as I was beginning to write this chapter. The race riots of the 1960s spurred the creation of employee resource groups (or ERGs, also frequently referred to as business resource groups, affinity groups, employee networks, and a variety of other name combinations). In fact, it was the CEO of the Xerox Corporation, Joseph Wilson, who helped start the first one after the violent race riots in Rochester, New York, in 1964.

I'm sure Wilson never imagined that over 50 years later we would be witnessing scenes all too similar to what he witnessed in Rochester.

At the time, Wilson and his black employees launched the National Black Employees Caucus to address discrimination in businesses across the United States. They initially established the group to advocate for equal pay and equal opportunity, a purpose that has expanded quite a bit over the years. Today, almost every Fortune 500 company has multiple ERGs.[2] Our research shows that two-thirds of companies with ERGs have seven or more, with some having dozens of groups. The most common type of ERG is Women (94 percent), Black/African American (87 percent), LGBTQ (87 percent), Hispanic/Latino (84 percent), Veterans (78 percent), and Asian (78 percent).

During our research on culture renovation, we were pleasantly surprised at how many organizations affirmed the importance of utilizing ERGs in their culture renovation efforts, particularly in leveraging them to maintain their culture. We've always known that ERGs are important; various i4cp studies have shown that they help support a more diverse and inclusive workplace, develop future leaders, and enhance engagement, among other benefits.

Over 40 percent that successfully changed their culture said that they relied on ERGs in the renovation process and leveraged them to strengthen the culture over time. It's not hard to understand why. ERGs can be especially influential in driving and maintaining a new culture by helping to develop better awareness of various employee groups throughout the organization and supporting and fostering inclusion. And by leveraging influential ERG members to act as culture ambassadors, organizations can promote and reinforce the new culture to ERG members as well as other employees.

There's no doubt that culture ambassadors are currently hiding in ERGs, undetected. So are future leaders. In fact, many organizations miss the incredible opportunity these groups provide as a leadership development platform. One of the most eye-opening findings in our ERG research is that two-thirds of companies felt these groups were more effective than other leadership development forums at developing leadership skills and competencies.

There are many leadership skills that are honed through participation in ERGs, but according to our research, the top five skills were:

1. Collaborative skills (87 percent)
2. Development of personal and professional networks (86 percent)
3. Inclusive behaviors (82 percent)
4. Ability to work with diverse employee groups (81 percent)
5. Cultural competencies (75 percent)[3]

Several other skills and competencies ranked high as well, such as agility, budget management, and innovative thinking. Given the leadership skills that ERGs help foster, these groups can serve a key role in fueling the leadership pipeline. They are surprisingly inexpensive yet effective leadership development platforms.

Top companies understand this, and senior leaders in those organizations aren't sleeping on the opportunity. In fact, high-performance organizations are nearly five times more likely to have executive sponsors observe and source ERG members for leadership potential. Many are using their ERGs as experiential career advancement and leadership development platforms, and since most ERGs are sponsored by senior executives, ERG leaders often say the exposure to senior leaders and recognition they receive from top executives is a top career benefit. Other benefits often cited, as shown in detail in Figure 19.1, are the increased opportunity to build an external reputation, the opportunity to speak on behalf of the company, inclusion on interesting or challenging projects, and the ability to strategically impact business results. Following the 2020 protests, many more organizations are looking at ERGs as an untapped resource for building a strong bench of diverse potential leaders.

Top six notable gaps between high- and low-performance organizations:

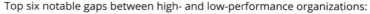

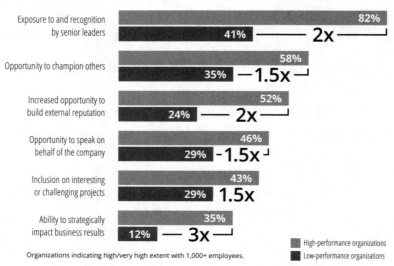

Organizations indicating high/very high extent with 1,000+ employees.

High-performance organizations
Low-performance organizations

FIGURE 19.1 Career Benefits Reported by ERG/BRG Leaders

Source: i4cp

In its culture renovation efforts, Sony Pictures positioned ERG leadership as a platform not only to influence organizational culture but also to engage and retain critical talent. And while Sony Pictures doesn't require employees to become ERG leaders in its leadership development programs, it has nonetheless seen a higher degree of career mobility within the organization among ERG leaders.

Executives at Sony have also noticed that employees with ERG leadership experience are more engaged and act as brand and culture ambassadors. Based on data from employee surveys, the company has consistently found higher engagement and net promoter scores among ERG leaders. While many high-performance organizations choose not to formally position ERG leadership as a springboard to other positions, tracking and reporting on the impact on these leaders' careers is a powerful tool for increasing group effectiveness and recognizing the skills group leadership helps to develop.

The Business Case for Diversity

While ERGs are effective forums for developing leaders, their primary benefit is to raise awareness of the different groups of people that make up the workforce of most organizations. This awareness promotes an inclusive work environment, and from a culture perspective, healthier cultures generally are more inclusive and diverse. Our research on healthy cultures showed that high-performance organizations outpaced their low-performance counterparts 70 percent to 40 percent in actively supporting diversity and inclusion initiatives.

Given this common understanding, the "business case" for diversity seems like it hardly needs to be made, but there's been a lot of effort to do so over the years. The *Wall Street Journal* published its own study at the end of October 2019, which showed that more diverse companies perform better in the stock market than companies with low diversity scores.[4] Our research on diversity and inclusion has always concurred with this conclusion. Greater diversity almost always correlates with greater market performance.

But making these links is not without controversy. Some argue that trying to make a business case for diversity is a dangerous path and that we should simply strive for a more diverse workforce because it's the right thing to do. There's little argument from most companies that greater diversity is better for the organization. Many point to the positive impact that diversity of thought and experience has on innovation, product development, marketing, and customer experience.

While all of that is true, the cultural impact might be even more important. When renovating culture, it's important to measure diversity throughout the organization, not just overall, but particularly at higher levels on the org chart. While some companies can tout impressive corporatewide diversity figures, they often look quite different among senior managers and executives, or (as has been frequently discussed) the board of directors.

The Business Case for Homogeneity

One of my favorite lines on the business case for diversity came from an African American executive I met at a conference. He scoffed at the whole notion and countered, "Can you make the business case for homogeneity? Of course not. No one asks that question."

That executive is Ken Frazier, chairman and CEO of Merck, one of the top five pharmaceutical companies in the world. Frazier is a revered leader, but when I met him, he was one of just four African American CEOs of Fortune 500 companies. *Four.* I was shocked when I heard that number from him at that conference, but after researching it, I know that number has changed very little this century. Since 2004, the number has fluctuated between four and seven each year, reaching seven only twice, briefly, over that time.[5] In fact, among all US companies with 100 or more employees, African Americans hold just 3 percent of executive or senior-level roles.[6]

Frazier and I met because we gave back-to-back keynotes at a forum for CEOs and CHROs as part of the CEO Action for Diversity and Inclusion coalition. I preceded Ken on stage and was flattered he used a few of my data points in his own presentation, a powerful and insightful keynote on the state of diversity in corporations. Frazier, who doesn't speak publicly very often, was vocal that day. He was just as vocal in the wake of George Floyd's death.

"What the African American community sees in that videotape is that this African American man, who could be me or any other African American man, is being treated as less than human," Frazier said in a *Squawk Box* interview on CNBC, his only interview following Floyd's death. "What the community saw was, until they went out into the streets, this officer—much less even the other officers—was not even going to be arrested for what was clearly inhumane treatment of a citizen," Frazier said.[7]

Frazier, whose grandfather was born into slavery in the Deep South, grew up in Philadelphia in the 1960s and was among inner-city African Americans bused out to schools more than an hour away. A lawyer by training, he joined Merck in 1992 as a general counsel and climbed the corporate ladder and was named CEO in 2011. "I know for sure that what put my life on a different trajectory was that someone intervened to give me an opportunity, to close that opportunity gap," he said. "And that opportunity gap is still there."

Frazier doesn't seem to care about ruffling feathers with his beliefs. In August of 2017 he quit Donald Trump's American Manufacturing Council after the president's response to white nationalist violence in Charlottesville, Virginia, and didn't worry about fallout from it. "America's leaders must honor our fundamental values by clearly rejecting expressions of hatred, bigotry and group supremacy," he tweeted at the time.[8] He was equally critical of the many bland statements that corporations issued following Floyd's death.

"People put out statements, they put out platitudes, they say this is terrible. The fundamental question is, do we do more than we're required?"

The organization that put on the conference where I met Frazier is one that I believe does more than required. CEO Action was started by Tim Ryan, US chairman of PwC (PricewaterhouseCoopers) in 2017, and has quickly become the largest CEO-driven business group to advance diversity and inclusion within the workplace. It was started in response to police brutality of a black man.

"The summer of 2016 . . . my first week as CEO, there was the Dallas [police] shooting that came on the heels of shootings in [Minnesota] and [Baton Rouge] Louisiana. At that point in time, I had really become engaged on the topic of diversity," said Ryan. "I saw how big of a gap there was in this country when it came to race and I decided to make that my top priority."[9]

I've heard Tim describe this story several times, but during that summer he heard the conversations within PwC and saw how affected his employees were by these incidents and the issue of diversity in general. That same summer, he launched a series of companywide meetings for employees to discuss race and share perspectives.

"You can have the best training in the world, but if you don't have an environment where someone can talk about what it's like to come to work and have these feelings in your head, the benefits to any of those [diversity] programs are muted," Ryan said.

Ryan recognized that while PwC had diversity and inclusion training, it wasn't enough. He was certain that was the case in most companies. To do something about it, he spearheaded the launch of CEO Action for Diversity and Inclusion, which was aimed at getting CEOs to advance diversity and inclusion initiatives at their companies. Initially, Ryan was hoping to get a few dozen CEOs to sign the organization's "diversity pledge." After a little over three years, over a thousand CEOs had signed on.

My organization and I were among the first to sign, and we have been involved from the start. CEO Action signatories have pledged to four core commitments:

1. Continue to cultivate workplaces that support open dialogue on complex, and sometimes difficult, conversations about diversity and inclusion.
2. Implement and expand unconscious bias education.
3. Share best known—and unsuccessful—actions.

4. Create and share strategic inclusion and diversity plans with
   our board of directors.

CEO Action has produced a great deal of educational material
and sponsored a number of public forums since that launch. It funded
a specially outfitted mobile home—a technology-enabled multimedia
experience—as part of a tour called "Check Your Blind Spots," which
shows up by request at companies and conferences around the country. It's created a "Day of Understanding," held each year by hundreds
of companies where employees convene within their organizations
to discuss bias in the workplace, much like PwC did originally. It's
also published around 500 best practices (discussion guides, educational quizzes, videos, etc.) for companies to utilize, and it has conducted several closed-door CEO-only meetings, as well as meetings
for CHROs and chief diversity officers, on how to improve diversity and inclusion efforts within their organizations. These meetings
have been keynoted and moderated by well-known figures such as
Van Jones, Magic Johnson, and W. Kamau Bell.

But mostly they bring together leading CEOs like Merck's
Frazier.

"Ken is just an incredible leader for the organization. And we
have benefited significantly from his leadership," said Tivonnia "T.J."
Harvey, an assistant vice president at Merck, to me over the phone one
day. Harvey has helped to spearhead Merck's own culture renovation.

"We're a company of significant history, and we're driven really
by our purpose," she continued. "I think not just because it sounds
good and it's got a nice beat and people can dance to it. But really
because of the mission of the organization . . . that medicine is for the
people. And if we focus on that, the profits will follow. So, I think for
an organization such as ours that's grounded in scientific medicine
and inventing breakthrough medicine, we're really focused on that
being a major driver for the organization."

Frazier earlier echoed Harvey's thoughts on purpose in an interview in 2018 with *Harvard Business Review*, where he said, "While a

fundamental responsibility of business leaders is to create value for shareholders, I think businesses also exist to deliver value to society. Merck has existed for 126 years; its individual shareholders have turned over countless times. But our salient purpose in the world is to deliver medically important vaccines and medicines that make a huge difference for humanity. The revenue and shareholder value we create are an imperfect proxy for the value we create for patients and society."[10]

Given Merck's long history of success, it's clear the company's focus on its purpose has served it well. But the company recognizes that to best serve its customer base, renovating culture to ensure future success needs to be a focus. With that in mind, Merck embarked on a culture renovation a few years earlier, and it maintains the new culture through attention to talent practices.

"With the transformation of the things happening in the world around us as well as the digital industrial revolution, we realized we had to change some of the things that we do, and we really did have to reimagine the way that we work," said Harvey. "I think though that has been a movement of changing the culture, and there's really been five components of it. It's moving from silos to networks, its controlling to empowering, its planning to experimentation, its knowing-it-all to learning, and withholding to sharing."

"But I don't think it's clearly that black and white," Harvey continued. "By that I mean, when you talk moving silos to networks, for example, I'm talking in generalities. In most organizations, we should be able to work much more collaboratively than we have in the past. In large organizations, you can imagine it's very easy to have silos build up within the organization. However, there are some clearly important places where we want silos. I want our sciences to be narrowly focused on what they're doing. That doesn't mean that they may not be looking to collaborate with other external partners or academic institutions . . . it's not an *either-or* but much more of an *and*. Those have been the five key elements to help to identify reimagining the way that we work."

For Harvey and the company, maintaining the culture they've renovated has encompassed several different talent practices.

"In the last two years, we started working on developing talent, and we deployed learning modules to individual contributors and their managers which focus on the difference between a growth mindset versus a fixed mindset. We also focused with managers on how you need to have continuous feedback discussion, and how feedback is not just a hierarchical thing, but across peers. That's something that we started a couple of years ago with our existing workforce, but we also applied these concepts to new people coming into the organization. To date, I think people have seen our efforts succeed. They moved from a silo mentality and found success because they talked to someone else in another department and found a better way of doing something. These kinds of success stories help to demonstrate to people that this is how we need to work in the future. There is a wonderful benefit to us as an organization and as an individual."

ERGs are another way that Merck maintains its culture. The company has more than 10,000 global members of its employee business resource groups (EBRGs) in 10 separate groups, and it invests in leadership development and diversity and inclusion capability through programs that include Foundations of D&I, Inclusive Leadership Executive Development, Diversity Leadership Program, and Unconscious Bias Education. The company's EBRGs have been recognized in the past for their success in different issues, such as taking on health literacy for at-risk populations.[11]

Whether it's standing up to the president of the United States or speaking out on police brutality of the black community, it's clear that Frazier—and Merck—value the power of diversity in the organization.

"Having a globally and locally diverse workforce makes us a more innovative and agile company," says Frazier, "and one better attuned to the needs of our customers, health care providers and patients who ultimately use our products."[12]

CHAPTER 20

STEP #17: INCREASE THE FOCUS ON TALENT MOBILITY

The less versatile you are,
the better you have to be at what you do well.
—BILL BELICHICK, NFL HEAD COACH

"The more you can do, the better . . . and that's what everyone's able to do on this team. If you look through the whole roster, there's not one person that only plays one position or one aspect. Everybody on the roster can play multiple positions . . . that's what we strive to be—to be a better player. Not just a single player, but to be an all-around player."[1]

That quote is from Lawrence Guy, probably someone you never heard of. Guy is an American football player in the NFL, and his quote was in response to being awarded a spot as one of the two defensive tackles on the New England Patriots All-Decade Team for the 2010s, a group that featured 12 offensive players, 12 defensive players, and four specialists. In fact, with names like Tom Brady, Julian Edelman, and Rob Gronkowski on this roster, it's more likely that you've heard of just about everyone else but Guy. To be awarded this honor is no small feat; Patriots teams in the 2010s won their division (the AFC East) every single season, in addition to winning three Super Bowls and playing in two others. No other team came close to this level of success, and many great players made up those rosters.

I grew up in Massachusetts and have been a Patriots fan my entire life. And for many years now I've admitted I'm a Patriots fan with some trepidation. Ever since they won their first few Super Bowls in the 2001, 2003, and 2004 seasons, they've become one of the most hated teams in professional sports, right up there with the New York Yankees and another favorite team of mine, the Red Sox. And that hatred seems to be universal outside of the six US states that make up the New England region. During the Patriots' amazing come-from-behind win over the Atlanta Falcons in Super Bowl LI (a game I was fortunate to attend in person), a friend texted me from a bar in California and said, "A third of this bar wants the Patriots to win, a third wants the Falcons to win, and a third wants the Patriots to lose."

But prior to the Patriots' dominance since Bill Belichick arrived as the coach at the turn of the century and Tom Brady was handed the reins at quarterback (a record six Super Bowl wins), the Patriots were generally pretty bad. When I was a kid, they won their division only once . . . and usually finished last. They were the least popular sports team in New England, so even back then it wasn't a time to boast that you were a Patriots fan either.

While many football fans will point to the brilliance of Brady at quarterback as the biggest factor in their rise to greatness, there's a characteristic of the Patriots that is often missed and is a key ingredient in their success: versatility. More than probably any other team, the Patriots value players who can play multiple positions. It's a Belichick specialty.

"There are reminders every year of how much value Belichick places on versatility," Phil Perry wrote for NBC Sports Boston.

"Versatile offensive linemen gain roster spots over specialists up front. Versatile defensive backs and receivers may get longer looks in the pre-draft process. Versatile linebackers are viewed as chess pieces who can handle multiple roles in Belichick's ever-evolving game plans. And those who can contribute in the kicking game have immense value to Belichick."[2]

"The less versatile you are," said Belichick, "the better you have to be at what you do well."[3]

In case you aren't aware, Bill Belichick is the winningest coach in the history of the NFL. He's a man of few words, but when he does talk, people pay attention. And what Belichick is saying in that quote is, unless you are the absolute best at what you do, you'd better be versatile. That matters a lot in American football, a brutal sport with injuries every game. With a limited roster of 53, and only 46 active players on game day, NFL teams must be ready at a moment's notice to substitute for an injured player. The old saying that "the most important player on a football team is the quarterback—the second most important player is the backup quarterback" is a truism on any game day. Under the Patriots' scheme, players must be able to play other positions on the fly. Effective player rotation wins games.

In fact, Belichick probably rotates more players during a game than any other coach. After one game, he told reporters: "Yeah, we've played a lot of players. I'm not sure whose snap count's up. I don't know. Maybe you guys can tell me that. We rotate a lot. We've played 20 players on defense the last four or five weeks." Belichick then added, "Show me how many teams in the league play 20 players on defense—not too many."[4]

Perhaps that is why he is the only head coach to win six Super Bowl titles and his career-winning percentage is the highest in NFL history. He has been a master at talent mobility and drafting and creating players who can play multiple positions. Under Belichick, the Patriots have generally shunned the superstar athlete and focused on team unity instead.

"There is an old saying about the strength of the wolf is the pack, and I think there is a lot of truth to that," Belichick once said. "On a football team, it's not the strength of the individual players, but it is the strength of the unit and how they all function together."

From Talent Hoarders to Talent Magnets

During a culture renovation, one of the most successful talent initiatives an organization can focus on is rotating talent to strengthen "the pack" and ensure the desired behaviors are exhibited throughout the organization. In fact, our research has shown several times that talent mobility is one of the most underutilized yet most effective organizational development and culture enhancement techniques in companies today.

Read that sentence again. Effective talent mobility is absolutely linked to high-performance companies, and yet I'm constantly surprised at how few companies encourage and formalize it. i4cp research has shown that those top organizations are twice as likely to emphasize talent mobility, but despite these findings, too few companies place a priority on moving talent or have a formal talent mobility program in place to operationalize the movement of talent internally (and externally).

If you are trying to win an NFL game or succeed at renovating culture, rotating talent is effective. Almost half of organizations that successfully changed their culture reported that an increased focus on talent mobility was a key to maintaining it.

Talent mobility is not merely moving people from one department to another. Top organizations view the practice as the capability to identify, develop, and deploy talent to meet the needs of the business. "Meeting the needs of the business" must happen both rapidly and strategically, just like in an NFL game. The ability to quickly deploy a different skill set, to staff at a minute's notice, to fill in for the unexpected—it's often the difference between winning and losing in football and in business.

Talent mobility is a general phrase that can cover a lot of movement types. It might mean moving someone laterally to another business group. Or a division. Or a subsidiary. Or perhaps to another geography. Or even to another company for a while. Or it might mean a promotion. It might even mean having someone transition down in order to eventually transition up.

All of this helps with recruiting and retention. An abundance of new career opportunities is a trait that both attracts and retains top talent in any organization and should be appealing to any manager of people.

But *should be appealing* is the elephant in the room. The main impediment to talent mobility is frequently the manager. Our research found that half of companies (and 74 percent of low performers) reported that managers' failure to encourage movement was their top obstacle to mobility. The reason? Too often they are "talent hoarders." They want to hang on to their top people. They don't want any other manager to get hold of them, and they even sometimes intentionally hide their top team members so no one discovers them.

It's hard to blame them for that. When managers are having success in metrics that the organization recognizes and rewards, they want to keep the talent that made them successful. It's human nature, and those who have managed people are guilty of wanting to retain the best talent within their group or department.

The key is how the organization recognizes and rewards managers. In a select percentage of some of the best companies in the world, it's understood that to rotate talent—especially high-potential talent—through the organization, they'd better make it worthwhile for the manager. So, they build it into the performance objectives, they loudly provide internal recognition, and they compensate managers for their ability to both develop people and provide them opportunities for further development. In short, they build a culture that relies on this movement. Building a culture of mobility—one in which managers are invested in both developing their people and offering them opportunities for new assignments—requires a mindset that prioritizes mobility as a talent development strategy and bases the performance reviews and incentives of leaders on how well they develop the next generation of talent.

A funny thing happens when companies make the cultural switch from a managerial attitude of talent hoarders to talent developers and talent movers: those same managers become *talent magnets*. Everyone wants to go work for the person who has a reputation of advancing employees' careers. It's like flipping a light switch on some of those former hoarders—as soon as they recognize they can continue to be successful because top talent wants to work with them, they immediately become mobility and development champions.

While those managers benefit from a focus on mobility, the organizational benefits are tremendous. Our research shows that, just like the Patriot's success on the field, organizations with strong talent mobility perform better than their competitors. Those high-performance organizations are more likely to reward the managers for developing their direct reports, defining talent mobility broadly, tracking their top talent, and making internal talent aware of job openings across the enterprise. They are also four and a half times more likely to report that the criteria for talent mobility are transparent to their entire organizations.

Borderless Careers

One of those companies is Schlumberger, the largest global supplier of technology and project management solutions to the oil and gas industry. At Schlumberger, the employee population is considered the foundation of its next generation of leaders.

"When we conduct talent reviews, we're not happy if managers have only looked at high-level people in the organization," said Janice Hyslip, global manager, employee experience and engagement at Schlumberger. "The idea is to look deep into the organization, at all the new, young people coming up, and to identify those top people early so we can make sure we give them the exposure they need and demand."

This type of formal strategy for talent mobility that identifies employees as soon as they are hired helps high-performance organizations hang onto top talent, while ensuring that their succession pipeline is well established. During the first three years of an employee's career, Schlumberger provides a structured training and development program that makes clear, level by level, the competencies needed to get to the next level. After that, the primary development mechanism becomes continuous movement into new jobs that offer increasing responsibility and diversity of assignments.

Hyslip said that most Schlumberger employees move to a new job every two years. Schlumberger's dedication to talent mobility has helped win high reviews on career sites such as Indeed and Glassdoor. *Business Insider* magazine named Schlumberger among the best companies to work for if your goal is to get promoted fast, citing employee feedback describing "unlimited career opportunities" as a leading benefit of employment.[5]

The only way for talent mobility to work is if management is invested in the development of its people. At Schlumberger, a significant part of the HR function's role is to partner with managers to make sure that the best people get exposure to new opportunities—without having to seek them out on their own. "A lot of the moves are done by pull," said Hyslip, noting that HR will help managers search the employee database for employees with the right skills and experience to move into new assignments. "As long as you're two years in your role, you're fair game for any other job in the company."

The leadership team believes that the best way to develop people for leadership roles is to give them exposure in three areas: cross-geography, cross-business, and cross-function. "The idea is to take risks on people," said Hyslip. "If you take risk on one axis, that's limited risk or reasonable risk. If you take risk on two axes, it's bigger risk, where you have to wait it out and maybe support the person more. So, we give people lots of different chances in lots of roles around the company." Schlumberger refers to this as the company's "borderless careers" philosophy.

One of the most successful features of the program is the company's commitment to giving employees global assignments. In the majority of the 85 countries where Schlumberger operates, leaders look for opportunities to give local managers a chance to take global assignments, then return to become regional leaders. They also seek out high performers in specific regions or nationalities that the company wants to develop and create a series of exposure assignments to develop their leadership skills before sending them back home. This helps the company grow its network of leaders and is an attractive feature for young talent coming into the company. "Many people join us because they are adventure seekers who want to move around the world and get that exposure," said Hyslip.

Global exposure is important to the company. Historically, Schlumberger's target was to have one-third of employees in their home countries, one-third moved to other geographies in their region (i.e., outside their home countries but still within the region), and one-third moved cross-region (e.g., a new hire in the Middle East might be sent to North America or Russia). This global mobility approach fosters cultural diversity, and ensures managers build strong networks that they can rely on as they move into regional leadership roles. "It's not just about pulling somebody to be a manager somewhere else," she said.

"Mobility at Schlumberger starts from day one at the individual contributor level, and we believe that global exposure is key."

Like Schlumberger, several other companies recognize the value of mobility to enhance an employee's skill set with new experiences. They don't just view talent mobility as a ladder; rather, it is a lattice through which employees are encouraged to move across the organization and into roles with stakeholder organizations to stretch their capabilities. Supporting lateral mobility and encouraging relocation assignments are talent mobility techniques that have high correlations to market performance. Our study found that high-performance organizations are more likely to support lateral moves (43 percent) and relocation assignments (40 percent) than low performers.

Celebrating lateral movement addresses one of the risks associated with mobility—hitting a glass ceiling. When companies only view mobility in terms of upward movement, it's important to have positions available. If organizations lack positions to move people into or have limited opportunities for upward mobility, they often leave employees feeling stuck. We found that 39 percent of employees cited lack of positions to move into as an obstacle to mobility.

This approach to mobility is not just about moving people; it's about changing the construct of the work to ensure the business has a diverse and engaged talent pool. The best companies make mobility a common part of their culture, and constant movement helps to improve collaboration, innovation, productivity, engagement, and retention—and ensure silos don't develop internally. Coupling talent movement with an organizational network analysis can also uncover influencers and blockers, and serve to strategically identify where to move talent to both infuse energy and help break down barriers.

Top companies prioritize talent movement (low-performance organizations are more than twice as likely to say the movement of talent doesn't matter), and they clearly articulate the process internally. They are also almost five times more likely to be transparent about that process, and they are better at moving talent across functions, projects, business units, geographies—and even external stakeholders.

Sharing Talent Between Organizations

That last group—external stakeholders—is one that often confuses business leaders, but it can be a very effective development tool. High-performance organizations are two and a half times more likely to plan movement of high-performing talent to external stakeholders, although very few companies develop talent using this method today. For the small percentage that do, they understand that a year or two with a client, a partner, a distributor, or a supplier can be incredibly educational and rewarding for some of their highest-potential employees.

Even if it's two organizations that you normally wouldn't associate together, sharing talent can be enormously beneficial.[6]

When Vice Admiral William F. Moran, the US Navy's chief of naval personnel, spent a day at Amazon's Seattle campus in the spring of 2015, he acknowledged that one of his goals—and a reason why he wanted to spend time at the company—is to keep the Navy competitive with employers like Amazon. This objective made sense to David Niekerk, Amazon's culture and engagement leader at the time.

"I said, 'We're happy to help you in that challenge, because we want people who come to Amazon to have made that decision with all the right data,'" recalled Niekerk, a West Point graduate and US Army veteran who had long championed the hiring of veterans at Amazon (the company has hired thousands over the years). The visit from Moran also gave Niekerk a chance to personally pitch an idea he'd been thinking about: to have the US Navy participate in a program of selecting commissioned officers to spend a year working at Amazon while still on active duty.

He thought the idea could work well for both sides. "We learn from them and from their military experience, and they go back into the service with the gained experience of working with a company like Amazon that reinvents and rethinks the way things are done," Niekerk rationalized.

Moran listened and liked the idea immediately, so much so that the Navy pursued the idea right away. The Navy's initiative, which is named "Fleet Tours with Industry," was partly modeled after that of the US Air Force's, which has been involved in partnering with private industry for decades. The US Air Force began placing active duty officers with companies as early as the 1940s, when pilots were placed with aircraft manufacturers to participate in the development and design of new aircraft.

"I didn't know the program existed in other branches of the service, but we had a former Air Force general at the time working in Amazon Web Services who I reached out to, and he told me about the Air Force's program," said Niekerk. "So, we decided to create a similar program in Seattle. The idea was that as a company we would be stronger for it and the military service people would gain great experience from it because it's such a different experience."

However, Amazon was a bit different from the types of companies the various branches of the military typically had worked with in the past.

"Traditionally with these programs, officers will go to work with big defense contractors and function in roles correlated to what they do in the military," Niekerk explained, "so to come to a company like Amazon that isn't directly related to the US military? That's a tremendous opportunity for learning in seeing how things get done differently. We have military officers in Seattle and in Herndon, Virginia, and it's an ongoing education both ways—we are constantly educating our own teams to think about how they will integrate these officers into their teams and what projects they will be assigned to.

"The other thing we're trying to do with them is give them a broader perspective of the company overall. They are all working on their own projects and delivering real results, but at the same time we want them to understand fully how the company operates at more strategic levels. So ideally, they leave after a year and not only understand how one business operates but have a strong understanding of how Amazon as a company operates."

Niekerk said he sees benefits to both organizations in this talent exchange.

"Number one, it's Amazon employees having daily interaction—sometimes for first time in their lives—with a military officer. I think the number is less than one percent of our civilian population ever having served in the military. The military officers wear civilian clothes when they're working at Amazon—they're not in uniform, so what the Amazon employees see is a colleague who also brings new experiences and ideas to the table, so it helps to educate and broaden views of the military for our employees.

"Second, Amazon benefits from the new perspective that the officers bring—they help us see around corners that we may not otherwise be able to. When you're used to thinking internally in a certain way and now you're introducing people who have a whole new or different experience or way of looking at something—they're going to help us get there.

"Third, frankly, our hope is that the officers will go back to their branches of service and be able to talk about their experiences and in the long-term be great sources for future talent as folks start to think about transitioning from military service to civilian life."

Additionally, he sees the military officers and the Navy as a whole gaining from the experience.

"In terms of the benefits for the Navy, and for the other services as well, first, I think they broaden the horizons and perspectives of their officers through participation in the program. I hear this in the feedback from the officers, that they're being exposed to ways of thinking about things that may have never entered their minds before in contrast to how they may have thought about something in the military.

"The second is speed of decision making and speed of delivery. Almost all of the officers talk about how impressed they are by Amazon's ability to quickly reach consensus decisions and move forward with them. In the military there are layers and layers of approvals and signoffs and so they're challenging bureaucracy and the broader structure in the military and looking at ways to get faster, quicker decisions made by using the Amazon approach to that.

"The third benefit, I think, is that they're taking back this lesson about focus from Amazon—how we have been able to grow the company and have a clear single focus on the mission—the mission at Amazon is to be Earth's most customer-centric company. All of the officers talk about how powerful it is to have a very clear single mission that everyone is focused on and how that helps drive the processes of making decisions. They're taking back new concepts about leadership principles and the tenets that we use in our decision-making process and introducing those into their services as methods of moving faster and making stronger decisions."

The officers under this arrangement are not considered Amazon employees; they draw their military pay while there. They are enrolled in Amazon's regular two-week training class to start, and initially spend a week with other new hires in operations leadership orientation. In the second week, they work on the floor of a fulfillment center performing jobs that the hourly workforce performs every day. They are also required to sign nondisclosure agreements to allow them to eventually work on high-level projects.

This type of talent swap is viewed as a retention tool for the military because it provides top military talent the opportunity to experience what it's like to work in a corporation without leaving the armed services. It also allows participants to return to duty with an expanded scope of professional experience, new skills, knowledge, and perspectives to share. For companies, the infusion of new ideas about how to approach decision-making and problem solving offered by the military is also quite meaningful. As one observer remarked, "Military officers don't view quitting as an option when things become tough—they don't figure they'll just go out and look for a new job—they're in it to win it."

In addition to Amazon, other companies like FedEx, Google, USAA, Siemens Corporation, Lockheed Martin, the National Football League, Caterpillar, Cisco, Microsoft, General Dynamics, and ExxonMobil, to name a few, have all shared personnel with the military. Assignments have been offered in the areas of artificial intelligence, aviation logistics, communications electronics, finance, marketing, security, procurement, public affairs, research and development, systems automation, and transportation.

"A big part of this is constantly working through the question of how we can make this opportunity the most effective for all parties involved," added Niekerk. Clearly both sides appear to have accomplished this mission.

A New Driver for Mobility

External partnerships that foster collaboration of key talent quite often result in innovations for both stakeholders as well. A fun example of this was the partnership created between Boeing and Callaway Golf. The two companies collaborated on the Callaway XR driver called the Speed Step, which changes airflow midswing, making the club more aerodynamic for a faster swing, resulting in more yardage on the course.[7]

"Usually if you make the head bigger, your aerodynamics get worse," said Alan Hocknell, Callaway's senior vice president of research and development. "Working with Boeing kind of unlocked that trade you might normally have to make. Now, it's a bigger body and still more aerodynamic than the head we already had."[8]

"We've been studying aerodynamics at Callaway for quite some time, but we knew if we were going to make the next big leap, we needed to partner with engineers who study aerodynamics full-time—the best of the best," added Evan Gibbs, manager of woods R&D at Callaway Golf.

"When an opportunity like Callaway comes up, Boeing likes to give new engineers a chance to apply their expertise outside their field," said Dr. David Crouch, senior technical fellow, Aero Flow Physics at Boeing. The partnership with Callaway was a unique one for Boeing, and especially interesting because it presented new sets of challenges. For example, Boeing engineers are accustomed to mul-tiyear timelines allotted to researching a problem; with this project with Callaway, they had only a few months.[9]

Members of both the Boeing and Callaway teams noted the par-allels between the problems of a golf club and the problems of an airplane. "There are a lot of similarities and a lot of differences. The physics are always the same," said Clark.

Gibbs says that Boeing's team learned quickly how difficult his job at Callaway can be. "They were actually kind of blown away by the constraints that our problem had," Gibbs noted. "It's a very dif-ferent process for them, but I think it's one of the things they liked, the idea of getting their guys to think faster, maybe not having every possible bit of data before we make a decision, put them out of their comfort zone a little bit."

Partnerships and programs like these will help redefine how tal-ent movement is viewed in the future. But to ensure success, com-panies need to recognize that a move of any kind probably requires the "new hire" treatment. Employees need onboarding and guidance as they move into each new role, even if it is a position they've held before. Our research shows that onboarding, reboarding, and repatri-ation of mobile employees is a next practice for talent mobility.

A final aspect to consider to effectively create a culture of talent mobility encompasses the metrics and review processes that ensure mobility is delivering value. Fifty percent of organizations measure the performance ratings of employees on new assignments to determine the success of the move. However, that usually doesn't determine if the mobility program is working or not. Our research found that two measures were important to track: first-year turnover rates of employees after movement versus overall turnover rates, and engagement scores post-movement versus overall engagement scores. Regularly monitoring and tracking those metrics, and adjusting if necessary, will help ensure the program is offering value.

To make sure the philosophy of talent mobility is adopted internally, it's also important to establish key performance indicators, track benefits, and capture success stories. These can go a long way toward convincing skeptical executives and managers of the benefit of mobility and encourage them to think more proactively about how moving key talent into new roles will benefit not only the culture, but also their teams. That "light switch effect" when talent hoarders flip to talent magnets can happen with not only the right key performance indicators and stories, but also the right incentives.

Getting talent mobility right certainly helps maintain culture change. It builds versatility. It improves collaboration. And it even develops character. In the words of the immortal Belichick: "Talent sets the floor; character sets the ceiling."

CHAPTER 21

STEP #18: DON'T UNDERESTIMATE THE VALUE OF EXTERNAL SENTIMENT

Your leaders are the megaphone for the
company's culture. In a world of sound bites
and tweets, our leaders have a moral obligation
in what they say and how they behave.

—MICHAEL FRACCARO, CHIEF PEOPLE OFFICER, MASTERCARD

The dot-com crash in 2000 gave rise to a new genre of website: the company review site. Like any restaurant, hotel, or other business review site, company review sites are populated by mostly anonymous ratings and comments by current and former employees. Those employees provide a critique of an organization's culture and offer a unique view from the inside that prospective employees can use to determine if the company is a good match. While that intent sounds logical and altruistic, many companies loathe these sites because the companies are often subjected to scathing reviews from disgruntled employees and caustic depictions of the employee experience, over which they have little control.

One of the first, more prominent company review sites created in 2000 had a very specific purpose: to document which dot-com companies were failing. It also had a very distinct name: F***ed Company.

F***ed Company (the name is a parody of Fast Company) was created by Philip J. "Pud" Kaplan as a "dot-com dead pool" that chronicled troubled and failing companies. I remember it being mainly an endless rant on companies and leadership. F***ed Company allowed employees to post anonymous comments on why their company was failing, or about how they mistreated employees, or about some other negative trait. Because of the caustic comments, the site was a target for frequent lawsuits. And like other dot-coms of the era, it struggled financially. In August 2007, the site ceased posting new content, and later it converted its main page to the simple message:

> F***edcompany is . . . f***ed.
> R.I.P. 2000–2007. If you're just now seeing this website for the first time, ask someone who was in the internet business during "round 1" to tell you all about it.[1]

However, the site's lack of success didn't deter others from launching their own review websites, the best known of which is Glassdoor. The company was founded in 2007 by former Expedia executives, including Expedia's founder, Rich Barton. The idea for the company reportedly grew out of an incident in which Glassdoor's CEO Bob Holman accidentally left the results of an employee survey on a printer while he was working at Expedia. While Holman retrieved the survey before anyone else noticed, it caused Barton and Holman to think about what would have happened if the results had gotten out into the public. This launched an idea to provide an anonymous forum for employees to comment on companies, bosses, and salaries and distill scores down to an easy, five-star system (not too far off what F***ed Company was doing). While Glassdoor is the most popular of employee review sites, there are many in existence, including Indeed (the number one job site in the world), Great Place to Work (better known for its awards), Comparably, FairyGodBoss (which caters to women), Vault, CareerBliss, The Muse, Kununu, and several others. Glassdoor was purchased in 2018 by Japan's Recruit Holdings for $1.2 billion (Recruit also owns Indeed).

Other software companies have created slightly different platforms loosely based on the same concept. For instance, Blind is a mobile app primarily aimed for internal use. It provides anonymous users a platform to talk about their experiences at a company. Once enough users sign up from a company, a channel opens in the app to confidentially discuss the workplace with coworkers. And while compensation information is often a big part of these sites, other sites such as PayScale and Salary.com cater specifically to compensation information and comparisons.

A Double-Edged Sword

Employee review sites can be an invaluable resource for job seekers to get a sense of what it's like to work for a company. Insights on leadership, compensation practices, benefits, and company policies can often be gleaned. Additionally, traits such as whether the culture seems inclusive or is more cutthroat can usually be assessed. While reviewers are anonymous, which introduces the likelihood of fake reviews or an overreliance on disgruntled ex-employees, most job seekers are looking for patterns from multiple reviewers and for clues on what to investigate further during the interview process.

For companies, these review sites are a double-edged sword. Most hiring managers and talent acquisition professionals begrudgingly acknowledge the importance of these sites to their employer brand, but they also feel helpless about what is being said. If they have good ratings, they often tout them; if bad ratings or negative comments, they will do what they can to improve or erase them. Several times all I've had to do is bring up the name "Glassdoor" in a room full of HR professionals, and the grumbling and disdain for the site will take up a major portion of the meeting.

And much of that is for good reason. Glassdoor is not at all a perfect barometer. Company ratings can be manipulated. In January 2019, the *Wall Street Journal* did an exposé on Glassdoor (titled "How Companies Secretly Boost Their Glassdoor Ratings")[2] and revealed that several companies had conducted internal campaigns to flood the site with positive reviews to offset negative ones.

"An analysis of millions of anonymous reviews posted on Glassdoor's site identified more than 400 companies with unusually large single-month increases in reviews," the article stated. "During the vast majority of these surges, the ratings were disproportionately positive compared with the surrounding months."

Generally, the flood of new positive ratings resulted in a 5 on a 1-to-5 scale. In the *Journal's* analysis, five-star ratings collectively made up 45 percent of reviews in the months where the number of reviews jumped, compared with 25 percent in the six months before and after. Well-known companies with large spikes included Slack, LinkedIn, Anthem, Clorox, SAP, and Elon Musk's SpaceX. When contacted by the *Journal,* spokespeople for Slack, LinkedIn, and Anthem admitted that their companies encouraged employees to give feedback. SpaceX and SAP took it a step further and said they conducted internal campaigns to leave reviews to help make Glassdoor's annual ranking of Best Places to Work. In another case, Guaranteed Rate asked employees to write positive reviews to raise poor ratings, according to interviews with current and former employees. The CEO later admitted that he and his management team felt Glassdoor ratings didn't accurately reflect the company's work environment and so they asked employees to post reviews.

In its defense, Glassdoor warns companies not to coerce or incentivize employees to post positive reviews and encourages reviews to be solicited from all employees. In a small percentage of posts, Glassdoor will delete reviews because they have offensive content or otherwise violate community guidelines. In a few cases, "ballot box stuffing" could also cause Glassdoor to remove positive reviews, according to the company. But that seems unlikely since, according to the analysis, more than a quarter of positive spikes came in October—right around the deadline for Glassdoor's annual ranking of companies.

That doesn't diminish the importance of Glassdoor or other employer review sites in influencing potential new hires or serving as as a source of information on the external employer brand. These sites are increasingly utilized and are more influential now than they have ever been. Most employers recognize this trend.

Glassdoor provides some compelling statistics. According to the company's own surveys, nearly three in four (74 percent) of Glassdoor users read at least four reviews before forming an opinion of a company.[3] The same number of people are likely to apply for a job if the employer actively manages its employer brand (e.g., responds to reviews, updates its profile, shares updates on the culture and work environment). And 62 percent of job seekers say their perception of a company improves after seeing an employer respond to a review.

Employer Brand

While it's clear that many job seekers conduct research on employer rating sites as part of their job-hunting process, companies can utilize external feedback to monitor the progress of efforts to renovate culture. To really gauge whether culture renovation is being maintained, companies need to be aware of what is being said about their employer brand externally. That external sentiment should be improving and moving in the direction the senior team envisioned when it originally embarked on a renovation of corporate culture.

The concept of "employer brand" has become especially important in recent years. The term describes an employer's reputation as a place to work as opposed to the more general corporate or consumer brand. While it was first introduced in the 1990s, the use of employer brand didn't become widespread until over a decade later, but its use eventually became ubiquitous. In fact, in 2008 Jackie Orme, the director general of the UK Chartered Institute of Personnel Directors (CIPD), said in her opening address to the CIPD annual conference, "When I started out in the profession, nobody talked about employer branding. Now it's absolutely integral to business strategy—resonating well beyond the doors of the HR department."[4]

As the HR profession often does, over time many competing terms have been created in the industry, such as "employment brand" or even "talent brand"—but they essentially mean the same thing. Another popular term that is very similar is "employee value proposition" (EVP), which represents the reasons people should care about employment at the company. EVP is more of an internal term and is usually used to describe what employees like best or value the most in the company. It's often described in the context of the financial and nonfinancial rewards available to employees and helps differentiate why one company is a more preferred workplace than another.

In the first few months of the pandemic, employer brand was heavily influenced by how companies initially reacted to an unprecedented event for which they had no contingency plans. Serial entrepreneur Mark Cuban warned companies several times that "how companies respond . . . is going to define their brand for decades,"[5] and "how you treat your employees today will have more impact on your brand in future years than any amount of advertising, any amount of anything you literally could do."[6]

Many companies heeded Cuban's warning. In research we conducted in late May of 2020—depicted in Figure 21.1—we found a somewhat surprising trend: 75 percent of respondents from hundreds of companies we surveyed said that their organization's culture had been affected during the pandemic *in a positive way*. The comments on why this was the case were uniform: the level of empathy shown by management to the employee base was at a level most had never seen. Flexible schedules were approved without a blink, benefits were increased, and work-from-home employees had much more autonomy than previously experienced.

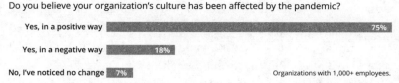

Do you believe your organization's culture has been affected by the pandemic?

Yes, in a positive way — 75%

Yes, in a negative way — 18%

No, I've noticed no change — 7%

Organizations with 1,000+ employees.

FIGURE 21.1 Impact of COVID on Organizational Culture
Source: i4cp

Many also commented on the "window" they were suddenly granted into the lives of coworkers and leadership. One survey-taker summed this up well:

> Though our organization has always been somewhat people-focused, the situation with the pandemic has increased enormously our level of empathy and understanding for how people have to cope with life outside of the workplace. It's been amazing to "live" in each other's homes and see a very different side of everyone from our CEO to—well—everyone. It allows us to appreciate how we are "one whole person" and not two different ones. Virtual working and the tools we use for meetings have been a great equalizer as well, bringing home an equality of participation that was not the same when some are in the meeting room and others are dialing in.

The good feelings around culture weren't ubiquitous, however. Layoffs, furloughs, and failing businesses created plenty of negative sentiments as well. As one survey respondent wrote: "Over 45,000 employees have been furloughed since April 1. Many are choosing to seek new jobs rather than waiting to be recalled," while another added, "Team members are more stressed; we had to furlough and RIF people which has created job security concerns." Another was even more succinct: "Economics first. Employees second."

The same was true during the social unrest following George Floyd's death. While our research found that almost 70 percent of companies sent out internal communication from their CEO, and close to 50 percent said their companies felt obliged to address the issue and take a stand, there were plenty of companies that remained quiet. I talked to one executive who was incredulous that his CEO refused to address it in any form internally.

While crises often spotlight organizational culture, it's *how* employees talk about the organization that is the biggest indicator of employer brand externally. High-performance organizations are much more likely than low-performance organizations to be tuned into (and actively engaged in shaping) perception about their organization.

High-performance companies actively measure their employer brand. For example, i4cp research shows top companies are:

- ► Six times more likely to track mentions in the media
- ► Two and a half times more likely to measure inclusion of employer brand in their marketing collateral
- ► Two times more likely to track social media engagement
- ► One and a half times more likely to track the ability of their employees to communicate the brand to others

High-performance organizations are also far better at getting top talent to refer friends to work at their organization by a factor of three and a half times versus low performers. Referrals have always been a top recruiting strategy, and these top performers are also twice as likely to measure employee referrals as an indicator of the effectiveness of their talent acquisition efforts.

While there are different ways to measure employer brand, our research shows that there is a definite difference between what is most popular versus what is most powerful. While measures like traffic to the career portal, number of "best employer" awards, and social media engagement are popular ways to look at employer brand, we find that the employee's ability to communicate the brand to others and the source of successful hires (usually from existing employees) are more indicative of top employer brands, as shown in Figure 21.2. It's tempting to tout the volume of traffic to your site, but that doesn't say much about the quality of applicants.

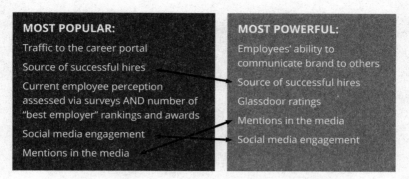

FIGURE 21.2 Popular Versus Powerful Brand Measurements

Employee Experience

As I referred to earlier in the book, "employee experience" has become a popular term in companies. It's meant to capture the entire life cycle of the employee, including the prehire experience; onboarding; learning and development opportunities; compensation and total rewards; the job itself; career opportunities and mobility; the social aspects of the workplace; and, finally, the experience at the end of employment. Like "customer experience," the employee experience is often used to determine where improvements can be made, programs enhanced, and synergies found. There's no question that the employee experience influences the employer and consumer brand.

High-performance organizations treat employee experience more seriously than low performers do. We found that almost 40 percent of high-performance companies had developed a formal strategic plan for employee experience versus 15 percent of low performers. But overall, employee experience is relatively new—over half of companies we surveyed said their employee experience program has been in place less than two years. Ominously, almost 70 percent said during the pandemic that they expected employee experience to be negatively impacted by COVID-19.

Mastercard is one company that understands the impact employee experience has on brand, as was outlined earlier in the comments of Ajay Banga, Mastercard's CEO. As the company developed that experience, Banga's partner over the second half of his tenure as CEO has been Michael Fraccaro, the chief people officer.

"We're working through the whole employee experience," said Fraccaro. "It's a wider continuum we're thinking about—starting from the time that candidates interact with our website to search for jobs or read thought leadership papers. And if it's clumsy or difficult to navigate, then it's a bad experience."

Fraccaro understands that talent increasingly comes from many different areas, and the relationship with employees will likely change over time for many organizations and ultimately will affect the employer brand.

"The shape and dimension of the workforce is changing, and the fact is you're going to have part of your work conducted by your employees, part of it by contingent workers, gig workers, and so forth," said Fraccaro. "It's going to be much more fluid. CHROs are going to have to think through this whole new paradigm. If you think about the future, the centennial workforce might have much longer careers, and it's more likely that they'll have more jobs in their careers. Therefore, it's highly probable they'll leave your organization. Maintaining that connection is really important to your employment brand."

At the start of the COVID-19 crisis, Mastercard understood deeply that it needed to be attentive to the needs of the workforce and take away as much uncertainty and fear about people's jobs as it could, given the other issues employees were encountering. Aside from telling the workforce there would be no layoffs, the company also addressed employee benefits.

"In the midst of the pandemic, we went out and announced that irrespective of your gender, irrespective of whether it's a natural childbirth or an adopted child or a surrogate child, we will give you 16 weeks of fully paid parental leave," said Banga. "Fully paid meaning no pro-rata, fully paid, including your bonus for the year."

Banga was cognizant that employees would be on the lookout to ensure benefits granted during the pandemic would be continued later.

"We don't change principles of dealing with employees based on COVID-19. We still think it's the right thing to do," Banga added. "I think that's the point. It's not just looking after them during a crisis. It's making sure employees realize we care for them no matter what might be happening in the world."

Defining and managing an employment brand starts with the employee experience, and as Banga and Fraccaro express, the CHRO and senior leaders need to feel responsibility for it. Fraccaro advises leaders to always be looking at the internal and external forces that can affect that brand.

"Your leaders are the megaphone for the company's culture. In a world of sound bites and tweets, our leaders have a moral obligation in what they say and how they behave. And we have to equip our leaders to lead and manage in a very different world than the one our leadership programs traditionally have," Fraccaro said. "What about your employee population? What are they saying on social media? Watch Glassdoor and similar sites. And clearly, you have to look to your customers, through surveys and the like. Always seeking this outside-in perspective is important to sustaining this kind of disruptive culture."

Analyzing social sentiment for employee feedback is something top companies are doing, often using natural language processing (NLP) tools mentioned earlier. While Glassdoor and related sites tend to skew more negative, they can be an important data source to analyze for common themes using NLP, particularly for inclusion or belonging. Like it or not, what is said on these sites affects perception among the talent pool.

Sentiment Analysis

Internally, one important finding from our research is that organizations that succeed at culture change make it safe for all employees to call out behavior that is counter to the desired culture change. A next practice in our analysis revealed that the use of "always-on feedback" platforms can help in the comfort, immediacy, and confidentiality for employees. Always-on can exist in different forms such as daily pulse surveys, hotlines, kiosks, mobile apps, or more often an online platform for sharing sentiment. Results from this sentiment should then be shared with leaders and teams to offer ongoing visibility and tracking toward deeper understanding to determine if the culture renovation has taken hold.

Regularly monitoring sentiment is important to make sure the culture hasn't slipped back to the "way it was," which has afflicted many culture change efforts. One company that makes sure it is on track with internal and external sentiment analysis is Workday.

Workday is a company familiar to many people, but especially to anyone in the human capital field. Probably the most successful HR software start-up in history, Workday provides enterprise cloud applications for human resources and financial management. In some ways, its story has elements of revenge.

In 2005, Oracle completed an acrimonious 18-month hostile takeover of PeopleSoft, a process that involved PeopleSoft's board rejecting five Oracle bids. In the center of it was Dave Duffield, a very successful entrepreneur (PeopleSoft was his fourth start-up) and the company's CEO. Powerless to stop the takeover, Duffield left the company after the takeover, determined to begin again. Duffield and former PeopleSoft senior vice president of product strategy Aneel Bhusri started Workday in that same year to compete head-on in the HR market with Oracle (and SAP), but this time as software as a service—in other words, a cloud computing platform—versus the clunky, on-premise application the competition was still supporting.

The two also did something else a little different. They structured Workday to have a dual-class stock that ensured they would have the ability to prevent an unwanted takeover in the future. In October 2012, Workday went public in an offering that valued the company at $9.5 billion and made Duffield one of the wealthiest individuals in technology. I always say this marked the first time HR technology became "cool." Workday's IPO woke up Wall Street to a whole category of software that it had largely ignored previously and ushered in a vast amount of fresh capital eager to capture the same magic.

While the valuation since has been impressive (the company's market cap quickly grew to north of $40 billion), Duffield and Bhusri were intent on creating a company that was the opposite of Oracle. As co-founders and co-CEOs, they not only took a significantly different path in application design and ownership structure; they also set out to design a contrary culture. Oracle, an operationally efficient company, has mostly been known for its cutthroat, competitive culture and traditionally hasn't been recognized by many award providers for its workplace environment. Workday, on the other hand, has prioritized its employee experience from the start and is a perennial leader on Great Place to Work's Best Workplaces lists and similar work culture lists. The company boasts one of the lower attrition rates in Silicon Valley and is known for employee perks and parties. Ninety-three percent of Workday's 12,000+ employees say the company is a great place to work.

"Our culture empowers our employees to achieve their organizational objectives, give their personal best, and work together as a team—ultimately defining who we are as a company and the customer experience we provide," boasts Bhusri, now sole CEO, on the company website. Workday ensures that it maintains the culture Duffield and Bhusri originally created by measuring employee sentiment regularly. The company conducts a weekly pulse survey known as the Best Workday Survey every Friday (what Workday calls "Feedback Fridays") that uses Workday's own software to ask all employees two to three questions.

The questions change every week, so that over the course of about four months, Workday has a comprehensive snapshot of its culture.[7] Survey prompts might include "My manager genuinely seeks and responds to suggestions and ideas" and "I am offered training or development to further myself professionally." If employees choose to participate, they can answer on a scale of 1 to 5 ranging from "almost always true" to "almost always untrue."

The process is run by a friend of mine, Greg Pryor, senior vice president, people and performance evangelist, and his team. They study the results to see overall trends in employee experience, but they also look at different demographics of the company. Greg reports to another friend, Ashley Goldsmith, the chief people officer. Ashley recalled to me one day how a few years earlier she and Greg noticed a small blip in their review of the culture data.

"It was 2016, and Greg and I were reviewing our internal and external data on culture and our employee experience, and we saw something we hadn't seen before . . . our data points weren't going up and to the right," said Goldsmith. "In fact, we noticed that several measures like our ratings on Glassdoor, LinkedIn, and others were going down slightly. It was small, like moving from a fraction of a percentage. A lot of companies probably would have ignored it, but we were concerned. Where there's smoke, there's usually fire.

"We were growing rapidly, and we knew it would be hard to maintain the culture completely, but we were concerned enough that we decided to bring it to Aneel. We put together a presentation. We weren't sure if he would think it's a problem or not, but we barely got through two slides before he immediately jumped in and said, 'OK, this might be an issue. Let's do something about this!' It's amazing to have leaders like this."

So, Aneel encouraged and supported us to have every single people leader at Workday come into San Francisco for two and half days and practice what it means to lead within values," Goldsmith continued. "The content was all taught by senior executives, and we had many great panel discussions and presentations. One of the top topics was empathy, and almost every topic showed some level of transparency and humility by our executives. It was powerful. So powerful, that now we do this every year—it's called the People Leadership Summit."

A year after the first summit, the measures started to improve. Today Workday conducts other summits for its leaders and employees and benchmarks its culture against other organizations, in addition to conducting the employee survey every Friday.

"We also enlisted several Culture Ambassadors, and now try to have one in every interview," said Goldsmith. "They've been trained on what does it mean to be a *culture add*, to make sure our values are aligned and to promote diversity.

"A positive employee experience ultimately improves performance and retention. This impacts the customer experience and helps increase a company's bottom line. We know that, but you can't assume your culture will always be great," reminded Goldsmith. "In order to maintain what you started and to keep improving, you need to always be intentional and keep focusing on talent practices. While I think we've done a great job, you have to always keep in mind that culture renovation is an ongoing effort.

"It never stops."

THEORY
VERSUS TACTICS

I t seems like every article I've read on culture change contains some variation of "Changing culture is hard," "It's deeply embedded," and "Change must come from the top." And it seems mandatory to quote Peter Drucker who may or may not have said "Culture eats strategy for breakfast." Or is it lunch?

Anyway, we all understand. Culture is critical, and changing it is difficult. Whether renovating a house or overhauling the culture of a century-old organization, it never goes completely as planned. The process demands optimism, patience, and perseverance.

This is likely quite obvious to most corporate executives. Even though most culture change efforts fail, everyone also knows it can indeed be accomplished—look no further than the organizations outlined in this book as proof. And clearly, it's not an easy process. But too many pundits enjoy pontificating on the nuances and challenges versus embracing what works. There are many CEOs who have thought to themselves, *Stop talking about how tough it is and just tell me how to do it.*

Culture conversations are often long on theory and short on tactics, and my hope is that you've appreciated the spirit of this book—a blueprint of proven tactics. The 18 actions detailed in this book were cultivated from i4cp's extensive research of thousands of companies and in-depth conversations with executives who have enabled culture change. Along with the real-life stories and data, I sincerely hope this book will be a guide that many who are initiating and sustaining culture renovation in their organizations can rely on for years to come.

While we've tried to capture the best and next practices of cultural renovation, we know there are more proven actions that others have used in their successful change efforts; we know that because we couldn't fit some of them in the book. But there also will be new innovations and new next practices. Like culture change itself, we never envisioned this book to be a one-and-done effort. It will evolve over time, and it will never really be finished.

To facilitate this ongoing discussion, we've created a place for those interested in culture renovation. Please visit and contribute to this ongoing effort at www.culturerenovation.com. There, we document new and additional tactics, case studies, and next practices on renovating organizational culture. We'd like to hear your stories, your insights, and the practical applications (both what worked and what didn't) that you've experienced. We also have exclusive content for purchasers of this book, among other useful items.

Together, we look forward to helping make your next culture change effort a renovation to be proud of.

N O T E S

Introduction

1. https://www.bloomberg.com/news/features/2019-05-02/satya-nadella-remade
   -microsoft-as-world-s-most-valuable-company.

Chapter 1

1. https://computerhistory.org/blog/the-hp-ways-lessons-on-strategy-and
   -culture/.
2. https://en.wikipedia.org/wiki/Lewis_E._Platt.
3. https://www.nytimes.com/2015/10/27/us/politics/carly-fiorina-was
   -contradictory-figure-at-hewlett-packard.html.
4. https://www.forbes.com/global/2007/0312/026.html#492880211919.
5. https://www.iedp.com/articles/why-corporate-culture-is-hard/.

Chapter 2

1. https://en.wikipedia.org/wiki/Unicorn_(finance).
2. Wikipedia.
3. *Organizational Behavior* by Ricky W. Griffin, Gregory Moorhead.
4. *International Business Times.*
5. https://www.inc.com/minda-zetlin/netflix-blockbuster-meeting-marc
   -randolph-reed-hastings-john-antioco.html.
6. https://hbr.org/2016/04/how-companies-escape-the-traps-of-the-past.
7. https://hbr.org/2016/04/how-companies-escape-the-traps-of-the-past.

Chapter 3

1. https://www.vanityfair.com/news/business/2012/08/microsoft-lost-mojo
   -steve-ballmer.
2. https://www.nytimes.com/2002/09/22/books/the-life-of-monkeyboy.html.
3. https://www.nytimes.com/2002/09/22/books/the-life-of-monkeyboy.html.
4. https://fortune.com/2014/05/31/steve-ballmer-crazy/.
5. https://www.trustedreviews.com/opinion/ballmer-s-balls-ups-5-misguided
   -moments-of-microsoft-s-ceo-2901826.
6. https://www.bbc.com/news/technology-23815316.
7. https://www.newyorker.com/business/currency/why-steve-ballmer-failed.
8. https://www.vanityfair.com/news/business/2012/08/microsoft-lost-mojo
   -steve-ballmer.
9. http://www.appocalypse.co/technology/the-top-4-microsoft-acquisitions
   -that-failed/.

10. https://www.reuters.com/article/us-qualcomm-ceo/qualcomm-promotes
-mollenkopf-to-ceo-ends-microsoft-talk-idUSBRE9BC0GC20131213.

11. https://www.wired.com/2014/02/microsoft-ceo-satya-nadella/.

12. https://www.langspace.com/en/video/10562091316414286.

13. https://www.usatoday.com/story/tech/2015/09/15/microsoft-ceo-nadella
-culture-everything/72330296/.

14. https://news.stanford.edu/news/2007/february7/dweck-020707.html.

15. https://www.businessinsider.com/microsoft-is-using-growth-mindset-to
-power-management-strategy-2019-11.

16. https://www.weforum.org/agenda/2020/01/all-the-books-microsoft-ceo
-satya-nadella-talked-about-at-davos/.

17. https://www.fastcompany.com/40457458/satya-nadella-rewrites-microsofts
-code.

18. https://www.businessinsider.com/satya-nadella-microsoft-mindset-book
-2019-1.

19. https://qz.com/work/1539071/how-microsoft-ceo-satya-nadella-rebuilt-the
-company-culture/.

20. https://qz.com/504507/a-lawsuit-claims-microsofts-infamous-stack-rankings
-made-things-worse-for-women/.

21. https://www.vanityfair.com/news/business/2012/08/microsoft-lost-mojo
-steve-ballmer.

22. https://www.forbes.com/sites/karenhigginbottom/2018/05/31/why-empathy
-matters-in-the-workplace/#6f5af1581130.

23. https://qz.com/india/1122336/microsoft-ceo-satya-nadellas-leadership-
mantra-is-all-about-empathy/.

24. https://qz.com/india/1122336/microsoft-ceo-satya-nadellas-leadership
-mantra-is-all-about-empathy/.

25. https://www.businessinsider.com/microsoft-satya-nadella-nonviolent
-communication-2018-10.

26. https://www.forbes.com/sites/roncarucci/2019/10/14/microsofts-chief
-people-officer-what-ive-learned-about-leading-culture-change/
#5657bdb6410d.

27. https://hbr.org/2016/10/how-microsoft-uses-a-growth-mindset-to-develop
-leaders.

28. https://www.bloomberg.com/news/features/2019-05-02/satya-nadella
-remade-microsoft-as-world-s-most-valuable-company.

29. https://www.bloomberg.com/news/features/2019-05-02/satya-nadella
-remade-microsoft-as-world-s-most-valuable-company.

30. https://www.forbes.com/sites/roncarucci/2019/10/14/microsofts-chief
-people-officer-what-ive-learned-about-leading-culture-change/
#5657bdb6410d.

31. https://www.fastcompany.com/40457458/satya-nadella-rewrites-microsofts
-code.

Chapter 4

1. https://fortune.com/2020/02/12/john-legere-will-go-down-in-corporate -history-as-one-of-the-greatest-turnaround-stories-of-all-time/.
2. https://fortune.com/2020/02/12/john-legere-will-go-down-in-corporate -history-as-one-of-the-greatest-turnaround-stories-of-all-time/.
3. https://hbr.org/2017/01/t-mobiles-ceo-on-winning-market-share-by-trash -talking-rivals.
4. https://www.storemypic.com/image/i-dress-act-behave-and-speak-same-if-im .RFW5.
5. https://hbr.org/2017/01/t-mobiles-ceo-on-winning-market-share-by-trash -talking-rivals.
6. https://hbr.org/2017/01/t-mobiles-ceo-on-winning-market-share-by-trash -talking-rivals.
7. https://www.t-mobile.com/news/the-dumber-championship.
8. https://hbr.org/2017/01/t-mobiles-ceo-on-winning-market-share-by-trash -talking-rivals.
9. https://www.theverge.com/2018/12/6/18128990/tmobile-slow-cooker -sunday-cookbook-ceo-john-legere.
10. https://hbr.org/2017/01/t-mobiles-ceo-on-winning-market-share-by-trash -talking-rivals.
11. https://www.geekwire.com/2016/listen-shut-f-tell-t-mobiles-john-legere -shares-leadership-advice/.
12. https://www.tlnt.com/weekly-wrap-720-million-spent-on-engagement-and -this-is-all-we-get/.
13. https://www.forbes.com/sites/roncarucci/2019/10/14/microsofts-chief -people-officer-what-ive-learned-about-leading-culture-change/ #320f8f6e410d.
14. https://www.forbes.com/sites/roncarucci/2019/10/14/microsofts-chief -people-officer-what-ive-learned-about-leading-culture-change/ #4274b9ca410d.
15. https://www.azquotes.com/quote/1588103.
16. https://www.storemypic.com/image/uncarrier-not-just-marketing-program -its-culture-its.p5Gv.

Chapter 5

1. https://money.cnn.com/magazines/fsb/fsb_archive/2003/04/01/341016/.
2. https://marketrealist.com/2016/06/15-rule-became-stepping-stone-3ms -innovation/.
3. https://money.cnn.com/magazines/fsb/fsb_archive/2003/04/01/341016/.
4. https://money.cnn.com/magazines/fsb/fsb_archive/2003/04/01/341016/.
5. https://en.wikipedia.org/wiki/William_L._McKnight.
6. https://money.cnn.com/magazines/fsb/fsb_archive/2003/04/01/341016/.

Chapter 6

1. https://historycenter.agilent.com/packard-speeches/ps1960.
2. https://www.huffpost.com/entry/the-seven-characteristics_b_11339884.
3. https://www.usatoday.com/story/tech/news/2017/02/20/microsofts-satya
   -nadella-counting-culture-shock-drive-growth/98011388/.
4. https://www.cnn.com/2014/02/05/health/cvs-cigarettes/index.html.
5. https://www.prosek.com/unboxed-thoughts/one-year-after-cvs-quits-selling
   -cigarettes/.
6. https://www.prosek.com/unboxed-thoughts/one-year-after-cvs-quits-selling
   -cigarettes/.
7. https://www.usnews.com/news/healthiest-communities/articles/2019-09-03/
   commentary-cvs-health-strengthens-commitment-to-help-end-tobacco-use.
8. https://www.gallup.com/workplace/236573/company-purpose-lot-words
   .aspx.
9. https://www.accenture.com/us-en/insights/strategy/brand-purpose.
10. https://www.cnbc.com/2020/01/17/what-a-1000-dollar-investment-in
    -mastercard-would-be-worth-after-10-years.html.
11. https://www.fastcompany.com/90424514/decency-quotient-how-this-ceo
    -frames-inclusive-capitalism-for-his-company.
12. https://www.youtube.com/watch?v=wIMVSJlN9ZE.
13. https://www.mckinsey.com/industries/technology-media-and
    -telecommunications/our-insights/microsofts-next-act.

Chapter 7

1. https://builtin.com/company-culture/types-of-organizational-culture.
2. http://www.nfl.com/news/story/0ap3000001089665/article/clocks-at-jaguars
   -facility-move-back-to-normal-time.
3. https://www.cnbc.com/2018/04/23/what-jeff-bezos-learned-from-requiring
   -6-page-memos-at-amazon.html.
4. https://www.wherewomenwork.com/Career/1580/F5-Senior-Vice-President
   -explains-company-name.

Chapter 8

1. http://informalnetworks.co.uk/wp-content/uploads/2014/10/Whitepaper
   -change-management.pdf.
2. https://www.vanityfair.com/news/2019/10/the-untold-story-of-the-sony
   -hack.
3. https://www.nytimes.com/2014/12/31/business/media/sony-attack-first-a
   -nuisance-swiftly-grew-into-a-firestorm-.html.
4. https://www.thewrap.com/greatest-hits-leaked-sony-emails-angelina-jolie
   -aloha-david-fincher/.
5. https://movieweb.com/interview-movie-2014-seth-rogen-looks-back/.

6. https://www.latimes.com/entertainment/envelope/cotown/la-et-ct-sony-hack-year-later-20151118-story.html.
7. https://www.reuters.com/article/us-sony-cyberattack-lawsuit/sony-to-pay-up-to-8-million-in-interview-hacking-lawsuit-idUSKCN0SE2JI20151020.

Chapter 9
1. NACD Blue Ribbon Commission on Culture as a Corporate Asset, 2017.
2. https://www.hrtechnologist.com/articles/compensation-benefits/employee-assistance-programs-have-low-utilization/.
3. https://www.i4cp.com/file/survey-analyses/next-practices-in-holistic-well-being-the-performance-advantage/download.
4. https://www.randstadrisesmart.com/blog/how-host-effective-employee-focus-group-meetings.
5. https://www.i4cp.com/productivity-blog/fords-culture-hackathona-next-practice-in-innovation.
6. https://www.wsj.com/articles/smile-your-boss-is-tracking-your-happiness-11583255617.
7. https://www.cnbc.com/2017/05/22/new-ford-ceo-promises-to-be-a-cultural-change-agent-bill-ford-says.html.
8. https://www.iso.org/news/ref2357.html.
9. https://read.nxtbook.com/nacd/directorship/january_february_2020/director_development.html.
10. https://read.nxtbook.com/nacd/directorship/january_february_2020/chros_suit_up_to_help_boards_.html.
11. https://www.citigroup.com/citi/investor/data/ethicsculturecharter.pdf.

Chapter 10
1. https://hbr.org/2016/09/how-wd-40-created-a-learning-obsessed-company-culture.
2. https://www.jmlalonde.com/accidental-soul-sucking-ceo/.

Chapter 11
1. https://www.businessinsider.com/nadella-letter-executive-shakeup-2014-3.
2. https://www.seattletimes.com/business/microsoftrsquos-human-resources-chief-lisa-brummel-leaving/.
3. https://anchor.fm/drew-kugler/episodes/Satya-Nadella-and-Kathleen-Hogan-ed7eva.
4. https://www.i4cp.com/interviews/kathleen-hogan-how-microsoft-is-transforming-its-culture?search_id=253607.
5. https://www.i4cp.com/interviews/kathleen-hogan-how-microsoft-is-transforming-its-culture?search_id=253607.
6. https://www.economist.com/business/2020/03/24/the-coronavirus-crisis-thrusts-corporate-hr-chiefs-into-the-spotlight.

7. https://www.cnbc.com/2020/04/22/the-coronavirus-is-elevating-the-role-of
-hr-chiefs-in-the-c-suite.html.
8. https://www.cnbc.com/2020/04/22/the-coronavirus-is-elevating-the-role-of
-hr-chiefs-in-the-c-suite.html.
9. https://guykawasaki.com/you_have_to_lov/.
10. https://www.forbes.com/sites/chunkamui/2012/02/15/forget-the-seven
-habits-but-remember-the-no-asshole-rule/#7350116c54b3.

Chapter 12

1. https://en.wikipedia.org/wiki/Qualcomm.
2. https://www.chieflearningofficer.com/2010/02/28/storytelling-drives
-knowledge-and-information-sharing-across-qualcomm/.
3. https://womensleadership.stanford.edu/stories.
4. http://www.alsinapublishing.com/2017/11/the-science-of-storytelling/.
5. http://www.alsinapublishing.com/2017/11/the-science-of-storytelling/.
6. https://en.wikipedia.org/wiki/History_of_Amazon.
7. https://en.wikipedia.org/wiki/Gatorade.
8. https://en.wikipedia.org/wiki/Trader_Joe's.
9. https://en.wikipedia.org/wiki/Yankee_Candle.
10. https://deerfieldattractions.com/yankee-candle-flagship-store-offers-holiday
-cheer-all-year/.
11. https://observer.com/2011/09/fuck-carol-bartz-a-brief-history-of-yahoos
-ousted-ceo-and-bad-words/.
12. https://www.cnet.com/news/bartz-lights-fire-under-yahoo-engineers/.
13. https://www.businessinsider.com/henry-blodget-carol-bartzs-f-bomb-2009-4.
14. https://www.theguardian.com/business/2011/sep/08/carol-bartz-blast-yahoo
-after-being-fired.
15. https://www.theverge.com/2014/2/4/5377318/microsoft-ceo-satya-nadella
-first-letter-to-employees.
16. https://gigaom.com/2014/04/25/nadella-gets-high-marks-on-his-first
-earnings-call-performance/.
17. https://www.businessinsider.com/ceo-outrageous-remarks-and-apologies
-2014-10#james-mcnerney-boeing-2.
18. https://www.seattletimes.com/business/boeing-boss-jim-mcnerneyrsquos
-turbulent-tenure/.
19. https://www.seattletimes.com/business/boeing-aerospace/muilenburg
-replacing-mcnerney-as-boeings-ceo/.
20. https://en.wikipedia.org/wiki/Boeing_737_MAX_groundings.
21. https://www.theatlantic.com/ideas/archive/2019/11/how-boeing-lost-its
-bearings/602188/.
22. https://www.theatlantic.com/ideas/archive/2019/11/how-boeing-lost-its
-bearings/602188/.

23. https://qz.com/work/1793377/how-boeings-new-ceo-dave-calhoun-can-fix -its-broken-culture/.

24. https://www.nytimes.com/2020/03/05/business/boeing-david-calhoun.html.

Chapter 13

1. https://www.accenture.com/_acnmedia/thought-leadership-assets/pdf/ accenture-competitiveagility-gcpr-pov.pdf.

2. https://blog.linkedin.com/2018/june/26/workplace-culture-trends-the-key -to-hiring-and-keeping-top-talent.

3. https://www.fastcompany.com/90280950/exclusive-patagonia-is-in-business -to-save-our-home-planet.

4. https://www.fastcompany.com/90280950/exclusive-patagonia-is-in-business -to-save-our-home-planet.

5. https://www.inc.com/scott-mautz/how-can-patagonia-have-only-4-percent -worker-turnover-hint-they-pay-activist-employees-bail.html.

6. https://www.inc.com/scott-mautz/how-can-patagonia-have-only-4-percent -worker-turnover-hint-they-pay-activist-employees-bail.html.

Chapter 14

1. https://www.businesswire.com/news/home/20060226005075/en/National -Grid-Acquire-KeySpan-7.3-Billion-Cash.

2. https://www.cbsnews.com/news/monk-works-in-good-company/.

3. https://www.fastcompany.com/48491/kenny-moore-held-funeral-and -everyone-came.

4. https://www.fastcompany.com/48491/kenny-moore-held-funeral-and -everyone-came.

5. https://www.cbsnews.com/news/monk-works-in-good-company/.

6. https://tompeters.com/cool-friends/moore-kenny/.

7. https://www.fastcompany.com/48491/kenny-moore-held-funeral-and -everyone-came.

8. https://www.i4cp.com/productivity-blog/fords-culture-hackathona-next -practice-in-innovation.

9. https://www.linkedin.com/pulse/culture-transformation-ford-julie-lodge -jarrett/.

10. https://en.wikipedia.org/wiki/Fluoropolymer.

Chapter 15

1. https://www.theguardian.com/business/2018/apr/19/starbucks-black-men -feared-for-lives-philadelphia.

2. https://www.theguardian.com/business/2018/apr/19/starbucks-black-men -feared-for-lives-philadelphia.

3. https://www.inquirer.com/philly/news/pennsylvania/philadelphia/starbucks -ceo-kevin-johnson-philadelphia-arrests-black-men-20180416.html.

4. https://money.cnn.com/2018/04/17/news/companies/starbucks-ceo-meeting
   -arrested-men/index.html.
5. https://time.com/5241426/starbucks-ceo-apology-philadelphia/.
6. https://www.forbes.com/sites/shephyken/2018/06/01/starbucks-closes-8000
   -stores-for-racial-bias-training-is-it-enough/#23a476ee2831.

Chapter 16

1. https://www.forbes.com/sites/85broads/2013/07/19/how-not-to-lose-your
   -new-employees-in-their-first-45-days/#537c25d93be3.
2. https://www.bamboohr.com/blog/onboarding-infographic/?utm_source=
   PT&utm_medium=MKP&utm_campaign=Bonu-TR-FreeTrialR-20180101
   -01&utm_content=blank&utm_term=blank.
3. https://www.forbes.com/sites/billconerly/2018/08/12/companies-need-to
   -know-the-dollar-cost-of-employee-turnover/#2dbd4dffd590.
4. https://www.gallup.com/workplace/238085/state-american-workplace
   -report-2017.aspx.
5. https://www.i4cp.com/file/survey-results/pulse-survey-results-onboarding/
   download.
6. https://www.freep.com/story/money/cars/2016/10/18/toyotas-move-texas
   -goes-far-beyond-moving-employees/92356352/.
7. https://www.freep.com/story/money/cars/2016/10/18/toyotas-move-texas
   -goes-far-beyond-moving-employees/92356352/.
8. https://www.dallasnews.com/business/local-companies/2018/07/31/after
   -toyota-moved-2800-workers-from-around-the-u-s-to-plano-how-is-texas
   -working-out/.
9. https://www.autonews.com/automakers-suppliers/toyota-relocation-houses
   -mattered.
10. https://www.i4cp.com/interviews/toyotas-onboarding-program-welcomes
    -and-inspires-new-hires.

Chapter 17

1. https://newsroom.accenture.com/news/people-and-work-connect-bring
   s-together-leading-companies-to-keep-people-employed-during-covid-19
   -crisis.htm.
2. https://en.wikipedia.org/wiki/Nordstrom.
3. https://www.linkedin.com/pulse/how-busboy-ended-up-becoming-president
   -nordstromcom-ray-cao/.
4. https://www.cnbc.com/2019/10/24/nordstroms-new-york-flagship-opens
   -heres-a-look-inside.html.
5. https://www.geekwire.com/2019/inside-nordstroms-new-7-story-flagship
   -nyc-store-digital-retail-meets-physical-brick-mortar/.
6. https://www.geekwire.com/2019/inside-nordstroms-new-7-story-flagship
   -nyc-store-digital-retail-meets-physical-brick-mortar/.

Chapter 18

1. https://www.workfront.com/blog/history-performance-management.
2. https://hbr.org/2016/10/the-performance-management-revolution.
3. https://en.wikipedia.org/wiki/Management_by_objectives.
4. https://en.wikipedia.org/wiki/Management_by_objectives.
5. https://finance.yahoo.com/news/10-great-jack-welch-quotes-223010106.html.
6. https://finance.yahoo.com/news/10-great-jack-welch-quotes-223010106.html.
7. https://hbr.org/2016/10/the-performance-management-revolution.
8. https://www.forbes.com/sites/petercohan/2012/07/13/why-stack-ranking-worked-better-at-ge-than-microsoft/#26f7d4343236.
9. https://en.wikipedia.org/wiki/360-degree_feedback.
10. https://en.wikipedia.org/wiki/Balanced_scorecard.
11. https://hbr.org/2015/04/reinventing-performance-management.
12. https://www.shrm.org/resourcesandtools/hr-topics/compensation/pages/ratingless-reviews-positively-affect-pay-practices.aspx.
13. https://www.shrm.org/resourcesandtools/hr-topics/compensation/pages/ratingless-reviews-positively-affect-pay-practices.aspx.
14. https://www.i4cp.com/productivity-blog/performance-feedback-culture-drives-business-impact.

Chapter 19

1. https://www.forbes.com/sites/isabeltogoh/2020/05/31/wave-of-protests-continues-into-sixth-day-as-more-us-cities-impose-curfews/#21333db17ab9.
2. https://en.wikipedia.org/wiki/Employee_resource_group.
3. https://www.i4cp.com/file/1763/download
4. https://www.wsj.com/articles/the-business-case-for-more-diversity-11572091200.
5. http://www.cristkolder.com/volatility-report/.
6. https://www.wsj.com/articles/why-are-there-still-so-few-black-ceos-11601302601.
7. https://www.cnbc.com/2020/06/01/merck-ceo-george-floyd-could-be-me.html.
8. https://www.ft.com/content/bee4c405-05df-4e9d-a93b-955366330e9e.
9. https://chiefexecutive.net/pwc-chairman-tim-ryan-top-priority-diversity-race/.
10. https://hbr.org/2018/03/businesses-exist-to-deliver-value-to-society.
11. https://www.diversitybestpractices.com/mercks-ebrg-impact-on-companys-global-health-literacy-strategy.
12. https://www.merck.com/about/featured-stories/powered-by-inclusion-how-we-celebrate-our-diverse-workforce.html.

Chapter 20

1. https://nesn.com/2020/04/how-this-lawrence-guy-quote-explains-patriots-2020-nfl-draft-strategy/.
2. https://www.nbcsports.com/boston/patriots/versatility-still-matters-bill-belichick-when-looking-players-nfl-all-time-team.

3. https://www.inspiringquotes.us/author/9436-bill-belichick.
4. https://www.masslive.com/patriots/2019/10/bill-belichick-flexes-a-little-on
-patriots-depth-show-me-how-many-teams-in-the-league-who-play-20-guys
-on-defense.html.
5. https://www.i4cp.com/file/surveys/talent-mobility-matters/download.
6. https://www.i4cp.com/file/white-papers/how-amazon-partners-with-the
-military/download.
7. https://www.i4cp.com/file/surveys/talent-mobility-matters/download.
8. https://www.golfdigest.com/story/callaway-teams-with-boeing-to-speed-up
-xr16-drivers.
9. https://www.golfdigest.com/story/callaway-teams-with-boeing-to-speed-up
-xr16-drivers.

Chapter 21

1. https://en.wikipedia.org/wiki/Fucked_Company.
2. https://www.wsj.com/articles/companies-manipulate-glassdoor-by-inflating
-rankings-and-pressuring-employees-11548171977.
3. https://www.glassdoor.com/employers/resources/hr-and-recruiting-stats/.
4. https://en.wikipedia.org/wiki/Employer_branding.
5. https://www.cnbc.com/2020/03/25/coronavirus-mark-cuban-warns-against
-rushing-employees-back-to-work.html.
6. https://www.wbur.org/onpoint/2020/04/07/mark-cuban-coronavirus
-corporations.
7. https://fortune.com/2019/01/17/how-workday-focuses-on-improving-its
-workplace-culture-every-day/.

INDEX

Kevin Oakes is a frequent author and international keynote speaker on next practices in human capital and works with business and HR executives on people practices that drive high performance.

He is the CEO and co-founder of the Institute for Corporate Productivity (i4cp), the leading authority on next practices in human capital. i4cp produces more research than any other human capital research firm on the planet, and many of the world's most prominent organizations and HR leaders turn to i4cp to better leverage emerging workforce trends. Supported by a powerful community of human capital practitioners, i4cp provides insights that help organizations effectively anticipate, adapt, and act in a constantly changing business environment.

Kevin is currently on the board of directors and advisory boards of several human capital start-ups. Kevin was previously on the board of directors of KnowledgeAdvisors, a provider of human capital analytics software, which was purchased by Corporate Executive Board in March of 2014. Kevin was also the chairman of Jambok, a social learning start-up company that was founded at Sun Microsystems and was purchased by SuccessFactors in March 2011. He also served on the boards of Workforce Insight and Koru prior to their sales.

Kevin is on the board of Best Buddies Washington and helped establish the first office for Best Buddies in the state in 2019. Best Buddies is a nonprofit organization dedicated to establishing a global volunteer movement that creates opportunities for one-to-one friendships, integrated employment, leadership development, and inclusive living for people with intellectual and developmental disabilities (IDD).

Kevin was previously the founder and the president of SumTotal Systems (NASDAQ: SUMT) which he helped create in 2003 by merging Click2learn (NASDAQ: CLKS) with Docent (NASDAQ: DCNT). The merger won Frost & Sullivan's Competitive Strategy Award in 2004.

Prior to the formation of SumTotal, Kevin was the chairman and CEO of Click2learn, which was founded in 1985 by Paul Allen, co-founder of Microsoft. Prior to joining Click2learn, Kevin was president and founder of Oakes Interactive in Needham, Massachusetts. Oakes Interactive was purchased in 1997 by Click2learn (then called Asymetrix), which Kevin helped take public a year later.